Illustrated Battles of the Napoleonic Age

Illustrated Battles of the
Napoleonic Age
Volume 2—1807-1811

Buenos Ayres, Eylau & Friedland,
Baylen, Finland, Vimiera, Aspern-Essling,
Corunna, Passage of the Douro, Talavera,
Tyrol-Innsbruck and Barossa

Arthur Griffiths, D. H. Parry,
Archibald Forbes
and Others

Illustrated Battles of the Napoleonic Age: Volume 2—1807-1811
Buenos Ayres, Eylau & Friedland, Baylen, Finland, Vimiera, Aspern-Essling, Corunna, Passage of the Douro, Talavera, Tyrol-Innsbruck and Barossa
by Arthur Griffiths, D. H. Parry, Archibald Forbes and Others

Leonaur is an imprint of Oakpast Ltd

Material original to this edition and presentation of the text in this form copyright © 2014 Oakpast Ltd

ISBN: 978-1-78282-243-1 (hardcover)
ISBN: 978-1-78282-244-8 (softcover)

http://www.leonaur.com

Publisher's Notes

The views expressed in this book are not necessarily those of the publisher.

Contents

Buenos Ayres by C. Stein	7
Eylau and Friedland by H. Sutherland Edwards	29
Baylen by Major Arthur Griffiths	59
The Winter Campaign in Finland by A. Hilliard Atteridge	79
The Battle of Vimiera by Major-General Sir E. F. Du Cane	97
The Battle of Aspern-Essling by D. H. Parry	125
The Retreat of Corunna by D. H. Parry	149
The Passage of the Douro by Lieut.-Col. Newnham Davis	167
Talavera by D. H. Parry	185
The Liberation of Tyrol and Three Captures of Innsbruck by A. J. Butler	203
The Battle of Barrosa by Archibald Forbes	229

July 5, 1807
Buenos Ayres
C. Stein

After the Battle of Trafalgar England had complete command of the seas, and, rightly or wrongly, her government had adopted the policy of striking at the European Powers which were actually in arms as her enemies, or whose interests were opposed to her own, by expeditions against their distant colonies and dependencies. The power of her navy could thus be thoroughly utilised, and her army, though used in comparatively small fractions, was generally, by its quality and discipline, able to act with success against any forces which it was likely to meet. Communication with different parts of the globe then demanded such long periods of time, and was at best so very uncertain, that naval and military commanders acted frequently on a general policy which had been imparted to them rather than on specific instructions which had to be exactly carried out.

When, therefore, in June, 1806, Buenos Ayres was seized by a small force of 1,700 men under Brigadier-General Beresford and Commodore Sir Home Popham, it is very doubtful how far that enterprise was directly authorised by the king's ministers, though from documents published at Sir Home Popham's subsequent trial it may be understood that it was countenanced both by Mr. Pitt and Lord Melville. Be that as it may, Brigadier-General Beresford found himself holding this new conquest with a wholly insufficient force in the midst of a numerous hostile population, and without any strong place of arms to which he could retire if menaced by an organised attack. Aware of his precarious position, General Beresford sent an urgent appeal to the Cape for reinforcements, pending the arrival of a sufficient army from England to make good the possession of one of the greatest and most valuable Spanish provinces in South America. Even from the Cape, however, no assistance could be expected for nearly four months, and a force from England could not land before double that time had elapsed.

The American-Spaniards were not long in discovering how feasible it was for a well-conducted insurrection to overpower the invaders, and, under the command of General Liniers, a Frenchman by birth, they attacked General Beresford so vigorously that after severe fighting, in which the English losses amounted to 250 men,, killed and wounded, his little army was obliged to surrender as prisoners of war. The captives included the whole of the 71st Regiment of infantry, 150 of the St. Helena corps, besides a few dragoons and artillery. The navy had been able to render little or no assistance, and Sir Home Popham was under the necessity of falling back to his cruising ground at the mouth of the Rio de la Plata. The expected reinforcements from the Cape arrived about the middle of October, consisting of two squadrons of the 20th Light Dragoons, a company of artillery, the 38th and 47th Regiments of infantry, and a company of the 54th. This armament sailed up to Monte Video, hoping, by a combined attack of the land and sea forces, to get possession of that town; but this was found impracticable, and it was deemed advisable to await the additional reinforcements from England before any great operation should be undertaken. As an immediate base of operations, however, the town of Maldonado at the mouth of the Rio de la Plata was seized and occupied, and here supplies could be easily procured, and a convenient harbour for shipping was available.

The news of the capture of Buenos Ayres had excited much triumph in England, and reinforcements for General Beresford had been at once prepared. It was not till October, 1806, however, that these could be despatched, and they did not arrive at the Rio de la Plata till January, 1807. They were placed under the command of Sir Samuel Auchmuty, and comprised the 17th Light Dragoons, the 40th and 87th Regiments of infantry, three companies of the newly-raised Rifle Corps, and some artillery. As we have seen, they were too late to save General Beresford from crushing defeat and captivity, but they found the Cape troops at Maldonado in the best condition, and fit for immediate service. These Sir Samuel Auchmuty at once embarked, and, at the head of a now formidable armament, sailed to the attack of Monte Video. Rear-Admiral Stirling, who had superseded Sir Home Popham in the naval command, protected the movement of the trans-

ports with his ships of war. A landing was effected about eight miles from Monte Video, and a brilliant action was fought with the Spaniards outside the town, in which the English were completely victorious. This action was remarkable as being the first occasion on which the Rifle Corps—afterwards the 95th, and now the Rifle Brigade—were actively employed. Their markedly gallant conduct then was an earnest of the long roll of distinguished services which the famous corps has since performed in all quarters of the world, wherever the honour of England has had to be maintained. After defeating the Spaniards in the open field Sir Samuel Auchmuty established batteries against the citadel and defences of the town, and landed heavy ship ordnance from the fleet wherewith to arm them, for no siege-train formed part of the equipment sent from England. From these batteries fire was opened, and continued for thirteen days, when a practicable breach was made. The town was summoned, and, as no reply was returned, the orders were given to storm. The defence of the Spaniards was tenacious, and their fire destructive and well-maintained; but, though they lost heavily, the columns of assault were everywhere successful in driving the enemy before them with the bayonet, and the place was taken.

After Sir Samuel Auchmuty had sailed from England, but before intelligence was received that Buenos Ayres had been retaken by the Spaniards, it was hoped by the Ministry that an expedition to the west of South America might meet with the same success as it was yet believed had attended British arms on the east coast. With a view to this object a force of 4,200 men was sent out in October, 1806, under command of Brigadier-General Robert Craufurd (afterwards the renowned leader of the Light Division in the Peninsula), accompanied by a naval squadron under Admiral Murray. The expedition was to be directed to the capture of the seaports, and the reduction of the province of Chili; and the course to be sailed, whether to the eastward by New South Wales, or to the westward by Cape Horn, was left to the discretion of Admiral Murray. It was hoped that, if Chili could be reduced, General Craufurd might communicate with Buenos Ayres, and that a complete chain of posts might be established across South America, which would then be opened up to English trade. When the news of General Beresford's disaster arrived, however, a swift sloop of war was sent after General Craufurd, with orders that he was to give up the attack on Chili, and to proceed to the Rio de la Plata, there to join the army of Sir Samuel Auchmuty. Craufurd was overtaken at the Cape, and, sailing at once, he arrived off Monte Video on the 14th June. The various corps under his command were two squadrons of 6th Dragoon Guards, the 5th, 36th, 45th, and 88th Regiments of infantry, five companies of the Rifle Corps, and two companies of artillery.

In view of the concentration of troops at the Rio de la Plata, it was determined to send out from England an officer of high rank to take command; and in an evil hour Lieutenant-General John Whitelocke was selected, who arrived at Monte Video on the 10th May with Major-General Gower as second in command, and bringing with him the 9th Light Dragoons, the 89th Regiment of Infantry, a detachment of artillery, and a number of recruits for the regiments already on the station. The total of the British force which in the middle of June was available for offensive operations amounted to more than 11,000 men, but the greater part of the cavalry and artillery were unprovided with horses. Most of the dragoons had to act as infantry, and the requirements of the guns were very insufficiently met.

Monte Video, on the north side of the great estuary of the Rio de la Plata, is nearly 150 miles from Buenos Ayres, which lies higher up the river on the south side; and in order to move the troops which were to undertake the attack of the latter town no vessels drawing above thirteen feet of water could be employed; but, as a strong garrison had to be left to secure the base of operations, it was possible, by doubling the number of men which each ship could properly carry, to find accommodation on board for all the rest of General Whitelocke's army. The embarkation was proceeded with rapidly,

EXPEDITION TO THE RIO DE LA PLATA, 1807.

and the troops were brigaded in the following order:—The Light Brigade, under General Crauford, included the Rifle Corps and a battalion formed of nine light companies from the various regiments; Sir Samuel Auchmuty commanded the 5th, 38th, and 87th; General Lumley commanded the 36th, 88th, and four dismounted squadrons of the 17th Light Dragoons; and Colonel Mahon commanded the 40th, 45th, two dismounted squadrons of the *carabiniers*, and four dismounted squadrons of the 9th Light Dragoons. There were also two companies of Royal Artillery. Twenty-eight guns of various calibres were embarked with an ammunition column for the conveyance of artillery and small-arm ammunition. Cavalry, acting as such, was hardly represented, only about a hundred of the 17th Light Dragoons being supplied with horses.

The first division of transports was able to get under weigh on the 17th June, but it was not till the 25th that a suitable place could be found for disembarkation. Below Buenos Ayres there extended for many miles along the bank of the estuary a broad morass, and it was necessary to select a landing-place from which a passage through this morass existed. Such a place was found at Ensenada, about thirty-two miles from Buenos Ayres, and here the landing was commenced at daylight on the 28th. General Craufurd's brigade was the first to gain the shore, followed by Sir Samuel Auchmuty's brigade, and the fiery Craufurd at once pushed forward through the morass to secure a position on firm ground. The Spaniards offered no opposition to the English troops, and under a capable commander the army might with ease have been formed and prepared for further operations. But from the outset neglect and incompetence were apparent, and neutralised at every turn the high qualities of the troops and the ability and courage of the subordinate generals. In regard to the supply of food to the army, the gravest errors were made. Rations for immediate use should, of course, have been carried by the brigades as they landed; and it had been intended that each man should have three days' food in his haversack, but no definite order had been given on the subject. Few had any provision made for them, and in default of instructions it was expected that the commissaries would meet all wants on shore. Reliance was placed also for the subsequent supply of meat on the herds of cattle which the country nourished, but it was forgotten that these half-wild animals could not easily be caught, and that they could only be brought to the butcher by men skilled in the use of the American lasso. No such men were attached to the various columns, which, with ample supply of meat constantly in view, were thus for the most part condemned to want.

The disembarkation was completed on the 28th, but none of the troops left the shore on that day, except the brigades of Craufurd and Auchmuty. The general forward movement began on the 29th, and

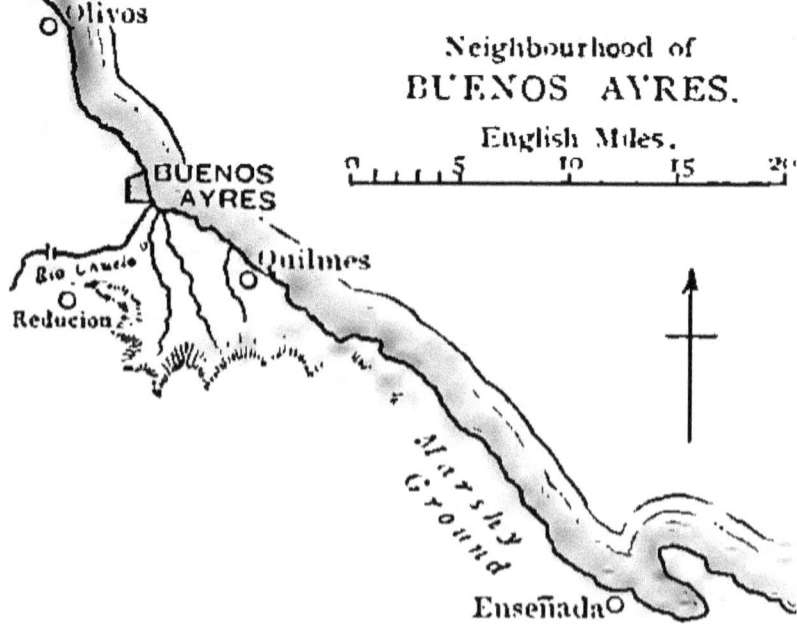

there was considerable trouble in passing the morass, some of the troops having to march for three miles up to their knees in mud and water. The artillery also were much delayed, only four field-pieces being dragged through the morass by the strenuous exertions of seamen and soldiers. Of the remaining guns only eight were subsequently brought to the front; the others were either destroyed, or left at Ensenada for want of means of movement.

The 30th June and 1st July were days of unrelieved toil and effort. The country was cut up by streams and swampy spots, and if opposition had been offered, it would have been much aided by these features; but no enemy was seen, except some detached bands of horsemen which hovered round, ready to cut off any fatigued straggler from the English columns. Craufurd still led the way, followed by Lumley's brigade, while the main body, with General Whitelocke, brought up the rear. Some of the men suffered terribly under the broiling sun, as, having been cooped up on board ship for months, they were in no condition for marching, and, ill-supplied with food from the uncertain sources which chance threw

BUENOS AYRES. 1807.

Scale of One Mile.

Churches.
1. Cathedral.
2. Santa Catalina.
3. San Domingo.

in their way, their strength was still further reduced by hunger. So general was the fatigue that on the afternoon of the 1st the men were ordered to throw away their blankets, as it was intended to push on that day to the village of Reducion. It was considered likely that there the enemy would hold the strong position, and would have to be driven from it by force. This village—about seven miles from Buenos Ayres—was, however, occupied easily, and the advanced brigades pushed through it to some high ground two miles further. Here their eyes were gladdened by the view of the city which they had come so far to attack, and which they hoped would ere long reward them amply for all their toils and privations. General Whitelocke, with the remainder of the army, occupied Reducion, and the night was passed without serious annoyance from the enemy, though the troops suffered greatly from exposure to a prolonged thunderstorm with heavy rain.

Between Reducion and Buenos Ayres, and about two miles from the former place, flows the Chuelo, a river which is fordable at few spots, and in the month of July, after the usual rains of the season, a very formidable military obstacle. Across it there was, in 1807, only one bridge, and from the English outposts could be seen the bivouac fires of a strong force evidently guarding this passage. Information was also received that the Spaniards had there constructed strong and well-armed batteries, and had concentrated a large number of men, in the expectation that the invaders would have no choice but to attack them. General Whitelocke appears to have had no very definite plan of action in his mind, and we may gather that, rather from a reluctance to engage in the assault of a strong position than from a well-studied strategical scheme, he resolved to seek for a ford said to exist farther up the river, instead of forcing his way by the direct route across the bridge.

At sunrise on the 2nd July the English force was under arms. Craufurd's and Lumley's brigades took the advance, as before, under the command of General Gower, to be followed by the main body of the army under General Whitelocke. Ascending the course of the Chuelo in search of a ford concerning which vague information had been received, reliance had to be placed in guides of doubtful trustworthiness, and there was uncertainty as to the objects of the march and the time it might be expected to require. Early in the day about 500 of the enemy's cavalry appeared, barring the road to the head of the column; but threatened in flank by the Rifles, and having received two or three rounds from the field-pieces, these quickly gave way, and were no more seen. It was not till half-past three in the afternoon that, following a scarcely distinguishable track which led to the river's bank, General Craufurd arrived at the sought-for ford, which even when found seemed to demand no ordinary hardihood to attempt its passage. At this place—the Passa Chico—the Chuelo ran thirty yards wide and four feet deep. Fortunately, the current was not rapid, and the bottom was a firm gravel. Craufurd's men, led by their impetuous general, plunged in, and, carrying the ammunition-waggon of the field-pieces shoulder high, safely effected the crossing.

Lumley's brigade followed. As the men were now formed in close proximity to the yet unseen enemy, with a formidable obstacle in their rear making retreat difficult, if not impossible, anxious eyes were directed over the extensive plain that had been passed, in the expectation of seeing the main body of the army following in support under General Whitelocke. Great was the wonder, bitter the disappointment, when no distant cloud of dust, no flash of steel, showed the appearance of the troops which should have been now closing on the advanced brigades. General Whitelocke had failed to preserve the communication with Lumley and Craufurd, and when the first serious encounter with the enemy was impending, either through incompetence or a more disgraceful motive, held himself aloof from the clash of arms.

About three-quarters of a mile from the ford which had just been crossed rose a long ridge of rising ground, and towards that ridge a strong column of the enemy could be seen moving as if with the intention of taking up a position of defence. The soldier's eye of Craufurd detected the danger which would result to the English from this movement if it was carried out, and he resolved to forestall it. General Gower gave him permission to act as he thought best, and promised to support him with Lumley's brigade. The light troops sprang forward, and the heights were quickly occupied without opposition. The enemy, confused and staggered by Craufurd's rapidity and dash, were obliged to forego their intention, and to seek another position still nearer to Buenos Ayres. The ground now became extremely intricate, covered with peach orchards and high fences; and the advanced parties of Rifles, threading their way through these obstacles, exchanged shots with the enemy's picquets, who were quickly driven in.

General Gower sent an order to Craufurd to halt; but, having his foe at last within striking distance, and confident in his judgment of the situation, that daring chief was not to be stopped on the threshold of success. Still he urged on the Light Brigade till the enclosures were

passed, and the great open space of the Coral was reached, the slaughtering-place or abattoir of the town. Lumley's brigade had now been far outstripped, but General Gower himself joined Craufurd. Not a Spaniard was to be seen. The advanced parties which had covered the forward movement of the English had fallen back, the column was halted for a breathing-space, and the generals with the staff-officers pushed along the broad road leading towards the city. Suddenly from cover on the other side of the Coral burst forth a discharge of grape and round shot. The Spanish position was developed, and

it was evident that the foe were here in strength, though their numbers were still hidden. There was a moment of surprise, almost of recoil, among the English, and General Gower made a suggestion to Craufurd about turning the enemy's flank. But this was no moment for a fine display of tactics, no occasion for well-regulated manoeuvre. Craufurd interpreted General Gower's words by the light of his own bold spirit, and he ordered a general direct charge. Undeterred by their ignorance of the strength before them, shaking off the fatigue of a long and toilsome march, the gallant Rifles and light battalion responded gladly to the call, and, cheering as they advanced, swept forward in irresistible assault. The South American Spaniards were not the men to meet the stern line of levelled bayonets, and everywhere gave way in panic-struck flight, leaving in the hands of the victors twelve pieces of artillery, with which their position had been armed. The Light Brigade followed hard in pursuit, and, firing no shot, smote the rearmost with the *arme blanche* alone. No halt was made till the outskirts of Buenos Ayres were reached, and at the very entrance to the streets Craufurd re-formed his men, who, flushed and excited with their prompt success, had fallen into some natural disorder.

Then was the time when Buenos Ayres should have fallen. A resolute advance at the heels of its disheartened and flying defenders would, it is very certain, have crushed every attempt at opposition, and the morning of the 3rd July ought to have seen the English flag again floating proudly over the town. If General Whitelocke, with the main body of his army, had followed closely the advanced brigades, and had now been at hand, no other blow need have been struck, no other shot fired.' If even General Gower had shared in a small degree the military insight and boiling courage of General Craufurd, and had boldly entered the streets with Lumley's brigade and Craufurd's light troops, the result would have been almost equally certain. But Whitelocke was still far distant, and, despite Craufurd's strongly-expressed opinion and readiness to crown the work so well commenced, General Gower resolved to do no more for the time. The advanced brigades were withdrawn to the Coral, and only picquets were left to mark the points where the tide of pursuit had been stayed, and whence the Rifles and light battalion, much against their will, had been ordered to fall back.

As the English soldiers lay upon their arms, the bivouac that night was wretched in the extreme. Overpowered with fatigue and hunger—for they had had no food for more than twelve hours—without fire or shelter, and drenched with tropical rains, believing, moreover, that if it had not been for the shortcomings of their generals they would even then be in Buenos Ayres, their cheerfulness was sustained by the hope that the entry into the town was only delayed till it could be effected by daylight on the following morning. But already the only gleam of success that was to shine upon the army in South America had died away, and nothing but disaster was left for the future.

Hopes were still entertained that General Whitelocke, with the main body of the army, must be near at hand, and would soon join the advanced brigades, and reconnoitring parties were sent out to try to establish communication with him. It was not, however, till the afternoon of the 3rd that—too late to profit by the discouragement which existed among the Spaniards on the evening of the 2nd— he made his appearance. He had not followed where the brigades of Craufurd and Lumley had led across the Chuelo by the Passa Chico; but, making a long detour of thirty miles, he had passed the river much higher up its course, and now brought in his men wearied with unnecessary toil, and, still worse, showing signs of discontent and loss of confidence.

In the morning of the 3rd General Gower sent a staff-officer into the town under a flag of truce, summoning General Liniers, commanding the Spanish forces, to surrender the place. But the panic of the previous evening had passed away and the answer returned was, "We possess sufficient strength and courage to defend our town." Closely following this answer came an attack in force upon the English picquets, who were obliged to give way until they were supported;

and after a desultory action lasting nearly two hours, in which both sides suffered some loss, the Spaniards again retired into the town.

Though General Whitelocke had now his army concentrated, though every hour added to the confidence of the enemy, and though delay seriously impaired the power of his own troops, both by the material losses which it involved and by the discouragement which it inevitably brought, the English general appears to have been in a painful state of indecision or irresolution. No plan of action was undertaken, and the Spaniards were able at will to insult and press upon the picquets, acting under cover of outlying houses, and to inflict losses for which adequate retaliation was difficult, if not impossible. Like the 3rd of July, the 4th was also allowed to pass in inaction, and it was not till the 5th that any forward movement was made.

The town of Buenos Ayres was, in 1807, about two miles in length by one in breadth. Its streets were rectangular, and the greater part of the houses were lofty, well-built, with roofs surrounded by parapets about four feet high. In the centre of the town was the castle, a small and feeble work, and near it was the great square. La Plaza. The principal buildings were, at the west end, El Retiro, the amphitheatre for bull-fights, and, at the east end of the town, an extensive building called Residentia, originally intended to be a royal hospital, and the church and monastery of St. Domingo. As has been told, the Spaniards on the night of the 2nd July were in a state of the utmost terror and confusion, prepared, if the English troops marched in, to receive them as conquerors. But the delays of Generals Whitelocke and Gower gave them time to recollect themselves, General Liniers exerted himself energetically to restore their courage, and, well seconded by his officers and by the clergy, whose aid he had invoked, he changed the spirit of the population from a weak and pusillanimous despair to a stern and patriotic determination to defend their town to the last. Active measures for defence were taken. Trenches were cut in the principal streets, cannon were placed in position, the slaves were armed, and even the women were inspired to assist in the coming struggle by throwing grenades from the housetops on hostile troops which might march below. The total number of defenders consisted of about 9,000 regulars, militia, and volunteer corps, all in some state of discipline, and about 5,000 men, formed in irregular companies, who had taken up arms for the occasion.

It has been told that the 3rd and 4th of July were allowed to slip away without any forward action being taken by General Whitelocke.

On the afternoon of the 4th, however, orders were issued for a general assault upon Buenos Ayres on the following morning. The available force was now, owing to losses and to the number of troops on various detachments, under 8,000 strong. No definite tactical plan appears

to have been formed. Objective points were indeed indicated to the commanders of columns, but the mutual relation which these points, if gained, were to bear to each other for assistance and support was entirely overlooked. No arrangements were made for communication

between the various portions of the force employed, or for receiving or asking for orders from the commander-in-chief. Above all, no lines of retreat were decided on in case resistance should be met too powerful to be overcome, and no reserve was kept conveniently at hand to support a success or neutralise a repulse. For the assault of a large town, held by a force of fair troops in addition to a numerous armed and fanatical population, the small army of attackers was divided into eight feeble columns, which were to enter the streets at different widely-separated points, without reasonably full instructions as to the general plan of the commander-in-chief, without cohesion as parts of one military body, and, except for a few entrenching tools, without any means of forcing the obstacles which might have been expected to be met with. On the morning of Sunday, the 5th July, the troops were under arms at four o'clock, and they hoped, at least, that they should have been let loose upon their task while darkness in some degree veiled their advance; but the sun was rising ere the signal was given to commence the attack, and the columns were put in motion.

Space does not permit that a detailed account should be given of the operations of each column. All did not encounter an equal amount of resistance, but everywhere the resistance was of the same character. Heavy fire was maintained from the roofs of the houses. Hand-grenades, stink-balls, brickbats, and other missiles were hurled from above on the English soldiers as they advanced. Breastworks, made of hide bags filled with earth, and deep ditches cut across the streets gave cover to the defence, while artillery opened a deadly discharge of grape at close range. Ever as the points were reached on which they had been directed the columns found themselves surrounded. The men through whom they had forced their way had again closed in, and they were circled by a ring of fire. On the left of the attack Sir Samuel Auchmuty, with the 87th and 38th, had bored his way, though with heavy loss, to El Retiro, and there established himself, taking a number of prisoners and three field-pieces, nor was the enemy able again to dislodge him. The 5th Infantry also penetrated to the convent of St. Catalina. The 36th made their way in the face of determined opposition as far as the beach of the Rio de la Plata, and their movement was signalised by the gallant conduct of Lieutenant-Colonel Byrne, who, with fifty men, charged and took two guns, driving their defenders, 300 strong, before him. Part of the regiment then managed to join Auchmuty, and the remainder, finding no tenable position in which to establish themselves, were obliged to retire. The 88th, acting in two wings under Lieutenant-Colonel Duff and Major Vandeleur, suffered almost more heavily than any other portion of the army. They fought with the brilliant courage which has always marked the "Connaught Rangers;" but exposed, outnumbered, with no hope of assistance, and having lost 17 officers and 220 rank-and-file, they were obliged to surrender at discretion.

The greatest disaster, the most overwhelming loss, was, however, suffered at the right centre. Here was the fiery Craufurd with the Light Brigade, which had already shown such undaunted determination, such a formidable warrior spirit. It was formed in two columns, of which the right was commanded by Craufurd himself and the left by Lieutenant-Colonel Pack, afterwards Sir Dennis Pack, the famous hero of the Peninsula. Craufurd had been ordered to make his way through the town to the Rio de la Plata, and to occupy any high buildings as near as possible to La Plaza. Two three-pounder field-pieces accompanied his brigade, and, though the victims of continuous musketry fire from the housetops, and the flanking discharge of artillery from their left front, they reached the great church of St. Domingo. By this time, besides the many losses in the main body of Craufurd's column, the officer commanding and the greater portion of the advanced guard had been laid low. It was essential to secure some cover from the withering storm of bullets, some post of vantage which might possibly be made good against the enemy, and serve as a base from which further operations might be undertaken, if the rest of the army had closed upon the city with the success which was hoped for. The door of the St. Domingo church was battered in and the building occupied. Unfortunately, its roof was sloping, and afforded no secure military position, as did the flat roofs of the surrounding houses, from which the Spaniards were still able to pour in a destructive and unceasing fire. Lieutenant- Colonel Guard, with the Grenadier company of the 45th, now joined Craufurd, and till twelve o'clock in the day there was no reason to believe that the rest of the army had not been also successful in establishing themselves close to the enemy's main position. At that hour, however, 1 Spanish officer with a flag of truce approached. Craufurd thought that he had come from General Liniers with an offer to capitulate. Bitter was his disappointment when the Spaniard informed him that the 88th had been taken prisoners, and summoned him to surrender. Craufurd could not believe that he had been abandoned by General Whitelocke, and still thought that if he could not be supported, at least some attempt would be made to com-

municate with him. He feared to compromise the whole situation of the army, and returned a peremptory refusal to General Linier's summons. As time wore on, however, it became more and more apparent that no succour was to be hoped for, and he resolved to take the first opportunity of withdrawing from the town. If a large number of the enemy could be engaged in the streets, Craufurd thought that the fire from the houses would be neutralised, as the Spaniards would be afraid of hitting their own friends. A considerable column of the enemy was now entering the street on the west side of the church, apparently intending to seize one of the English field-pieces which had been left outside the building. The Rifles were ordered to form up ready for a sally, and while they were doing so the enemy's column was gallantly attacked by Lieutenant-Colonel Guard with the Grenadiers of the 45th, and by a small party of light infantry under Major Trotter. The column gave way, but the fire from the surrounding houses was so severe that Major Trotter and about forty of the attackers were killed or wounded in two or three minutes. It was evidently impossible to retire, and there was nothing for it but to continue the defence of the church, hoping against hope for some favourable turn of events.

At half-past three there could be no longer any doubt that the attack on Buenos Ayres had failed. His men were falling fast, the enemy were bringing heavy guns into position to batter the church, and Craufurd felt that further sacrifice of life could not be of any advantage. Repugnant to his brave spirit as was the duty, he surrendered himself, with the shattered remnants of his brigade, as prisoners of war at four o'clock.

It only remains to tell how it fared with the right of the English attack on Buenos Ayres. The 45th Regiment, on the extreme right, under Lieutenant-Colonel Guard, obtained possession of Residencia, after meeting with some opposition from a body of Spaniards stationed with some artillery in an open space. The guns were soon abandoned, however, and, there being no resistance from the neighbouring houses, the extensive building was crowned with the colours of the regiment. Lieutenant-Colonel Guard then, as has been seen, joined General Craufurd with his Grenadiers, and shared the fate of the Light Brigade. Major Nicholls was left in command at Residencia, and, though the Spaniards made repeated attempts to recover the building, he maintained his post by skilful defence and occasional sallies, in one of which he took four pieces of cannon. Between the 45th and the Light Brigade, the *carabiniers* entered the town and penetrated some distance, but they were unable to overcome the resistance which they encountered and were forced to retire after severe loss, Captain Burrell being among the killed and Colonel Kington severely wounded.

The result of the disastrous 5th July was that the English army lost above 70 officers and 1,000 men, killed or badly wounded, and 120 officers and 1,500 men were taken prisoners. Abandoned by their chief—who took no active part in the day's operations, who gave no command, who had shown no forethought, and who failed to afford either counsel or example—the subordinate leaders and the men of the various columns had fought with a bravery and discipline worthy of the best traditions of the English army. If disgrace and shame there was, at least their honour was untainted, their valour had shown itself to be unquestionable. But, though General Whitelocke's army failed not in doing its best to accomplish a task given to them in a manner which rendered it impossible of fulfilment, they would not have been men if they had not felt acutely and expressed emphatically their mortification and disgust at the way in which they had been commanded. Craufurd himself publicly called Whitelocke a traitor, and even told his men to shoot him dead if he was seen in the battle; and Sir Samuel Auchmuty afterwards said that the soldiers of his column had so greatly lost confidence, and were speaking of their general in such terms, that he did not think they were to be relied upon for further effort under his command.

General Whitelocke put the seal to the story of his ineptitude and disgrace by making a treaty with the Spanish leaders, giving up all the advantages which had previously been gained on the Rio de la Plata, and engaging to withdraw from and deliver up the town and fortress of Monte Video. He only stipulated for an unimpeded retreat and embarkation, and that all the prisoners of war should be restored. In January, 1808, General Whitelocke was tried by court-martial at Chelsea Hospital, and was sentenced "to be cashiered, and declared totally unfit and unworthy to serve His Majesty in any military capacity whatever."

So keen and widespread was the national and military feeling of indignation at the way in which the South American campaign had been conducted that, for long after that period, the common toast in canteens and public-houses was, "Success to *grey hairs*, but bad luck to *white locks!*"

FEBRURY 7-8 AND JUNE 14, 1807
Eylau and Friedland
H. Sutherland Edwards

The battles of Eylau and Friedland were closely connected with one another and with the Treaty of Tilsit (July 7th, 1807), to which they led. At the beginning of 1807 it seemed that the destinies of Europe were about to be decided on the shores of the Baltic, where a mighty struggle was pending between the resources and genius of the North in conflict with those of the South; between Alexander, Emperor of Russia, and the King of Prussia on the one part, and on the other Napoleon—or "Bonaparte" as he was then called—Emperor of France and King of Italy. The latter derived support from the nations hg had subdued: Italy, Spain, Holland, and a great portion of Germany. The former were dependent, in a measure, on the goodwill and co-operation of Great Britain and Sweden. The Battle of Eylau, however—the first in which Napoleon received a check, though not a defeat—was fought by the armies of Russia and Prussia against those of Imperial France.

The Russians in a general sense occupied, as they always must in conflict with the nations of the West, a very advantageous position; for, even if unsuccessful, they could be sure, in their retreat, of drawing the enemy into an inhospitable and barren country, while they on their side would be able to obtain both reinforcements and supplies. The battle of Eylau was claimed both by the French and by the Russians as a decisive victory; though it really decided nothing. Napoleon's immediate object in attacking the Russians was to drive them back, and advancing upon Königsberg occupy the ancient capital of Prussia and seize the king; which he failed to do. But the more important aim of

the Russians and Prussians was to drive the French from the country they had invaded; and towards this result they made no effective step. The French at the end of the second day's fighting occupied the field

of battle, tended the enemy's wounded, buried the dead, and remained in their positions for upwards of a week; after which they returned, unmolested, to winter quarters.

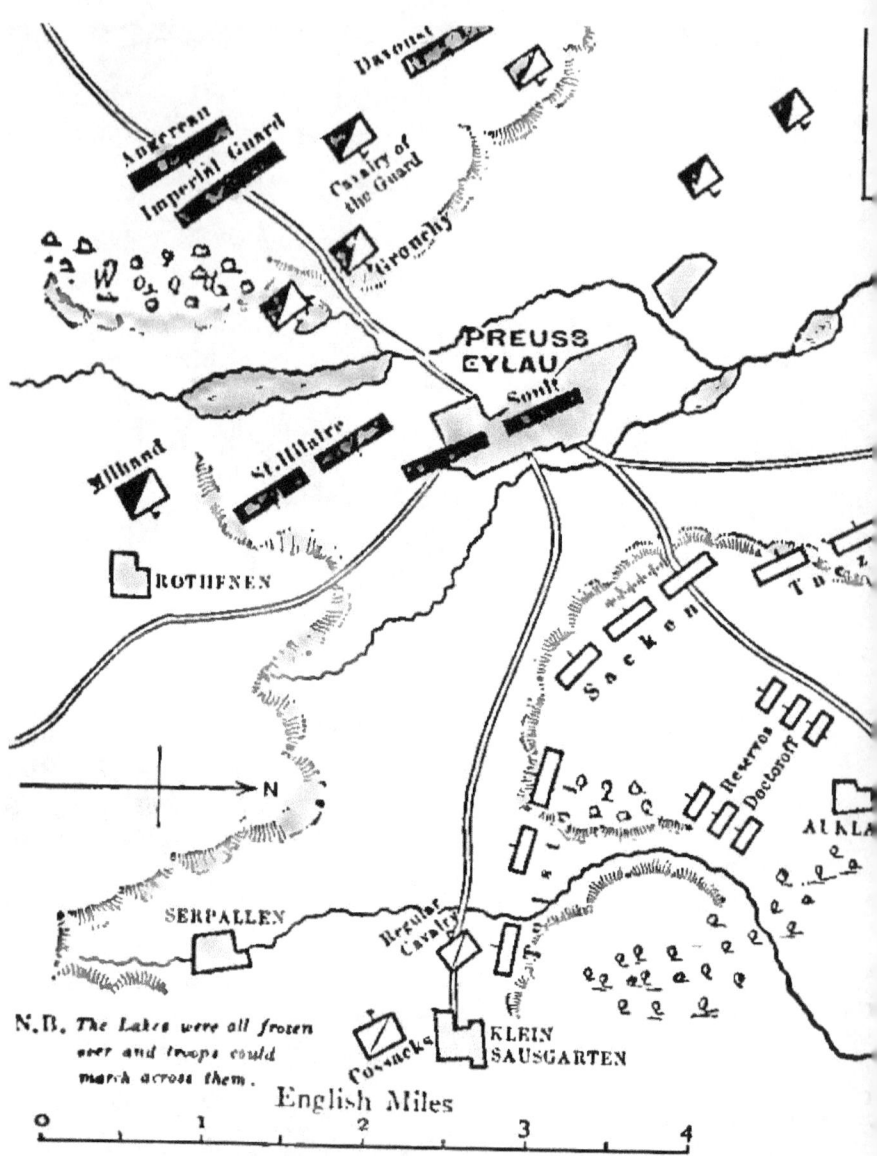

In numbers the French were superior to the enemy, in the proportion of 75,000 to 70,000; but they had the climate against them, and Napoleon found but little opportunity of employing his infantry. This can scarcely be taken into account in reckoning up the opposing forces. But as a matter of fact, the battle was won by the French cavalry and artillery; and in both these arms, Napoleon was stronger than the allies. Though Napoleon's infantry took but little part in the action,

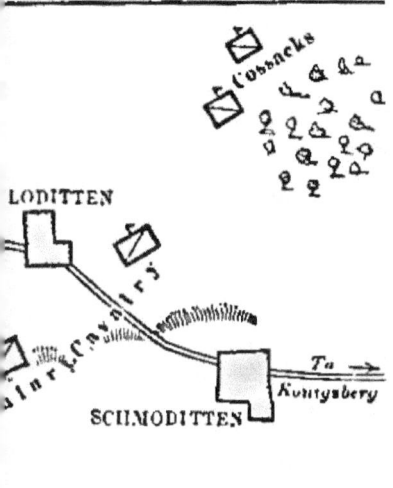

tions are those occupied on the of Feb. 7. 1807: The French in on the ground from which they ven the Russian rearguard. The is on the ground on which they the French attack next morning.

CAMPAIGN OF 1807
English Miles
0   50   100

one particular regiment, the 25th, suffered so severely that it lost nearly the whole of its officers. "To the officers of the 25th regiment," says the brief monumental inscription recording the fact. One other peculiarity of this remarkable battle may be noted: some of the Tartar regiments in the Russian army were armed with bows and arrows—to the great amusement, it is said, of the French artillery. An English publicist, writing soon afterwards of this sanguinary encounter, found cause for satisfaction in the fact that although our political interests demanded the defeat of the French, the troops of civilisation had shown themselves able to put back the northern hordes. Considering, however, that the French were superior in numbers to the Russians, that they were better armed, and that they were commanded by Napoleon in person (whose presence on the field was estimated by Wellington as equivalent to an additional forty thousand men), the wonder is that the Russians, who formed the bulk of the allied army, were able not only to hold their ground against the French for two successive days, but when they at last retired, to do so without being seriously pursued. For if at the end of two days' fighting the French occupied the field of battle, they took care not to advance beyond it.

After the fatal day of Jena, King Frederic William of Prussia found himself reduced to one province and 25,000 soldiers. He and his court retired to Königsberg, there anxiously to await the arrival of the Russians; and no sooner had Prussia's powerful allies come within reach than Napoleon prepared to attack them. After several reconnaissances in force and partial encounters, Napoleon by a skilful and formidable flank movement forced Benningsen, the Russian commander-in-chief, to retreat to Eylau, a small

town on the Pasmar, about twenty-two miles south-east of Königsberg. Marshal Soult, in rapid pursuit, entered the place at the head of his corps almost at the same time as the Russians. A collision took place in and around the Eylau cemetery, where the fighting was kept up with fury on both sides for several hours, until night came on. The Russians then fell back behind the town, but lighting their camp fires, showed that they had no intention of retreating further. They evidently meditated a renewal of the conflict on the following morning.

Napoleon lost no time in ordering Marshals Ney and Davoust to take up their positions—the former on his left, the latter on his right; and Davoust was on the right of the French early the next morning, ready to fall upon the Russian flank. Ney's corps, however, being at some distance, it was impossible to communicate with him in time for the next day's battle.

On the following morning, February 8th, the Russians commenced the attack with a brisk cannonade on the village or town of Eylau, held only by one division under St. Hilaire. To the emperor's military eye a hill commanding the town presented itself as the most important object of attack. Until this was carried the centre of the army would be unable to act offensively against the enemy, for it would be impossible to execute the necessary operations of extending it in the plains. Marshal Augereau was therefore ordered to advance with his corps and to open a cannonade against this commanding spot. He was suffering from rheumatism and fever; and unable to sit firmly on horseback, had caused himself to be strapped to the saddle. He directed, however, a vigorous artillery-fire upon the key of the position; and the armies being now within short distance of one another, every shot took effect. The slaughter was terrific. At one moment it appeared from the movements of the Russians that, impatient of suffering so much without any decisive result, they wished to outflank the French on the left wing. But at that moment Marshal Davoust's sharpshooters appeared, and fell on their rear. Upon this Augereau's corps filed off in columns to attack and occupy the centre of the Russian army, which might otherwise have overwhelmed Davoust by its superior numbers. At the same time the division commanded by General St. Hilaire filed

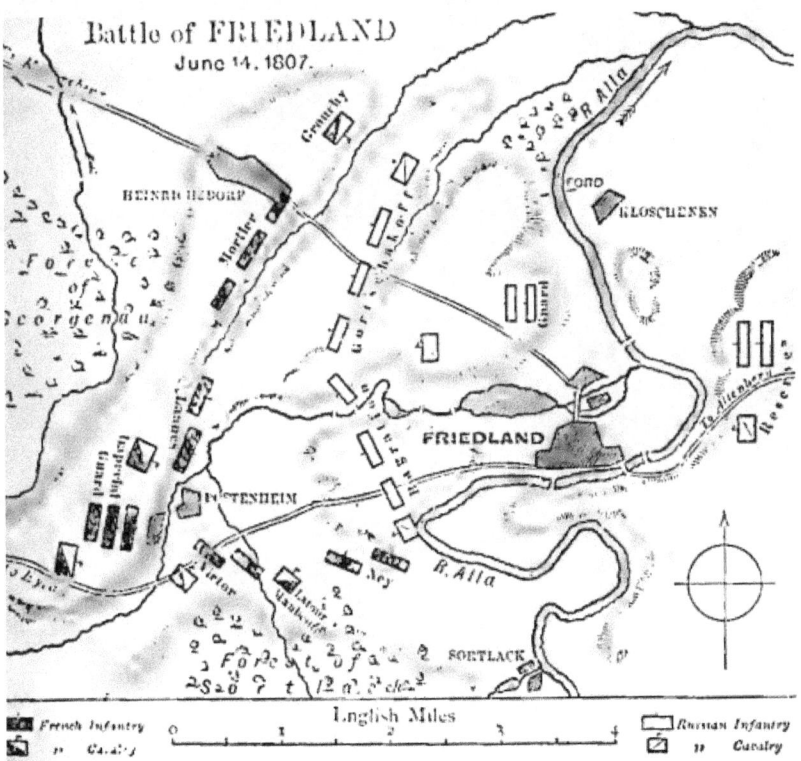

off to the right in support of Davoust, and in order to facilitate eventually a junction between Davoust and Augereau.

No sooner had these movements been begun than so thick a fall of snow covered the two armies that neither could see beyond the

distance of two feet. The point of direction was lost, and the French columns, inclining too much to the left, wandered about in uncertainty. This darkness lasted half an hour. When the weather cleared up, 20,000 Russian infantry, supported by cavalry and artillery, were on the point of executing a turning movement, with the view of cutting off the division of General St. Hilaire. The French Army was in the most critical position. It was without cohesion. Its columns were straggling about in all directions, incapable of supporting one another. Many superior officers, including Augereau, had been wounded. The latter, assisted into Napoleon's presence, complained bitterly of not having been adequately supported.

Napoleon saw the danger, and calling for Murat, said to him: "Are you going to let us be devoured by these people?" He then ordered a grand charge to be executed by the cavalry of the whole army. Eighty squadrons took part in it, and the masses of French horsemen broke through the lines of the Russian army, to sabre the enemy right and left. The Russian cavalry, in endeavouring to oppose this movement,

were routed with great slaughter. But it was the Russian infantry, against which the charge had been directly made, that especially suffered. Its two massive lines were utterly broken. The third, falling back, rested for support upon a wood.

The fortune, however, of the battle was not much changed until Davoust, whose progress had been greatly impeded by the weather, was at last enabled to fall on the rear of the enemy and drive them from the hilly ground. The Russians, after repeated attempts to regain the ground they were constantly losing, beat a retreat, leaving behind them masses of killed and wounded and a portion of their artillery.

The battle seemed won. But at this moment took place what Napoleon had been constantly fearing might occur: the arrival on the scene of a Prussian force, from 7,000 to 8,000 strong, under General Lestocq. The Prussian commander was being pursued by Marshal Ney. But he

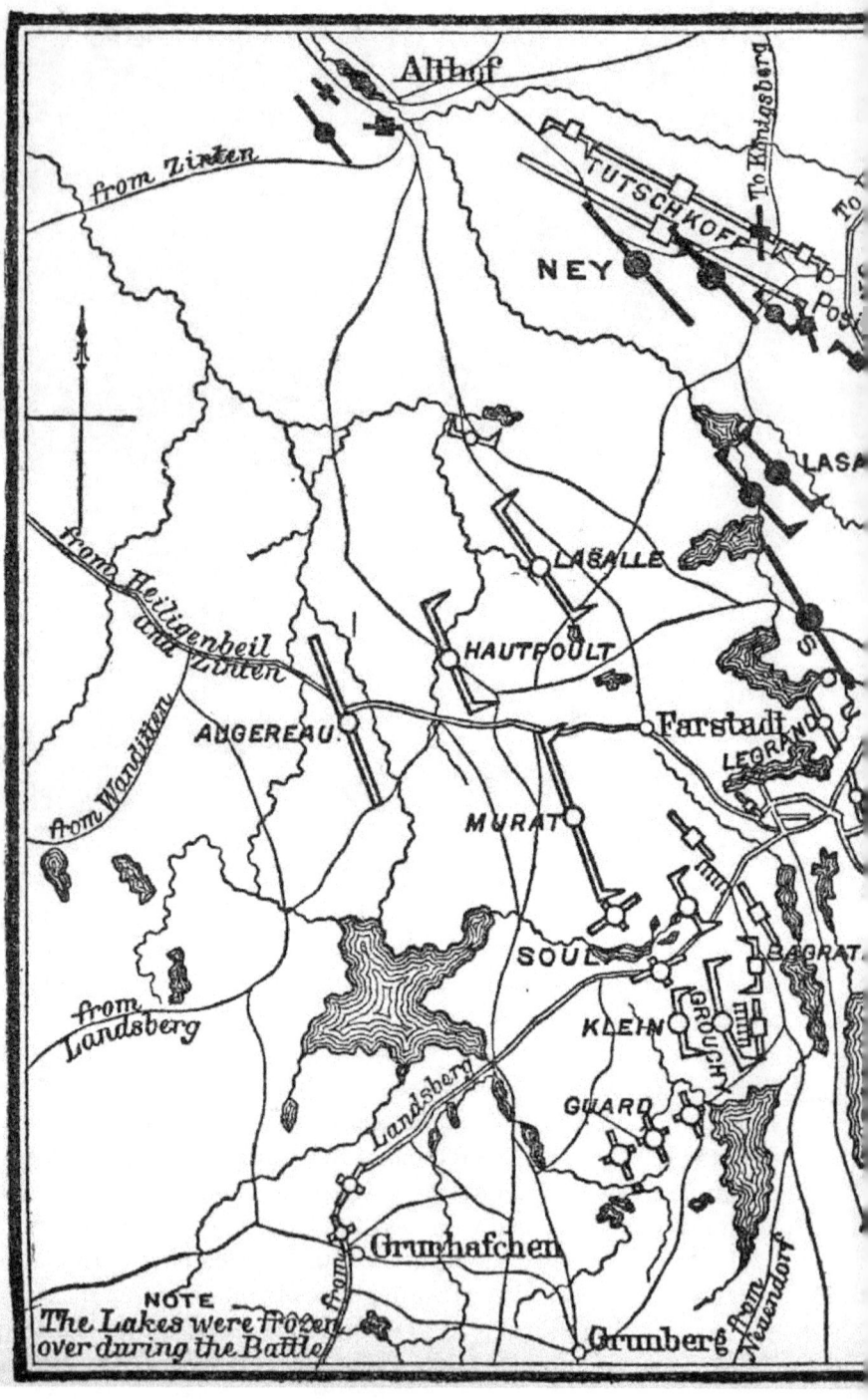

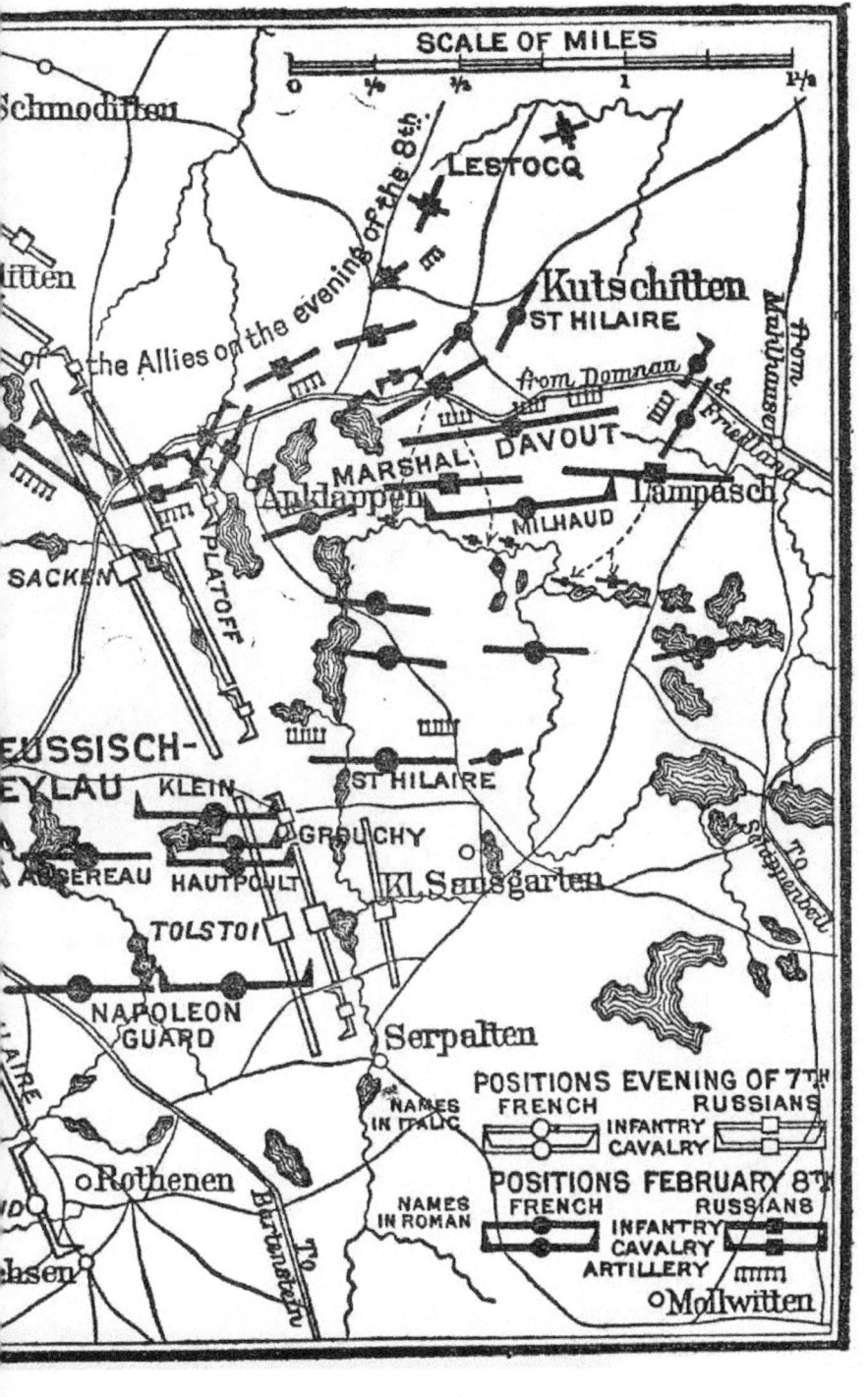

was some two or three hours ahead of his enemy, and the battle would certainly be decided before Ney could come up. The rapid entry into action of new troops has often had a determining effect upon a battle of which the issue was previously doubtful. The part played by the Prussians at Waterloo, by the French at Inkerman, are cases in point. But eight years before Waterloo the sudden appearance of Prussian reinforcements at Eylau had no effect, except perhaps to modify the character of the French victory and of the Russian defeat. But for the assistance rendered by the Prussians, the French might have routed the Russians and executed the meditated advance upon Königsberg. As it was, General Lestocq held the French to some extent in check; and the balance had in some measure been restored between the contending forces, when

Benningsen, just as he was proposing a final attack, received news of the approach of Ney, who was about to fall on his left flank as Davoust had previously turned his position on the right. A final retreat was now ordered, and Benningsen was at least able to boast that his line of retreat was the one chosen by himself. He marched, that is to say, in the direction of Königsberg without being seriously pursued by Napoleon, who throughout the battle had kept Königsberg constantly in view, and more than once had sought to encourage his troops by pointing to the just visible steeples of the ancient Prussian capital.

It had been the design of Bonaparte to take Königsberg, but he was forced to fall back on the Vistula. It had been the design of the Russians to drive back the French beyond the Vistula, to retake Ebling and Thorn, and to force them to raise the sieges of Colberg, Gaudenz, and, above all, Danzig. But by a series of successive actions they were themselves driven back by the French as far as Eylau, and, on the day after the great battle, beyond the Pregel.

Sixty-three years later, a similar question arose as to which side had gained the victory in a battle fought at Bapaume, in the north of France, between the French under General Faidherbe and the Germans under General von Goeben. The French drove back the Germans, and occupied at night the positions held by the Germans in the morning. This looked like victory. But the object, said General von Goeben, of the French attack was to break through the German lines and march towards Paris for the relief of the siege; and this the French did not do.

The doubtful victory of Eylau not being sufficient for the emperor's glory, there was now no possibility of Napoleon's returning to Paris until after the accomplishment of an unmistakable conquest. Danzig, it is true, had fallen. But the Russian army was still in a threatening position, and had to be disposed of.

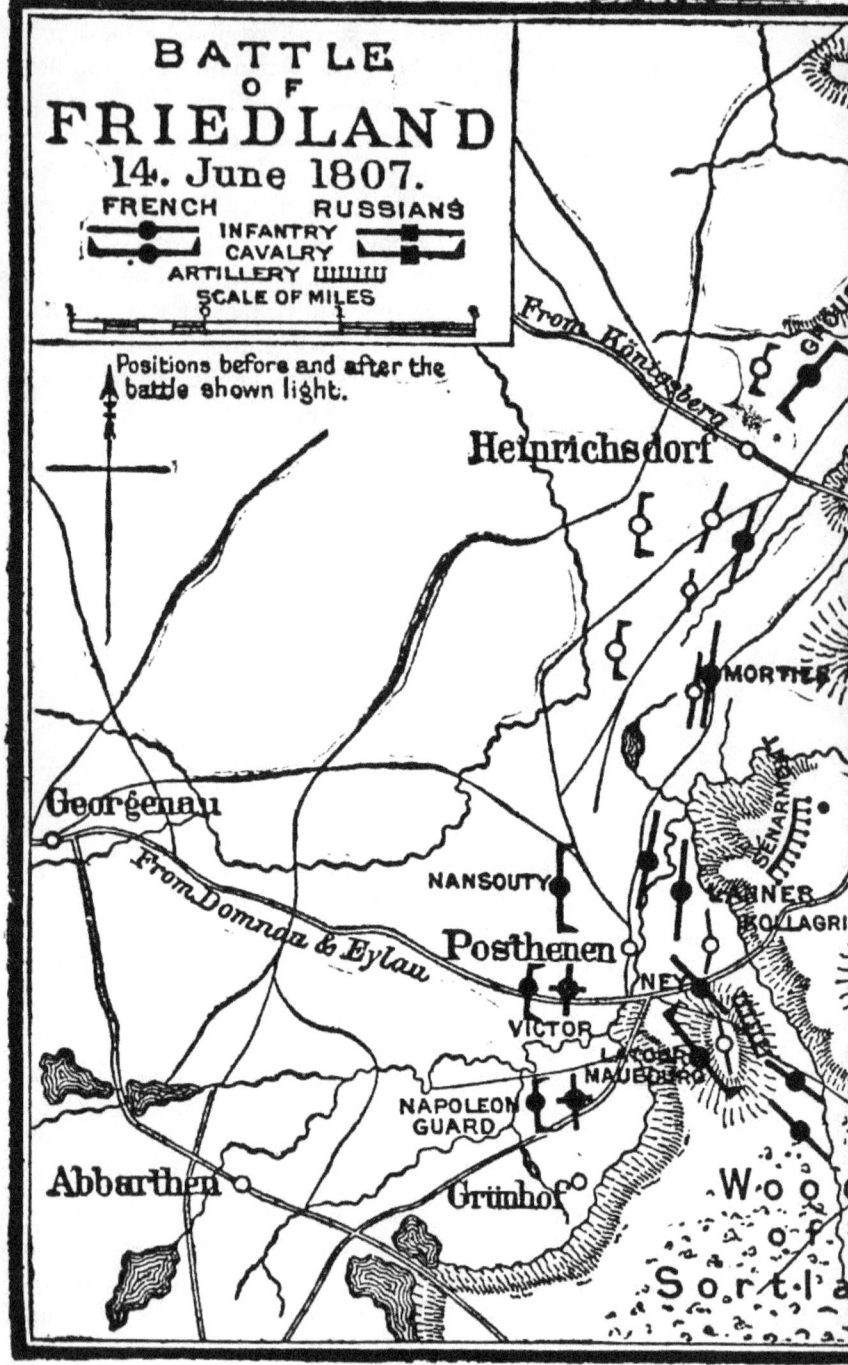

Napoleon's army, meanwhile, had been increased, through the fall of Danzig, by more than 30,000 men; and, though there was neither truce nor armistice, he did not take any immediate measures for opening the campaign and surprising the enemy, according to his usual system, by the promptitude and rapidity of his movements. He, on the contrary, manifested every symptom of a sincere and even somewhat earnest desire that hostilities might be, for the present, terminated by negotiation. Till this could be arranged, Napoleon seemed determined to remain on the defensive. The ambassadors attending his court at Finkenstein were witnesses of the proud eminence on which he now stood, and abundant care was taken that they should fully understand the importance of his recent conquest—the great bulwark of the Vistula. When the ambassador of the Porte was presented, on the 28th May, by the Prince of Benevento, Napoleon declared that he and the Sultan Selim would be forever after as inseparably connected as the right hand and the left. The offices and administration of the government were now transferred from Warsaw to Danzig, which seemed at this time to be intended for the capital of the French dominions in those parts. The recently captured city was visited on the 30th May by Napoleon, at the head of the greater part of his staff, together with his Minister for Foreign Affairs, and all his Court. The emperor reviewed his troops, and gave orders for the reparation of the works demolished in the course of the siege. General Rapp— a great favourite—was appointed governor, and Le Febvre created Duke of Danzig. Each soldier who had been engaged in the siege received a gratuity of ten francs.

In the meantime the light corps of the army advanced in various directions in order to pass the Russians, and get between them and their magazines, by cutting off their retreat to Königsberg; and soon afterwards the headquarters of the French army arrived at Eylau. Here the fields were no longer covered with ice and snow, but, on the contrary, presented one of the most beautiful scenes in Nature. The country was everywhere adorned with beautiful woods, intersected by lakes, and enlivened by handsome villages. On the 13th, while the Grand Duke of Berg and the Marshals Soult and Davoust had orders to manoeuvre in the direction of Königsberg, Napoleon, with the corps of Ney, Lannes, Mortier, the Imperial Guard, and the 1st Corps, commanded by General Victor, advanced on Friedland. On the same day the 9th regiment of Hussars entered that town, but was driven out of it again by 3,000 Russian cavalry. On the 14th the Russians advanced on the bridge of Friedland, with the intention of pursuing their march to Königsberg, and at three in the morning a cannonade was heard.

"It is a lucky day," said Napoleon; "it is the anniversary of the Battle of Marengo."

Different movements and actions now took place, by which the Russians were stopped on their march. A mighty struggle was una-

voidable, and both armies prepared for a decisive battle. By five in the evening, the several corps of the French were at their appointed stations. Marshal Ney was on the right wing, Marshal Lannes in the centre, and Marshal Mortier on the left. The corps of General Victor and the Guards formed the reserve. The cavalry, under the command of General Grouchy, supported the left wing; the division of dragoons of General La Tour Maubourg was stationed as a reserve behind the right; and General La Housay's division of dragoons, with the Saxon *cuirassiers*, formed a reserve for the centre. The whole of the Russian army was also drawn up in the best order that the place and circumstances seemed to admit. The left wing extended to the town of Friedland, and the right wing a league and a half in the other direction.

The position taken up by General Benningsen was apparently one continued plain, which, however, was intersected by a deep ravine full of water, and almost impassable. This ravine ran in a line between Domnow and Friedland, where it formed a lake to the left of that place, and separated the right wing of the Russians from their centre. A thick wood at the distance of about a mile and a half from Friedland, on more elevated ground, fringed the plain nearly in the form of a semicircle, except at its extremity on the left, where there was an open space between the wood and a narrow river. In front of the wood about a mile from the town of Friedland, and nearly opposite to the centre of the army, was the small village of Heinrichsdorf. The field of battle lay between the left of this village and the river, to the south of Friedland.

Bonaparte, having reconnoitred the position of the enemy, determined to take the town of Friedland. Suddenly changing his front and advancing his right, he commenced the attack with the advanced part of that wing. The firing of twenty cannon from a battery was the signal of battle. At the same moment the division under General Marchand, supported on the left by another division, advanced upon the enemy, the line of direction being towards the steeple of the town. When the Russians perceived that Marshal Ney had left the wood in which his left wing had been posted, they endeavoured to surround him with some regiments of regular cavalry and a multitude of Cossacks. But General La Tour Maubourg's division of dragoons rode up at full gallop to the right wing, and repelled the attack. In the meantime General Victor—who commanded, as has been mentioned, a corps of the Grand Army erected a battery of thirty cannon in the front of his centre; and his works, pushed forward more than four

hundred paces, greatly annoyed the Russians, whose various manoeuvres for producing a diversion were all in vain. Marshal Ney was at the head of his troops, directing the most minute movements with his characteristic intrepidity and coolness. Several Russian columns that had attacked his right wing were received on the point of the bayonet and driven into the river. Thousands were thus lost, though some escaped by swimming.

In the meantime Marshal Ney's left wing reached the ravine which surrounded the town of Friedland. But the Imperial Guard of Russia, horse and foot, had been placed there in ambush; and it now rushed suddenly on Marshal Ney's left wing, which for a moment wavered. Dupont's division, however, which formed the right of the reserve, fell on the Russian Imperial Guard and defeated it with great slaughter. Several other bodies were sent from the centre of the Russian army for the defence of the all-important position of Friedland. But the impetuosity, the numbers, and the prompt and skilful co-operation of the assailants with an immense artillery prevailed. Friedland was taken, and its streets bestrewed with dead bodies. The attempts of the Russians on the left wing of the French being defeated, they made repeated attacks on their centre. But all the efforts of their infantry and cavalry to obstruct the progress of the French columns were exerted in vain. Marshal Mortier, who during the whole day had exhibited the greatest coolness and intrepidity in supporting the left wing, now advanced, and was in his turn supported by the fusiliers of the Guard, under the command of General Savary. The French columns pressed forward on the Russians, chiefly along the sides of the ravine; which was thus as advantageous to the French as disadvantageous to the Russians. Victory, which had never, in the judgment of the French generals who drew up the bulletin, been for a moment doubtful, now declared decidedly in their favour.

The field of battle presented one of the most horrible spectacles of wounded, dying, and dead men and horses that was ever beheld. The number of the dead on the side of the Russians was estimated by the French at from 15,000 to 18,000, and that of the dead on their own side at less than 500. But they admitted that the number of their wounded amounted to 3,000. Eighty cannon and a great number of covered waggons and standards fell into the hands of the conquerors. The Russians were pursued in their retreat towards Königsberg till eleven o'clock. During the remainder of the night the cut-off columns endeavoured to pass, and part of them did pass, the river at several fordable places. But next day covered waggons, cannon, and harness were everywhere seen in the stream. The French bulletin says:

"The Battle of Friedland is worthy of being numbered with those of Marengo, Austerlitz, and Jena. The enemy were numerous, had fine cavalry, and fought bravely."

Next day, June the 15th, the Russians endeavoured to reassemble on the right bank of the river, while the French army manoeuvred on the left bank to cut them off from Königsberg. The heads of the hostile columns arrived at Wehlaw, a town situated at the confluence

of the Alia and the Pregel, nearly at the same time. The Russians at daybreak on the 16th passed the Pregel, and continued their retreat to the Niemen. The French bulletin says that:

"Having destroyed all the bridges, they took advantage of that obstacle to proceed on their retreat."

If, however, there were several bridges on the Pregel, they must (as was pointed out in reply) have left one at least standing till they had crossed the river themselves, though the French gazetteers would insinuate that they escaped only by means of the demolition of all the bridges.

The consistent and true account of the matter seems to be that which is given by an eyewitness of the campaign, who says that:

"At Wehlaw the Russian army passed the Pregel, without any loss or even annoyance, on a single bridge. A detachment of 4,000 French troops watched their movements, but did not oppose their retreat. The bridge was then burnt, and the Russians continued their retrograde movement to Pepelken, where they were rejoined by the Prussian corps under General Kaminskoy, who had been detached to Königsberg on the 10th, for after the defeat of the main Russian army Königsberg was untenable."

At eight in the morning Napoleon threw a bridge over the Pregel, and took up a position there with his army. Almost all the magazines which the enemy had on the Alia had been thrown into the river or burnt. At Wehlaw, however, the French found an immense quantity of corn. Possession was taken of Königsberg by the corps under Marshal Soult. At this place were found some hundred thousand quintals of corn, more than 20,000 wounded Russians and Prussians, and all the arms and ammunition that had been sent to the Russians by England, including 160,000 muskets that had not been landed. The French bulletin continued as follows:

"It was on the 5th of June, that the enemy renewed hostilities. Their loss in the ten days that followed their first operations may be reckoned at 60,000 men, killed, wounded, taken, or otherwise put *hors de combat*. They have lost a part of their artillery, almost all their ammunition, and the whole of their magazines on a line of more than forty leagues. The French armies have seldom obtained such great advantages with so little loss."

Over the conduct of this short campaign on the part of the Russians, as well as its commencement after the reduction of Danzig, there still hangs a mysterious cloud. After this important event, and the addition that was made to the French army by the liberation of between 30,000 and 40,000 fighting-men, it was universally supposed that General Benningsen would *"play the part of Fabius."* As the possession of Danzig and the peninsula of Nehrung gave great facilities to the French for turning the right flank of the Russian army on the north, it was supposed that instead of making an attack, he would fall back behind the Pregel, and support his right on Königsberg, where he would be nearer his resources, and the French further from theirs. Thus, also, time would have been afforded for the execution of those military plans which were projected in Swedish and Prussian Pomerania. The conduct of the Russian general, which had been so much extolled when his operations were supposed to have been successful, was now, as commonly happens to the unfortunate, severely condemned. The grounds of censure appear, indeed, to have been at least very plausible. But the world did not then know, nor do we now know, the whole of the case. That the Russians should have lost in the course of ten days 60,000 men, while the French had only about 1,200 killed and 5,000 or 6,000 wounded, appears so monstrous an exaggeration that even the policy of it may reasonably be questioned. Yet the losses and disasters of the Russians were admitted by themselves to have been immense. General Benningsen did not attempt to conceal the real situation of affairs after the battle of Friedland, as he had done after that of Eylau; and he did not hesitate to give it as his opinion that any further contest with the French on the field of battle would be hopeless.

It was computed by the most dispassionate and competent judges that the French commenced this short campaign of ten days with 160,000 men, including all kinds of troops stationed between the Oder and the Alia; and that the allies had about 100,000 effective men, infantry and cavalry, besides Cossacks, Bashkirs, and other irregular troops. It was acknowledged by French officers that from the 5th to the 14th June the Grand Army had lost in killed and wounded at least 20,000 men.

On the 19th, at 2 o'clock p.m., Bonaparte with his Guards entered Tilsit.

Although the Russians were completely beaten at Friedland, they had presented such an obstinate resistance both at Friedland and at Eylau that Napoleon now thought it worth his while to make peace with them in the first place at the expense of Prussia, Russia's powerless ally, and secondly at the expense of all Europe, with a special view to the injury of England. Overtures of peace were accordingly made, and the result was a meeting of the two emperors at Tilsit. Prussia was now entirely sacrificed, the king losing all his possessions, with the exception only of Memel. Without abandoning the Duchy of Warsaw, formed out of the Polish provinces taken from Prussia, to which was afterwards added the whole of western Galicia (the best part, that is to say, of Austrian Poland), Napoleon arranged, beyond doubt, with Alexander a partition of the continent of Europe. The treaty was, of course, not made public. But in reference to its provisions Napoleon in his speech to the Senate, in August, 1807, said:

"France is united to the people of Germany by the laws of the Confederation of the Rhine, to those of Spain, Holland, Switzerland, and Italy, by the laws of our federative system. Our new relations with Russia are cemented by the reciprocal esteem of these two grand nations."

Many were the stories told of the peaceful, conversational collisions between Napoleon and Alexander at Tilsit, sometimes during the conferences, often when the conferences were not taking place, and the two monarchs were talking privately together. Alexander declared himself a disbeliever in the hereditary principle, to which he owed everything. Napoleon, on the other hand, who had in no way profited by this principle, was its warm partisan.

Once when the French and Russian Emperors were walking out together, they met a French sentinel of the Imperial Guard, whose face was terribly disfigured.

"What do you think of soldiers" asked Napoleon, "who can survive such wounds?"

"And what do you," replied Alexander, "of soldiers who can inflict them?"

"*Ils sont tous morts!*" interrupted the sentinel.

"Your side is always victorious," said Alexander, with a smile.

"Thanks to the timely support of my Guard," answered Napoleon.

This sort of military *marivaudage* is reproduced by M. Thiers in his *Histoire du Consulat et de l'Empire*, though the light, *vaudevillistic* style of repartee was not at all in harmony with the character of Napoleon's mind.

Numbers of persons professed to know, almost immediately after the event, what had taken place at Tilsit; and one political agent sold what he declared to be the secret articles of the Treaty to the English Government, which, according to M. Thiers, wasted its money in buying them. What, however, could two such powerful sovereigns do—already masters of nearly the whole continent of Europe—but develop a project for uniting their forces and perpetuating their dominion!

July 20, 1808
Baylen

Major Arthur Griffiths

One morning in Spain, in the ancient capital of Valladolid, Napoleon was holding a grand review. A grenadier regiment of the Imperial Guard had paraded for his inspection in front of the grand old palace of Charles V. Napoleon passed slowly down the ranks, followed by a glittering staff; then, returning to the saluting point, he came upon a group of superior officers anxious to make their bow before their Imperial master. Suddenly he halted before one of them, whom he addressed in a voice of thunder:

"Can it be possible that you dare to come into my presence?—that you can show yourself in public branded with infamy, with disgrace which affects every brave man in the army? And your right arm there—why does it not hang withered by your side? It was with that hand that you affixed the seals to the capitulation of Baylen!"

The wretched man who stood there speechless and abashed while he was thus cruelly apostrophised was General Legendre, who had been General Dupont's chief of the staff when that general surrendered to the Spaniards at Baylen on the 20th July, 1808.

Napoleon never forgot or forgave this capitulation. It is said that in after years he could never think of Baylen without a shudder—never speak of it without an outburst of the fiercest indignation. No one ventured to talk of it, even to mention the name, in his presence. Long after the occurrence it was kept a profound secret. When King Joseph, Napoleon's brother, was forced by it to retire from Madrid, the *Moniteur* explained the retrograde move by a far-fetched story: it was publicly announced that the French headquarters in Spain had moved "to

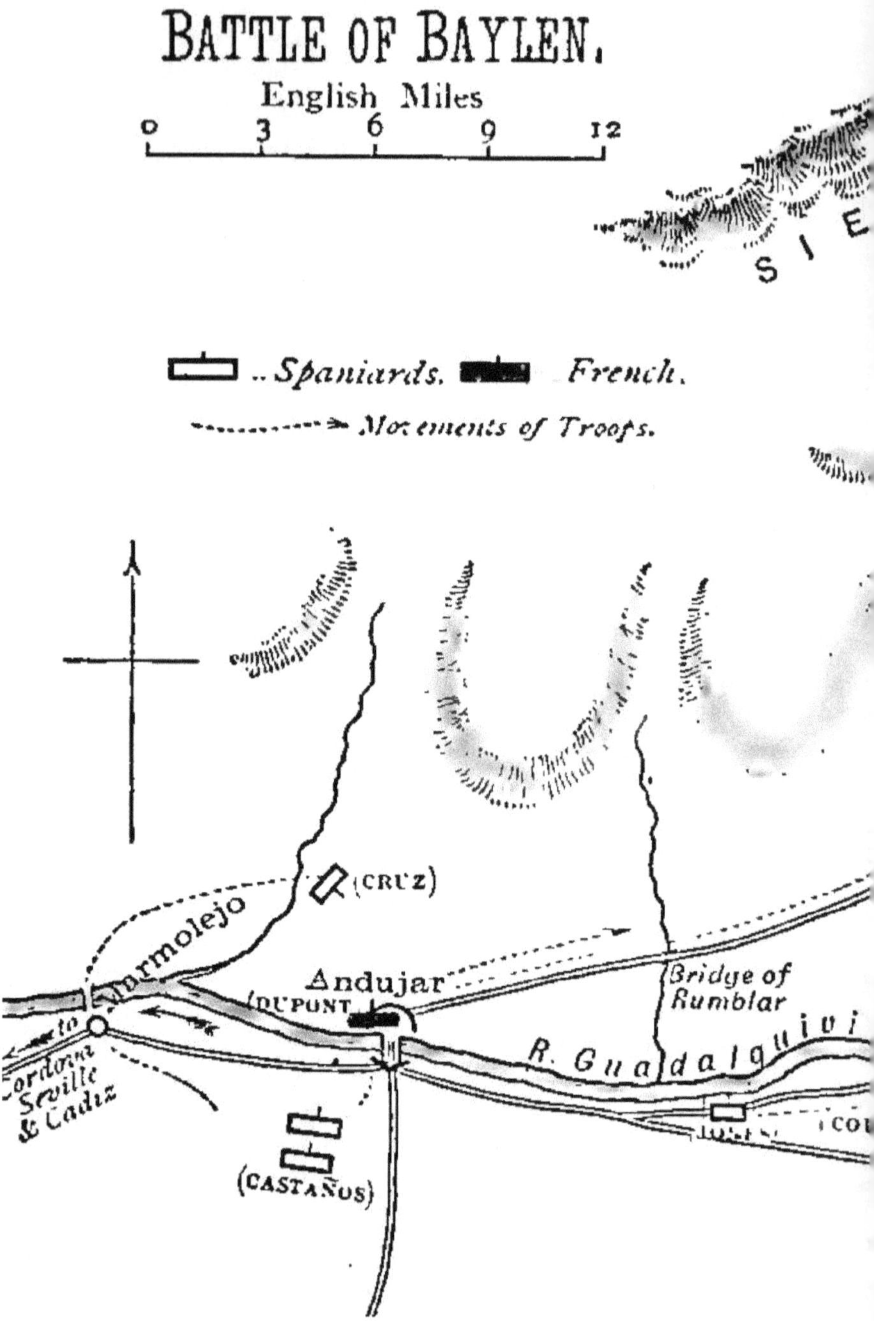
BATTLE OF BAYLEN.
English Miles
0 3 6 9 12
Spaniards.
French.
Movements of Troops.
(CRUZ)
Andujar
(DUPONT)
Bridge of Rumblar
R. Guadalquivi
Seville
& Cadiz
(CASTAÑOS)

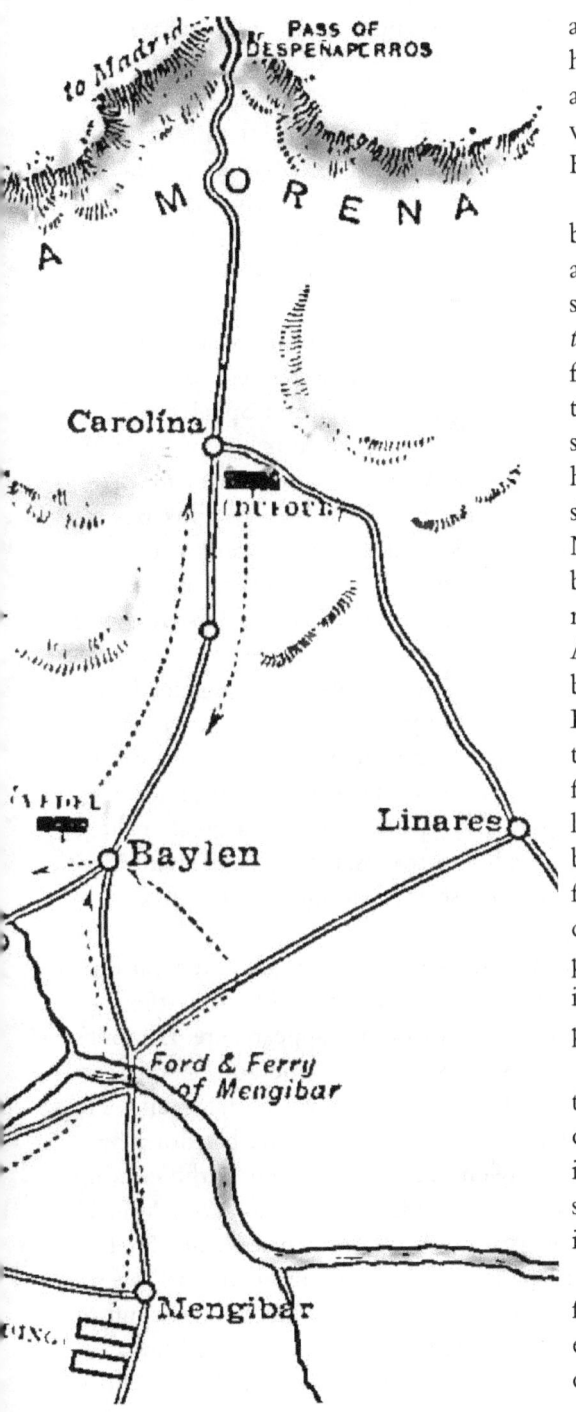

a place where it would have the benefit of milder air and better water." This was Bayonne, within the French frontier.

That Napoleon should be shocked and humiliated by Baylen was not strange. It was the first *contretemps*—the first real misfortune—that had befallen the French arms since the star of the great Corsican had risen over France. The shame of it eclipsed in Napoleon's mind his most brilliant victories. The glory of Marengo, Wagram, Austerlitz, and Jena faded before the dishonour of Baylen. Nor was it the actual fact alone that a large force of French soldiers laid down their arms in a battle which was not yet fully decided; it was the consequences of the capitulation that give it such immense importance. Napier says:

"In its moral effects the battle of Baylen was one of those events which, insignificant in themselves, cause great changes in the affairs of nations."

Not in itself, for the fight was small, the forces engaged on either side comparatively few, the generalship indifferent; but Baylen was a new point of departure in the Napoleonic struggle. Till then the emperor had triumphed all along the line. His hold of Spain, although shaken by the tardy but fierce revolt of the Spaniards, was tightening. He had crushed the insurrection, north, east, and west; his brother's Court was established at Madrid. The English expeditionary force, which was to change the whole current of events, had not yet landed in the Peninsula; and it is more than probable that but for Baylen, Arthur Wellesley would never have become the Duke of Wellington.

To understand and fully appreciate the momentous issues that hung around this battle it is necessary to hark back to the beginning, when Napoleon's restless ambition led him to interfere in Spanish politics. The dissensions at the Court of Madrid gave him his opportunity; his troops poured across the Pyrenees, and, on the plea of replacing one detested king by another of the people's choice, he took possession of the country. The principal Spanish fortresses were secured by treachery. One army corps occupied Catalonia, another old Castile; Junot crossed the entire Peninsula and entered Lisbon; Bessières, with movable columns, ranged the northern provinces and was ready to attack. Galicia. A part—and not the least part—in the general plan was the invasion of Andalusia in the south, the conquest of which was of paramount importance. It was a rich province, amply endowed by Nature; in one of its principal cities—Seville—was a cannon foundry, and in another—Cadiz—a large arsenal, from which a great artillery train could be equipped. It was full of troops, mostly well-disciplined, veteran troops, probably the only serious opponents left to be encountered in Spain.

The movement against Andalusia was entrusted to General Dupont; and, as this officer was soon to become notorious through his misfortunes, some account of him should appear here. Dupont's failure and collapse are not easily explained. Napoleon, in his rage, condemned him as having shown "inconceivable incapacity. He seemed to do very well at the head of a division; he has done horribly as a chief" But, up to Baylen, Dupont was one of the coming men: it was confidently said of him when he started from Madrid that he would find his baton as a Marshal of France at Cadiz. He had already done good service, had earned many laurels in early years, and he was still in the prime of life. He had fought at Valmy and in the Argonne, when Dumouriez made such successful resistance to the Prussian invasion of France; he contributed largely to the victory of Marengo, which was one of the first foundations of Napoleon's fame. At that battle it was Dupont who, as chief staff-officer of the reserve, had rallied and sent forward a number of beaten troops. Again, in commanding the right wing of the army of Italy, he had seized Florence, had defeated 45,000 Austrians with 14,000 men, and had earned for himself the sobriquet of "the bold general" (*le général audacieux*). At Jéna he had given further proof of his right to the epithet by holding a bridge with five battalions against 22,000 of the enemy, supported by powerful artillery—a feat characterised as one of tremendous daring. "I would not have attempted it," said the great leader, "with less than 60,000 men." Once more, at Friedland, he showed great courage and determination, and was decorated with the grand cordon of the Legion of Honour on the field.

Yet this was the man who later surrendered at Baylen, who "stained the French flag," who was "guilty of cowardice" in this "horrible affair." Such are the vicissitudes of fortune that wait on all who follow the profession of war. It has been urged in Dupont's defence that at the time of the catastrophe he was suffering from illness, as indeed were many under his orders; and that he had been badly wounded was reason sufficient to account for a temporary loss of head. Napoleon himself long afterwards, at St. Helena, admitted that Dupont had been more unfortunate than guilty, yet previous to the great final catastrophe it was plain that his fortitude was breaking down and that in his conduct he had lost all his old enterprise and audacity. A more serious complaint against him was that he thought more to preserve the plunder he had recently amassed than to fight through his foes. Dupont was no doubt largely tainted with the brigandage and love of "loot" which disgraced so many of Napoleon's greatest subordinates in the field, especially in Spain.

To return to the operations in Andalusia. Dupont left Madrid in the latter end of May, crossed the rugged mountains of the Sierra Morena by the great pass of Despeñaperros, and reached Andujar on the 2nd of June, 1808. He had with him an infantry division—Barbou's—Fresia's cavalry, some Swiss regiments, and a marine battalion of the Imperial Guard—in all about 24,000 combatants. On arrival at Andujar he first learnt that all Spain had risen, that war to the knife had been proclaimed against the French, and that all Andalusia was in arms. He knew that to reach Cadiz he must fight his way there; and, according to the best critics, he should now, in the face of this entirely new situation, have demanded fresh orders from Madrid, and

meanwhile waited in a strong position of observation backed up by the hills. But he decided to push on at once to Cordova, which he summoned to surrender, stormed, carried at the point of the bayonet,

and then proceeded to pillage. It was at Cordova that the treasure and valuables which were afterwards to prove such a fatal encumbrance were chiefly secured.

The loss of Cordova spread consternation in the neighbouring city of Seville, where a sort of provisional government for the south of Spain was established, and a general stampede very nearly followed. No serious resistance would have been offered Dupont if he had boldly continued his advance, and all Andalusia would probably have been easily won. But here his weakness and vacillation first showed themselves. He sat still where he was and hurried back courier after courier to Madrid with despatches full of despondency and fear, earnestly imploring reinforcements. Many of these letters fell into the hands of the Spaniards and gave them heart of grace. All could not be quite lost if such was the situation of the French. Castaños, the captain-general of whom Napier writes as "the first Spaniard who united prudence with patriotism," was in command of the Spanish forces. Even he had despaired at first. Although he had gathered men together, including those of his own camp, at St. Roque, originally intended for the siege of Gibraltar, he had been so little sanguine that he had already embarked all his heavy artillery and stores. But as troops joined him, he began to hope that he might yet get the better of Dupont. His strength was first doubled, then quadrupled—all classes had taken up arms, high and low, rich and poor. In a few weeks an army of 39 battalions and 21 squadrons, with a well-formed and well-organised artillery, was collected about Seville. Castaños was supported by two capable officers: one a French *émigré*, Coupigny, the other a Swiss soldier of fortune named Reding. An Irish general called Felix Jones was also under the orders of Castaños, so that he and his lieutenants were representatives of four different nationalities.

The Spaniards now prepared to take the offensive against Dupont, both by front attack on Cordova and by menacing his communications through the passes of the Sierra Morena. Their impatience to attack was forestalled by Dupont's frantic anxiety to retreat. Finding he could not regain the golden opportunity lost by his ten days' inactivity of Cordova, he exchanged the forward for a retrograde movement, and from that moment his troubles and embarrassments began. On the 17th of June he evacuated Cordova and fell back on the Guadalquivir at Andujar, the Spaniards pressing him with their advanced guard. It is possible that Dupont's fears were aggravated by the horrible nature of the contest, and the ferocity displayed by his Spanish enemy. All along his line of retreat he came upon ghastly proofs of their bloodthirsty and implacable character: they cut off and butchered his stragglers, seized and slew his sick in hospital, his doctors, couriers, and all non-combatants. One French officer. Colonel Rene, returning from a peaceful mission in Portugal, was taken prisoner, mutilated, placed alive between two planks, then his body was sawn in two. A timorous general (yet this was Dupont *l'audacieux!*), not strangely, was greatly affected by these terrors. His despatches, while magnifying his dangers, were filled with the most painful misgivings and the most piteous appeals.

So desperate did he conceive his situation that he wrote as follows to Madrid from Andujar—a letter which was intercepted, and which, no doubt, greatly increased the confidence of his enemy:—

"We have not a moment to lose. We must immediately fall back from a position where we are unable to subsist. My men being always under arms have no time now as heretofore to reap the corn and bake their own bread. . . .

"For Heaven's sake hurry up reinforcements with all haste! What we imperatively require is the assistance of a firm and compact body of men, able to support me and to support each other. . . . Send me medicines with all speed, and linen for my wounded. The enemy for a whole month has intercepted all supplies both of food and ammunition."

Yielding to Dupont's repeated applications, General Savary, who was Joseph's military right hand at Madrid, had ordered Vedel's division to push through the pass of Despeñaperros; and that general; although harassed in his march by Spanish irregulars, got past safely and reached Baylen (soon to become historical) with some 14,000 men. Another general, Gobert, had also been sent in support by Savary, anticipating Napoleon's permission. Dupont was now strong enough to have resumed the offensive—Napoleon fully expected him to do so. The emperor could not believe him to be really in danger. Commenting upon the situation from a distance, he wrote:

"Dupont, with 2.5,000 men, ought to accomplish great things. As a matter of fact, with only 21,000 the chances would be eighty *per cent*, in his favour." This opinion was dictated at Bayonne on the 21st of July—the very day of Dupont's capitulation.

There was no vigorous initiative left in Dupont: a bold stroke might have got him out of his mess, but he remained inactive, clinging tenaciously to a vicious position. He had entrenched himself at Andujar on the far side of the river, fortifying the bridge against attack. He thought to cover the pass and his communications, but he was too far forward, and his defensive line was weak, easily to be turned on either flank. The river Guadalquivir was nearly dry, and fordable at many points; below him on the right was the bridge of Marmolejo; higher up, his left, his weakest flank, was assailable by the fords of Mengibar, and pressure along this line would make his whole position untenable. In fact, he was altogether in the wrong place. His excuse is that he held on to Andujar because Napoleon had approved of his halt there; but the emperor was not then in possession of the latest news, and he always hoped that Dupont would not remain idle. His safest course would be to fall back, concentrate at Baylen, strike the Spanish columns as they showed; and then, even if defeated, his retreat through the mountain passes would have been secure.

At that time, no doubt, Dupont's army was weak and in wretched case; and this added greatly to his

anxieties. The soldiers were mostly conscripts, young unfledged recruits, barely formed as soldiers, having hardly learnt discipline, ignorant even of their drill. They were half-starved, too, and suffered greatly in health. It was the height of the "dog days," the heat almost tropical; the supplies were very short; there was no wine, vinegar, or brandy; only half-rations were issued, often only quarter- rations of bread. The banks of the river were dangerously unhealthy, the "eternal home of malarious fever." Six hundred men went to hospital in less than a fortnight, and the rest lost all heart and strength. Dupont occupied a position too wide for his numbers. He himself was at Andujar, Vedel at Baylen, Gobert away back at Carolina, just as he had come through. Being besides continually harassed by guerillas threatening his communications, he was obliged to break up his force into fragments, and keep them constantly moving to and fro in large patrols along his whole front. This greatly increased the sufferings and hardships of the French troops, who, always marching to and fro, badly nourished and under intense heat, became greatly exhausted and fatigued.

The Spaniards so far had failed to realise the faulty dispositions of their opponent. Castaños, of his own accord, would not advance to attack; he did not even prepare to do so until he received positive orders to that effect from Seville. Then he slowly approached the Guadalquivir: even now, notwithstanding the strength of his very mixed force of regulars and irregulars, which numbered some 50,000, he was so little in earnest that he still talked of retreat. He could not see that Dupont, by holding to Andujar, was giving himself into his hands. No doubt what Castaños presently did was just as a skilful general would have acted; but it was more by luck than good management, the mere chance of the lie of the land than wise action following profound military forethought and science.

At last, in accordance with the definite decision of a council of war, the Spaniards began active operations on the 18th July. The plan arrived at was, as it happened, the best possible. Dupont's false position was his enemy's opportunity. The true system of attack was to encourage him to remain at Andujar by strong feints in his front, while the real stress was laid on his left—his extreme left, far away where his line of retreat lay exposed. This, in effect, was what happened. On the 13th, General Reding advanced from Mengibar towards the ford of that name, and drove the French outposts across the Guadalquivir; next to him, on his left, came Coupigny, then Felix Jones. This movement was threatening enough, but, as it was not persisted in, Dupont seems to have neglected it, mistaking its dangerous intention. Moreover, Castaños now strengthened him in his unwise resolves to hold to the right, for the Spanish general began serious demonstrations against Andujar; he covered the heights opposite with a great multitude, and apparently "meant business." Dupont, terrified, stood fast, and only sent frantic appeals to Vedel for help. Then Castaños opened with his artillery against the Andujar bridge, and despatched a body of irregulars across the river at Marmolejo lower down with orders to manoeuvre around Dupont's right rear.

Now Reding, pressing forward, forced a passage at the Mengibar ford. Dupont, hearing this, countermarched Vedel, who was approaching him, and directed him to protect Baylen, which was now exposed and within easy reach of Mengibar. Vedel, having made one useless march, was again to be of no service; for Reding having crossed the direction of his march, indicated an intention to strike at Linares and the pass beyond. Accordingly Dufour, who commanded after Gobert's death, hurried off to Carolina, hoping to forestall Reding; and Vedel, equally anxious, quickly followed Dufour. Thus, these two French generals with their divisions were separated on the 17th July by five-and-twenty miles from their chief and comrade, Dupont, at Andujar. All this was enormously to Reding's advantage. He was joined on the 17th by Coupigny, and now the two together, 20,000 strong, seized Baylen. Here Reding, after throwing out a detachment towards Carolina, took up a position facing Andujar and the west.

In order to fully appreciate this most complicated state of affairs, it will be necessary to recapitulate the positions of the opponents. Dupont, with one-half of the French forces, was at Andujar, the extreme end of a front of forty-five miles; Vedel and Dufour were at the other end, quite cut off from him, about Carolina. Reding was in between the two ends, holding Baylen, the key of the position. Castaños was in strength opposite Dupont, having thrown troops across the river to threaten Dupont's exposed right flank. Whether intentionally or not, it was clear that the Spaniards had quite outmanoeuvred the French, and, if not absolutely masters of the situation, they had undoubtedly the best of it.

Dupont only learnt in the course of the 18th, and with the deepest dismay, that an enemy's force was established at Baylen, thus severing his communications and cutting him off from the rest of his army. He knew nothing of Reding's strength, but he saw that he must at all costs regain touch with Vedel and reopen his line of retreat. Possibly he now awoke to the grave military error he had committed in holding on to

he moment of DUPONT'S third attack.

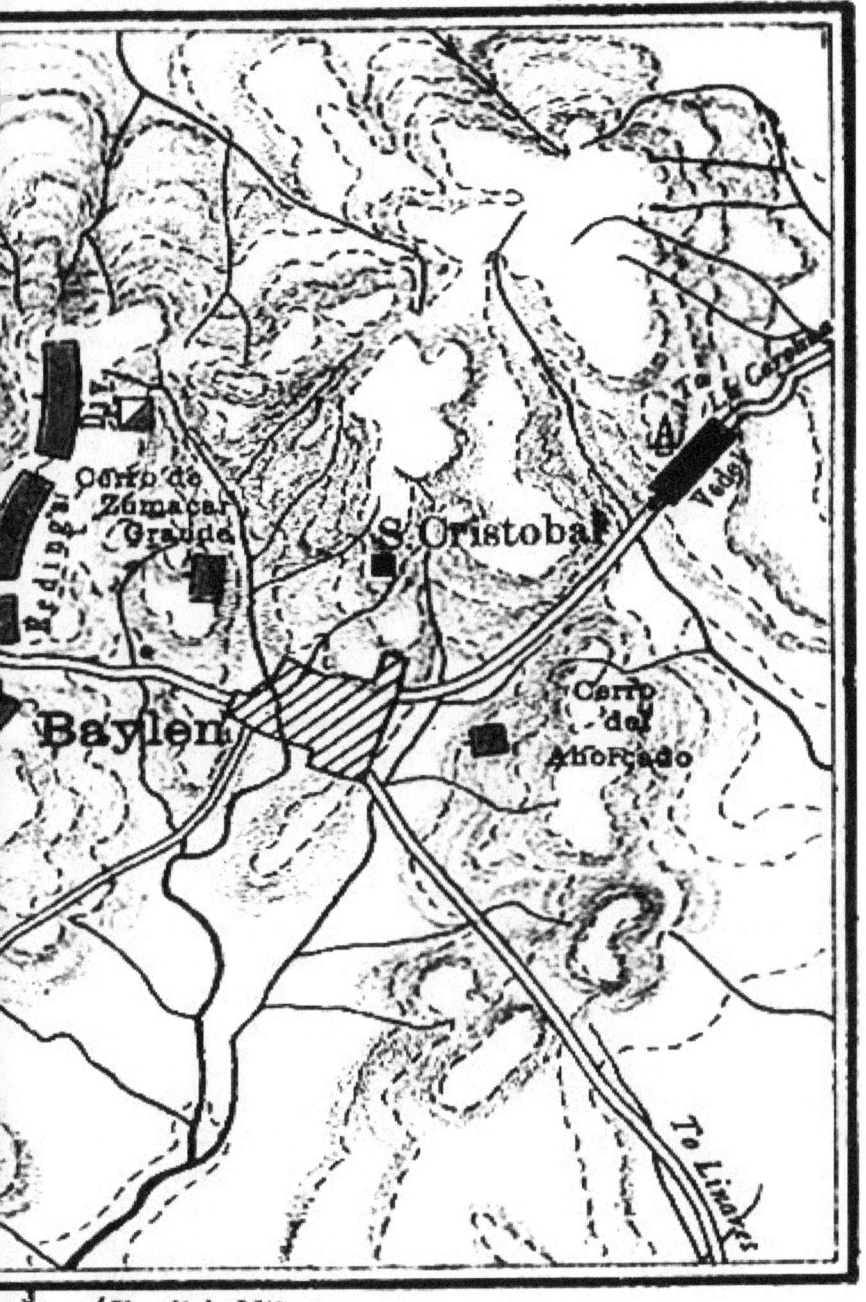

Andujar for so long. At any rate his preparations were made with great secrecy and in all haste: the move was an escape rather than a retreat, carried on in the depth of the night and with extreme precaution. The force, some 11,000 strong, was divided into two portions—half for the advanced-guard, half for the rear-guard—both protecting the precious train of 800 waggons, laden with plunder and sick, which, thus guarded, dragged along in the centre of the column. Dupont feared most for his rear, believing Castaños more formidable than Reding, and therefore the head was weaker than the tail of his force.

Castaños—negligent, dilatory, slow to move—had no inkling of Dupont's withdrawal for many hours after the Frenchman had started, and too late to interfere with his march. By daybreak, about 3 a.m., Dupont's advance reached a mountain torrent called the Tiedras, and got touch of Reding's outposts. By 4 a.m. the French, leaving a force at the bridge of Rumblar to watch for Castaños behind, were engaged with the enemy in front. It was of the utmost importance to drive back Reding and get through before Castaños could come up; and to secure this Dupont should have attacked immediately with all his strength, eager only to get on. But he paused to make elaborate dispositions, thus wasting the precious hours, and only charged Reding with the puny efforts of small successive columns. Nevertheless, the French, fighting with their customary gallantry, gained ground at first and drove in the first line of defence; but in the second the Spaniards stood firm, and their artillery fire being heavier, overmastered the French guns. At 10 a.m., Reding made a counter attack, advancing with great energy, to be checked in turn by the brilliant charges of the French cavalry. Yet now the Spanish reserves restored the fight, which, as the day grew on towards noon, manifestly slackened on the French side.

Dupont's men were horribly exhausted. They had been marching all night, fighting all the forenoon; they were covered with dust and exposed to a tropical sun; they were mad with thirst and there was no water to be had. Already 1,500 men had been struck down, the Swiss regiments in the French service had gone over to the Spaniards, large numbers of officers were wounded, Dupont himself included. At this time the French general declared he could not dispose of more than a couple of thousand men, although it was never properly explained why his forces had dwindled to so few. Thousands could never have fired a shot, and it was openly said afterwards that the care of the general's personal baggage, swollen with church plate and plunder, so fully occupied a great part of his whole force that it was never brought into action.

Now at this critical moment the guns of the pursuit were heard in the rear about the Rumblar bridge. Castaños had come up at last, and the French were taken between two fires. Poor Dupont had no news of Vedel, and was in despair. He proposed a suspension of arms, which Reding willingly granted, because, as a matter of fact, he himself could hardly hold his own ground. Nevertheless, Vedel was really near at hand. He had been aroused by the distant sounds of battle, and had left Carolina that morning at 5 a.m., working, as a good soldier should, towards the noise of guns. Yet now, although time was of the utmost consequence, he tarried by the way and halted for several hours six miles short of Baylen to let his men breakfast and rest. He only resumed his march when the firing had ceased, to arrive on the ground after Dupont had asked for an armistice. Being ignorant of this, Vedel attacked Reding to good purpose, and captured 1,500 prisoners. Then an *aide-de-camp* from Dupont came and told him to desist, informing him that negotiations with the enemy were in progress.

Thus the battle was lost when on the point of being won. It would have been easy enough to reopen the strife, and with every prospect of success. Vedel clamoured for a joint attack on Reding, and was supported by his subordinates. Dupont would not consent, ordered Vedel to give up the prisoners he had taken and withdraw to Carolina. This did not please Castaños, who insisted that Vedel should also surrender, and threatened in default to massacre all Dupont's force. Here was an opportunity of quashing the negotiations and resuming hostilities. Dupont and Vedel together, 18,000 French soldiers, were strong enough to give a good account of a raw Spanish army; and if Dupont was caught between Castaños and Reding, Reding was in equally critical condition between Vedel and Dupont. It was an occasion when a bold stroke for freedom would probably have resulted in triumphant victory. Had Dupont been the man of Marengo, Jena, and Friedland he would have cut his way through his difficulties sword in hand. But he was completely broken down, and could only assemble a council of war, upon whom he threw the responsibility of decision. Heroic resolutions such as alone could have saved the French were not to be expected from a number of different opinions, and the council came to the conclusion that further resistance was hopeless.

Negotiations recommenced, and now Castaños imposed harder terms. At first he would have permitted the French troops to return to Madrid, but at this moment a letter from General Savary, recalling Dupont to Madrid, fell into the Spanish general's hands. Castaños not strangely declined to carry out Savary's views, and insisted that the whole French force—Dupont's, Vedel's, and Dufour's—should lay down their arms and surrender at discretion. Meanwhile, Vedel had again drawn off, but Castaños demanded his return, and that he should be included in the capitulation. Extraordinary as it will appear, Dupont sent Vedel peremptory orders to come back; and Vedel, although well out of danger, and at the head of a force armed and intact, actually returned. Nor was this all. A French officer with a Spanish escort scoured the country to pick up small parties and outlying French garrisons, and include them in the surrender. As Napier says:

"And, these unheard-of proceedings were quietly submitted to by men belonging to that army which for fifteen years had been the terror of Europe."

Twenty thousand French soldiers gave themselves up at one stroke of the pen to an enemy for whom they had had the greatest contempt. There is no more pregnant truth in military art than that the conduct of soldiers depends greatly upon the character of their immediate chief.

General Dupont undoubtedly failed when put to a supreme test. It was the first occasion on which he had been in independent command, and he was unequal to it and its peculiar difficulties. According to all accounts he was a man of lively imagination, apt to vary between the two extremes of enthusiasm and despondency. He is described as an affable, agreeable person, a good talker, with strong literary tastes, and, even when a general, he had competed for poetical prizes. His writings are full of fine rhetoric, but his military despatches were wanting in force and decision. Whatever his faults were, he expiated them to the full. On his return to France he, with the other generals concerned in the capitulation, were arraigned before a special commission and treated with the utmost rigour. Dupont himself was sentenced to be degraded from his rank; he was to give up all his medals and decorations, to forfeit the rank of count and all money grants made him, and to be imprisoned indefinitely. He lingered on in a state prison until the fall of Napoleon in 1814, when the Bourbons, on return to power, released him, and he was at once made Minister of War. A special royal ordinance restored him to his rank and honours, and he occupied a prominent military position until his death in 1838.

It only remains to be said that this capitulation, "shameful in itself, was shamefully broken." The French prisoners, on their march down to Cadiz, where, according to the treaty, they were to be embarked

and sent home to France, were treated barbarously by their Spanish captors. Many were murdered in cold blood: eighty officers were massacred at Lebrija, but not before they had kept their cowardly assailants at bay sword in hand, to be shot down treacherously from houses around. All who survived to reach Cadiz were there cast into the convict hulks and subjected to horrible ill-treatment. The wretched remnant were afterwards transported to the desert island of Cabrera, where "they perished by lingering torments in such numbers that few remained alive at the termination of the war."

Baylen is a dark spot in history, disgraceful to both sides engaged. Yet from it started the career of one of England's greatest generals, and it was the first serious blow that assailed the fabric of Napoleonic power.

1808
The Winter Campaign in Finland

A. Hilliard Atteridge

In the opening years of the century, when Europe echoed with the thunder of Napoleon's great battles, many minor campaigns passed almost unheeded. Yet some of these have had more lasting effects on the world's history than some of the more famous battles with which they were contemporaneous. How few have ever heard anything of the war between Sweden and Russia in 1808, the marches and battles amid the northern snow and ice, and the siege of Sweaborg! Yet the result of these operations was the annexation of Finland to the imperial crown of Russia, and the predominance of that Power on the shores of the Baltic.

The war was brief but eventful. If success finally rested with Russia, notwithstanding hard-fought Swedish victories in the field, it was because the policy of King Gustavus made the efforts of his generals unavailing, and because a weak and irresolute commandant prematurely yielded the chief fortress of Finland and of the Swedish crown to the invaders. Sweaborg, a mass of granite forts and ramparts, built on a group of five rocky islands, in the midst of the sea, was till then supposed to be impregnable. It was the chief arsenal both of the Swedish armies in the north end of the kingdom and of the flotilla maintained for operations in the shallow waters of the gulfs of Bothnia and Finland. In war time a fleet stationed there was already at the gates of St. Petersburg, and could blockade and menace the Russian capital. No wonder that its possession had long been coveted by the *Czars*.

By the secret articles of the Treaty of Tilsit, it was agreed between Napoleon and the Emperor Alexander that Russia should take possession of Finland. The ministers of the *Czar* proceeded at once to press various complaints against the conduct of the court of Stockholm. Gustavus Adolphus, the king of Sweden, was warned by friends that he was to be attacked in Finland; but he obstinately refused to believe that there was anything more serious than diplomatic friction with Russia. In any case, he expected that there would be no war till the summer. Bur the Russians had planned a winter campaign. In the summer they would have had to reckon with the opposition of the Swedish fleet, probably reinforced by a British squadron; but in the winter months, the frozen northern seas made naval warfare impossible. It is true that on the land the intense cold would add to the difficulties of campaigning; but the advantage of being secure from an attack by sea was so great that the winter campaign was decided upon.

The banks of the frozen river Kymen, which then formed the frontier of Swedish Finland, were only held by a feeble line of detached posts, the usual guard maintained in time of peace for Customs and police purposes, and nothing more. On the Russian side of the frontier in the first half of February, 1808, 16,000 men were concentrated under the command of General Count Bouxhoevden. The troops were specially equipped for winter campaigning. The infantry were provided with snow-shoes, the guns and stores were mounted on sledges. As soon as everything was ready war was declared, and the little army of invasion crossed the Kymen in three columns at Aberfos, Stromfos, and Keltis.

The Swedes were in no position to make an effective resistance on the frontier. Everywhere they fell back before the Russians. The first blood was spilt at Aberfos, where the Swedish post fired upon the cavalry of the Russian vanguard, and killed a dragoon officer who was anxious to distinguish himself by being first across the Kymen bridge.

The left column of the invaders, under General Gortschakoff, moved parallel with the shore of the Gulf of Finland. The little town of Lowisa was occupied; a detachment of 1,800 men was left to besiege the fort of Swartholm on an adjacent headland; and Gortschakoff pushed n towards the defile of Fosby, strongly held by Swedes under Colonel Palmfeld, who hoped to stop the Russian advance at this point where the coast road passed through a rocky ridge. In summer the position would have been a good one; but now the ice on Permo Bay enabled the attacking force to work round the headland and turn the defile. As the Russians marched out upon the ice, a squadron of Swedish dragoons attempted to check them by threatening a charge, but they were in their turn charged by the Cossacks of the Imperial Guard; and the strange spectacle was seen of a fierce cavalry fight upon the frozen waters of the bay. The Swedes were thus forced to abandon their position, and on February 26th the Russian left occupied Borgo, the most ancient town in Finland. Two days later the right, under Prince Bagration made a night attack upon Artsjo, held by a Swedish detachment, and captured the place after a hard struggle in the snowy streets. The Russian centre column met with no resistance worth noting. In summer the numerous lakes and marshes would have rendered the Russian advance more difficult, but now they were able to move across lake and marsh more rapidly than through the rocks and woods of the solid land between the lakes.

The Swedish Government was taken by surprise. There were about 15,000 regular troops and some 4,000 local militia in Finland,

SWEABORG.
English Miles

but they were scattered in various garrisons, and no army was ready to act against the Russians. Seven hundred men were blockaded in Swartholm, 7,000 held Sweaborg, and about 4,000 under General Klercker were at Tavastheus, the principal town in the south-west. To Tavastheus General Count Klingsporr, whom King Gustavus had appointed to the command in Finland, hurried as quickly as relays of horses could convey his sledge. When he arrived there he heard that the Russians were already in possession of all the south-east of the country. They had occupied Helsingfors without resistance, seizing a number of guns and a quantity of valuable stores in the town. The siege of Sweaborg had begun; a column of invaders under General Toutchkoff was overrunning the east of the country; throughout nearly one-half of it the reserve men and the militia could not be called out; Bagration was advancing upon Tavastheus with a force superior to that under Klercker and Klingsporr, so that the Swedish commander had to begin his campaign by retiring northwards to Kurvola, while the Russians occupied Tavastheus on March 6th. By a bold initiative, a series of forced marches and a few unimportant engagements, they had secured enormous advantages. At first Klingsporr had an exaggerated idea of their numbers, for the detachments they pushed forward in so many directions acted so boldly, that the Swedes took them for the vanguards of strong *corps d'armée*.

Bouxhoevden, the Russian *generalissimo*, while maintaining the blockade of Swartholm and of Sweaborg, sent a detachment to seize Abo, the old capital of Finland, and with his main body pursued Klingsporr. The latter could not do more than delay the Russian advance by some show of resistance. His rearguard made a stand at Bjorneborg, but the place was stormed by Bagration's division. Tammerfors was abandoned, after a cavalry fight on the neighbouring lake. Klingsporr could have retired from Wasa (now known as Nikolaistadt) across the ice of the Gulf of Bothnia into Sweden, but he decided rather to draw the Russians after him to the northward, retiring along the west coast of Finland, and receiving his supplies from Sweden through Tornea at the head of the gulf, by which route also some reinforcements reached him. His hope was to prolong the campaign until the breakup of the ice in the spring would enable the Swedish fleet first to relieve Sweaborg, and then to co-operate with him against the invaders.

Swartholm surrendered on March 18th, after five or six days' bombardment. The garrison had plenty of corn, but they were short of water, and sickness had broken out in the crowded and ill-ventilated casemates. Seven hundred prisoners and 200 guns and mortars were the prize of the victors. The detachment under Chepeleff occupied Abo, and seized sixty-four galleys which were ice-bound in the harbour. Finally, on April 12th, the Cossacks marched across the ice of the Baltic and occupied the Aland isles. Klingsporr all the while was retiring slowly northwards, skirmishing among the rocks and woods. It was not till the middle of April that he felt strong enough to make a serious stand. Meanwhile, all unknown to him, the fate of Sweaborg had been sealed—Sweaborg, on which his hopes for the defence of the province finally rested.

The defence of the famous fortress had been entrusted to Admiral Count Cronstedt, a veteran officer of the Swedish navy, although the force under his command included only about 200 sailors among

more than 7,000 combatants. Half the garrison were Swedes, the rest Finns. A large flotilla of galleys and gunboats lay in the creeks between the islands, protected by the works, but themselves unable to take any part in the defence of the fortress, for they were frozen fast in the ice. The same thick ice joined the islands to the coast, and extended in a solid sheet far out to seaward.

The Russian force which was detached from the army of invasion for the siege of Sweaborg, was directed by an engineer officer, General Suchtelen. When he approached the place in February he had not quite 3,000 men at his disposal, but he was gradually reinforced until, in the first week of March, he commanded eleven battalions of infantry, four squadrons of cavalry, four field-batteries, a company of garrison artillery, and two companies of engineers. Heavy guns for the siege-batteries were taken from the Russian fortresses on the frontier of Finland, packed on sledges, and dragged slowly across the snow ice to Helsingfors, the busy commercial town which stands on a point of the mainland west of Sweaborg. Naturally, there was a limit to the number of guns that could be thus brought up, especially as for every gun a quantity of ammunition would have to be conveyed to the front in the same laborious fashion. Thus it was that Suchtelen had never more than thirty heavy guns and sixteen mortars in his batteries, though there were some 2,000 cannon, mounted and unmounted, in the forts and arsenal of Sweaborg. Nor was the want of ordnance the only

difficulty of the attack. Suchtelen had to construct the batteries for the few guns he possessed with logs, bundles of brushwood, gabions filled with snow, and other light materials; for the bare rocky ground of the islands and capes made it impossible to dig, and between the capes and the fortress there was only the level ice of the Gulf of Finland, covered with frozen snow, and broken here and there by a ridge of rocks. To carry parallels and zigzags across such a surface, and erect breaching batteries upon it, was out of the question. Suchtelen, therefore, decided that this singular siege should be chiefly a blockade, varied with an occasional bombardment, when his limited supplies of ammunition would permit of such a display of fireworks.

He mounted his heavy guns and mortars at Cape Helsingfors and on Skandetlandet island, and some adjacent rocks. Back Holm, on the east of Sweaborg, was held by a detached force, and the expanse of ice to the northward covering the great roadstead was continually patrolled by night and watched by day. There was not much chance of the garrison breaking out to the southward, where the ice covered the open sea for miles. At first Suchtelen had thought of attempting a *coup-de-main*, in the shape of a sudden assault with scaling-ladders; but, considering the great risk and the certain cost in life of such an enterprise, he decided that it should be attempted only if other means failed.

The first cannon-shots were exchanged on March 6th. At daybreak a Swedish working party, several hundreds strong, was seen to be busy on the west side of Sweaborg, breaking up the ice in front of the fortifications. It was a difficult piece of work; for blocks of ice had to be sawn out and carried off, so that it was more like quarrying than the ice-breaking we see on an English pond or river. Count Cronstedt was trying to secure a barrier of open water, or at least of thin ice, for the forts that he believed to be most exposed to attack. A Russian battery on a rocky island between Sweaborg and Helsingfors opened fire on the ice-cutters, and they ran back behind the nearest forts, which promptly replied to the Russian fire. Laid with a high elevation, the Swedish guns sent most of their projectiles over the Russian battery and into the town of Helsingfors behind it, where roofs and walls were soon crashing down. On this Suchtelen ceased firing, and sent an officer with a flag of truce across the ice to Sweaborg. The officer was brought to Admiral Cronstedt's quarters, and told the Swedish commander that he had been sent by General Suchtelen, out of motives of humanity, to remonstrate with him as

to the damage his guns were doing to the peaceful inhabitants of Helsingfors. Most of them, he pointed out, had relations and friends in the garrison; and if, nevertheless, the governor was so unfeeling as to destroy their homes and expose them to the horrors of a northern winter, the Russian army would make reprisals on Swedish towns that were already in its possession. The old sailor replied that the destruction of Helsingfors was necessary for the security of his garrison; and, sorry as he was for the poor people of the town, he must think first of the defence of the fortress. But Cronstedt was anything but a determined man, and after giving this decision he consented to take the advice of a council of war on the point. Now, councils of war, almost without exception, avoid strong measures and disagreeable courses, so the result was that later in the day Cronstedt agreed to a compromise suggested by Suchtelen. On the one hand, the Swedes agreed not to fire upon Helsingfors; on the other, the Russians pledged themselves not to erect any batteries in the direction of the town. There was to be no fighting on the north-west front of Sweaborg, "from motives of humanity."

But the old sailor had been outwitted by the wily Russian, who had gained a tremendous advantage out of this humanitarian compact. To quote Suchtelen's own words in his report on the siege:

"Our ammunition trains, our hospitals and stores, could thus be placed in perfect safety at Helsingfors. The town afforded at the same time to the headquarters, and to the troops carrying on the siege, the only shelter from the weather that was to be found in the neighbourhood."

Having thus secured a base of operations, the Russians proceeded to harass the garrison by day and by night. The heavy batteries bombarded the fortress, taking aim at the mills and the masts of ships that rose above the ramparts, and especially firing at the great snow-covered roofs of the shipbuilding-slips and workshops of the arsenal. Day after day fires broke out in the place. Even at night the garrison was allowed no rest. Troops would march out upon the ice from the Russian lines, with drums beating and torches flaring, only to disappear as the first gun was fired from fort or rampart. The Russian field-artillery added to the alarms of the garrison. Colonel Argoun, who commanded it, was always playing a gigantic game of hide-and-seek among the rocks around Sweaborg. His guns would slip along from rock to rock, appear suddenly where they were least expected within point-blank range of the ramparts, send a shower of grape over them, and retire just as the garrison beat to arms to repel a supposed attempt to storm the works. For, with all this activity in the Russian lines, Cronstedt was persuaded that Suchtelen was meditating an assault. The result was that the garrison turned out to its alarm posts several times every day and night, besides having to work continually at putting out the fires in the dockyard and arsenal. Exposed to bitter cold, working hard by day, deprived of proper rest at night, no wonder the men began to break down. Cronstedt had no idea of the weakness of the force opposed to him, or of the strength of his own position. To his mind, Sweaborg was an island fortress depending on the sea for its security; and now, thanks to the ice, the sea was traversed even by field-artillery, and a column of assault could march right up to the ramparts. Yet all the while, if he had abandoned his attitude of passive and irresolute defence, he was himself in a position to seriously menace the besiegers with disaster.

Soon he began to be anxious about the supply of food. On the approach of the invaders a large number of the people of Helsingfors had fled to Sweaborg. Cronstedt would have liked to get rid of these "useless mouths," and he sent some of them out to try to reach their old homes. The Russian outposts drove them back at the point of the bayonet. But General Suchtelen sent in a courteous message to the admiral under a flag of truce. He could not allow him to increase his supplies by sending out hundreds of the civilian inhabitants of Sweaborg, but he would be happy to give a safe conduct and an escort to the admiral's own family, in order to spare them the sufferings of the siege. Cronstedt nobly replied that he and his must share the lot of the garrison. He would accept no special privileges for his wife and children.

The Russian general further showed his. courtesy by sending into the governor gazettes, newspapers, and letters for the families of officers and men. But all the papers and letters had been carefully examined beforehand, and only those were allowed to pass out of Helsingfors which contained depressing news for the Swedes about the progress of the Russian arms and the sufferings of the rest of the country. All good news was carefully kept back. Flags of truce were thus always coming and going, and the Russian staff arranged, on one pretext or another, to have as many conferences as possible with the admiral and his officers. They soon found out that he had no confidence in his position, no expectation of the siege being raised, and that, he was particularly suspicious of the promised English naval succour in the spring. He thought that if the British came it would be to get possession of the Swedish fleet. Hopes were artfully held out to him that it might be possible to save the flotilla at Sweaborg by negotiating a separate capitulation for the fortress, and on April 3rd Suchtelen and Cronstedt met on the Isle of Loman and signed a convention for an armistice. It was a curious document. It provided that the cessation of hostilities should last till May 3rd. and then went on to provide that:

"If at noon on the 3rd of May the fortress has not been succoured by at least five ships of the line, it shall be given up to H.M. the Emperor of Russia. Be it understood, that it is necessary such succour shall at that hour have actually entered the harbour of Sweaborg, and that if it should only be in sight of the fortress it shall be considered as not having arrived."

On the ratification of the armistice, the Swedes were to give up to the Russians, as a guarantee, the island of Langorn, with its batteries. The one advantage which was held out to the old admiral as the price of this convention was the preservation of the flotilla. But even this was only conditional, for the article referring to it ran thus:—

"The flotilla shall be restored in its actual condition to Sweden, after the peace, provided always that England shall restore to Denmark the fleet taken from that Power last year."

Next day the Russians were given possession of Langorn, the batteries of which commanded the entrance to the great harbour, and they immediately took precautions to prevent any rescuing squadron from getting in when the ice broke up. Additional guns were mounted. Furnaces were prepared and kept ready day and night for firing red-hot shot, and the gunners slept in shelters beside their guns. But the ice held on, and no relief appeared; so on May 3rd Admiral Cronstedt surrendered, and the Russians took possession of the fortress, with 2,000 guns, over 300,000 projectiles, and a great store of arms and ammunition, 2 frigates, 19 transports, and 100 galleys, sloops, gunboats, and small craft, besides a considerable supply of rigging and naval stores. Two hundred and eight officers and 7,368 men laid down their arms.

Suchtelen wrote:

"The Russians had hardly enough men to occupy the place and see to the dispersion of the enemy's garrison."

There were rumours that Cronstedt had been bribed to surrender the fortress, but both Russian and Swedish writers deny that there was any ground for such a charge against him. Without supposing anything of the kind, his conduct is explained by the fact that, though a brave sailor, he was quite out of place as the commandant of a mixed garrison of soldiers and militia in an ice-bound fortress; and, above all, the simple-minded old man was no match for a soldier diplomatist like Suchtelen. Cronstedt was weak and vacillating at a time when victory was within reach of a determined man, and so the great prize of Sweaborg fell into the hands of adversaries who were full of resource, enterprise, and determination, the very qualities in which he was deficient. On May 8th the Russian flag was hoisted on the forts, with a salute of 101 guns, and a *Te Deum* was solemnly celebrated in the great square of the citadel. The Black

Eagle has flown there ever since. In the Crimean War Sweaborg defied the attacks of our Baltic fleet.

Its surrender to Suchtelen came at a most unfortunate time, for not only was the ice breaking up, so that very soon a joint Swedish and British fleet would have been in the Gulf of Finland, but the Swedish armies in the field, under Klingsporr, had been winning decided victories over the Russian army of invasion. The first serious fighting took place in the second week of April. On the 13th the Swedes were in and about Pyhajoki, at the mouth of the river of the same name. Klingsporr's headquarters were in the town, and Colonel Gripenberg, with about 200 men, covered it by holding the strong position of Ypperi, on the coast a little to the south. On the 13th, Gripenberg was attacked in front by the Russian vanguard, while another column, led by General Koulneff in person, moving on the ice of the Gulf of Bothnia, turned his right flank. In this way Gripenberg was driven out of three positions in succession. His fourth stand was made close to Pyhajoki, and here Klingsporr came to the rescue of his rear-guard. His artillery checked the Russian advance on the coast road, while his chief-of-the-staff, Colonel Count Löwenhjelm, with a brigade of infantry and some squadrons of dragoons, charged Koulneff's Russians on the ice. In one of these charges, which he led sword in hand, Löwenhjelm had his horse killed, and was himself wounded and taken prisoner. This caused some confusion among his followers, but the result of Klingsporr's attack was that he disengaged his rear-guard, stopped the Russian pursuit at the mouth of the Pyhajoki, and was able to continue his retreat unmolested.

The Russians occupied Brahestad on April 18th, and drove the Swedish rear-guard out of Olijoki. But a few miles to the northwards, near the church of Sikajoki, Klingsporr made a more determined stand than he had yet ventured upon. At the mouth of the Sikajoki River, the Russians tried to repeat the manoeuvre which they had so often found successful, by moving out on the ice to turn the position of the Swedes on the land. But this time Klingsporr was ready for them, and they were beaten back with heavy loss by the Swedish artillery and cavalry. The frontal attack made no more progress. The Russians came on again and again, but the Swedes doggedly held their ground. The fight went on for eight hours, the whole length of the short northern day. Towards sunset General Adlerkreutz, who was now acting as Klingsporr's chief-of-the-staff, noticed that the Russian fire was slackening, and abandoning the defensive attitude for the attack, charged them all along the line, and drove them from the field. The fight had cost a loss of about 1,000 killed and wounded, among the former the Swedish general Fleming. One of the chivalrous incidents of the struggle is worth noting. In those days of smoothbore flintlocks, men fought at a range of from 100 to 200 yards, and so it was that Koulneff, who commanded the Russian attack, noticed a Swedish officer who was recklessly exposing himself to danger, and, admiring his courage,  he told the Cossack sharpshooters not to fire at the brave fellow. The officer bore a name now famous in Scandinavian literature—he was a Captain Björnsterne. But the Swedes were equally generous, for, in the same fight. Adlerkreutz was so struck by Koulneff's intrepid bearing, that he gave orders that care should be taken not to shoot down the Russian general.

Klingsporr withdrew next day northwards to Lumijoki. where he waited for reinforcements, which soon gave him the advantage of numbers over the Russians, who now made no further attempts to disturb him. In the last week of April he felt strong enough to assume the offensive. He had good information, for the peasants were all friendly to the Swedes, and he learned in this way that two Russian columns, under Generals Boulatoff and Toutchkoff, were marching to unite their forces near Revolax in his front. He resolved to delay one of them while he overwhelmed the other with a sudden attack, and on April 27th he set in motion two columns. The smaller, under Adlerkreutz, was to keep Toutchkoff engaged, while the larger, under General Cronstedt (a relative of the admiral), was to interpose between his force and Boulatoff, and try to break up Boulatoff's corps. The attacks were to have been simultaneous, but Cronstedt's march was delayed by deep snow drifts, and Adlerkreutz was in a very serious position, engaged with Toutchkoff's force (which repelled all his attacks), and at the same time exposed to the danger of Boulatoff's corps coming up. But in the afternoon, when Boulatoff, marching towards the sound of his colleague's guns, was approaching Revolax, he suddenly found him-

self attacked by a Swedish column, which, to his utter surprise, debouched not from a road, but from the hollow of a frozen stream, the ice of which it had used as a roadway. At the same time a sharp fire from the edges of all the fir-woods on both his flanks told him that Cronstedt, before showing his hand, had lined all available cover with his sharpshooters. He saw he was caught in a trap. Forming his brigade into a solid column, he tried to bear down the Swedish main attack, but as this first effort failed, he cut his colours from the staff, and giving them to one of his officers, told him to try to get through to Toutchkoff, and tell him that the brigade would fight to the last. Wounded several times, Boulatoff did not give the word to cease fire till he was actually dying. In this condition he fell into the hands of the Swedes, who took

800 prisoners and four guns. Some hundreds more of the Russians got away in the gathering darkness, and the wreck of the brigade rallied to the standard of Toutchkoff, who, on hearing of his colleague's fate, retreated to Pyhajoki, leaving a rear-guard at Brahestad. His force was a little over 5,000 men, with nineteen guns. Klingsporr had now 12,000, but there was a good deal of sickness in his army.

He followed the Russians with his main body, sending a flying column under Colonel Sandels to recover possession of the lake-land of central Finland. The Russians had declared that they came to deliver the Finns from Swedish tyranny, but now the peasants were rising in insurrection on the flank and rear of the invaders and cutting off their convoys. It was thus difficult for them to get supplies, or to maintain their communications. The Russians abandoned Brahestad and retreated to Gamle Carlaby before the advancing; Swedes, Klingsporr crossing the Pyhajoki in triumph, while the insurrection spread eastwards, supported by Colonel Sandels' column, and the Russians had to rapidly take precautions for the defence of their own frontier.

Then with the first days of May there was a pause in the operations. For the thaw had begun, and every river was a torrent of rushing water and whirling masses of ice; the streams of melting snow made watercourses of the roads; and marsh and lake were no longer passable for the flying columns. To Count Klingsporr it must have seemed that victory was now assured for Sweden. He had recovered the north of the kingdom. Even with the forces at his command he could drive the Russians back to the south, where, as he supposed, Sweaborg was defying their attacks. The thaw would bring to his aid not merely the Swedish fleet, but the English squadron, which had reached Gothenburg, escorting transports that conveyed 14,000 British troops under Sir John Moore. It looked as if the summer would see the disastrous retreat of the invaders from Finland.

But all these hopes were dashed to the ground when news came, first that Sweaborg was in the hands of Russia, and then that King Gustavus was quarrelling with his English allies. He was dreaming of vast schemes of conquest—of repeating the exploits of his great namesake, the Gustavus of the Thirty Years' War, by throwing himself into Denmark at the head of his Swedes and Sir John Moore's troops, and intervening in Germany with decisive effect. When Sir John would not listen to these wild schemes, the king refused to co-operate with him in any other direction, and after useless debates, the British troops re-embarked, and Sir John Moore sailed away to find victory, death, and fame in the Spanish peninsula. Even the king's Swedish forces, after a long delay, were frittered away in ill-directed enterprises against the Russian fortified positions in the south of Finland. In the shallows among the islands Gustavus carried on, with varying success, a kind of amphibious warfare, where his own galleys and troops acted against the Russian batteries and the galleys and gunboats taken by the invaders from his own arsenals. Had he used his resources to reinforce Klingsporr, that brave and capable soldier would have accomplished more.

Even as it was, Klingsporr inflicted further defeats on the invaders, recovered all the west of Finland from them, and, co-operating with Sandels, freed the centre, where at one time all the Russians held was the fortified town of Kuopio, strong in its position in the midst of a labyrinth of lakes and creeks.

Meanwhile the joint Swedish and British fleet had defeated the Russian fleet off Hango Head, and blockaded it in Baltsch Port till the autumn. It lay there under the protection of some shore batteries, until one day a violent storm forced the blockading squadron to stand out to sea, when the Russians ran out also and got safely into Cronstadt. No attempt was made by the allied fleet to recover Sweaborg, or even to menace it. With the key of Finland thus in their hands, the Russians held the south of the country through the summer.

Then came an armistice; divided counsels among the Swedes, quarrels and dissensions among the leaders, which were the prelude or the revolution in the following year; and 1809 saw the fall of Gustavus, and the treaty signed which gave Finland to Russia.

AUGUST 21, 1808
The Battle of Vimiera

Major-General Sir E. F. Du Cane

Napoleon's great project for the invasion of England, in 1805, was frustrated by the failure of De Villeneuve to carry through the profound naval strategic operations which were intended to procure for him the necessary command of the Channel. It was indefinitely postponed by the subsequent destruction of the French and Spanish fleets at Trafalgar, on the 21st October, 1805. His persevering and fertile mind at once was directed to devising some other plan for humbling and ruining the nation whom, ten years later, he called " the most powerful, the most constant, the most generous of my enemies."

England was turning to account her preponderant sea power by carrying out a blockade of the whole line of French coast. As Napoleon could not retaliate by a naval blockade of the English ports,' he believed that her commerce might equally be interrupted and blockaded at the other end of the voyage, if she was not allowed to land her goods at their destination. He therefore conceived the plan, called "the Continental system," of closing the ports of the Continent against us, which his superior power on land would, he thought, enable him to do. He hoped by this means to distress and impoverish her; and that, gradually building a new navy, and possessing himself of those of other Powers, he might obtain command of a fleet large enough to overwhelm the English force, and ultimately carry out his scheme of invasion. This Continental system was embodied in the Berlin decree of November, 1806, and the Milan decrees of 1807. It required, in order to its full success, not only the obedience to his decrees which he might expect from those countries in which his power and influence

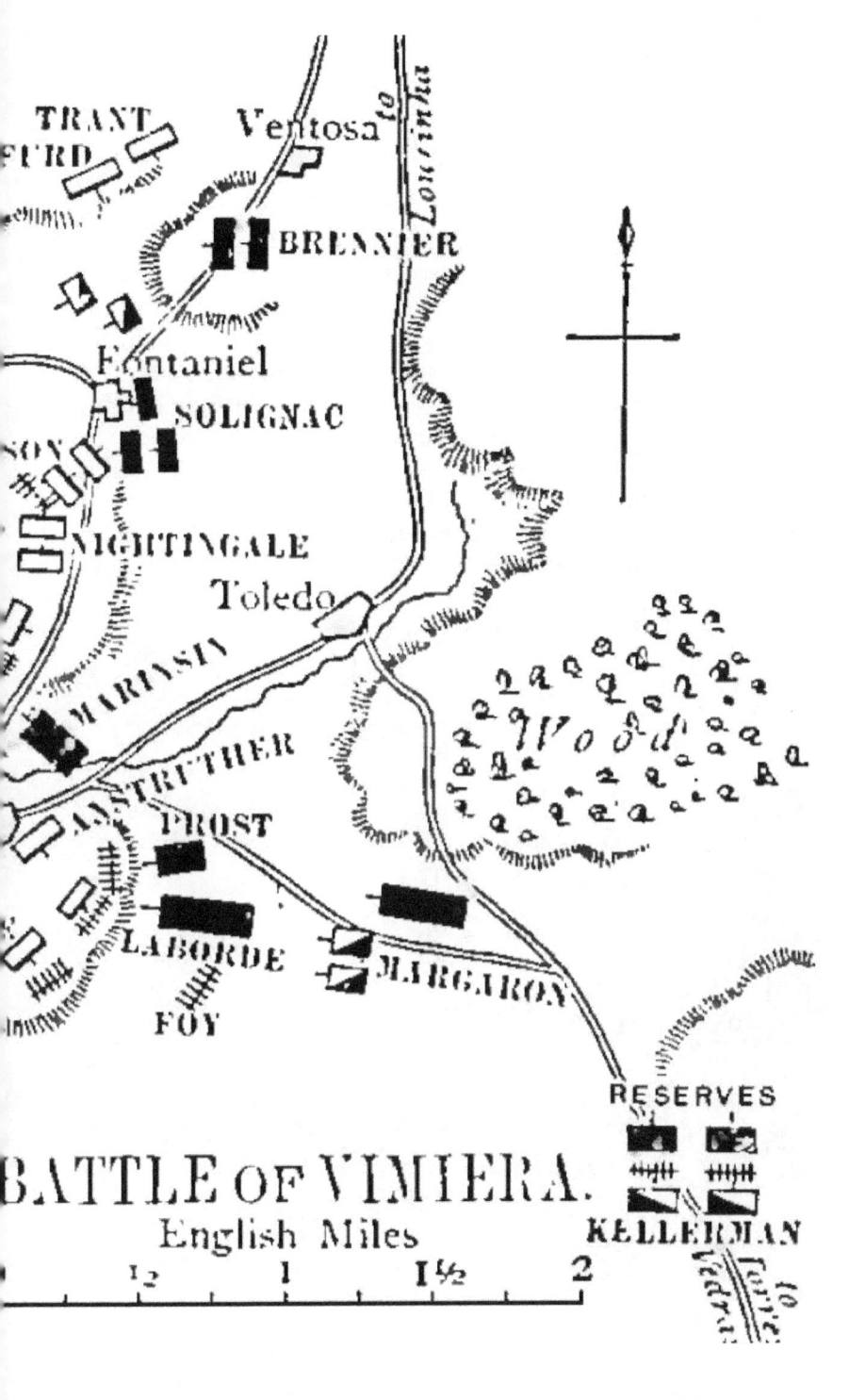

were direct and predominant, but also the co-operation of other Continental Governments which still retained their independence; and his course of action for the rest of his career was largely influenced by his determination to force them to follow his policy in this respect.

Great Britain naturally resolved that countries which excluded her trading ships from their ports should not obtain the merchandise they needed in any other way, and her command of the sea enabled this resolution to be effectually carried out; with the result that all the countries which submitted to Napoleon's influence endured the hardship of being deprived of all commerce, of having no outlet for their own surplus produce, and no means of obtaining the comforts and necessaries they had been accustomed to obtain from other countries. These hardships were so unendurable that they came to be corrected by a system of licences—or tolerated smuggling—which was employed on both sides; but the feeling they gave rise to had a large share in the ultimate combination which led to Napoleon's overthrow. Meanwhile the system of compulsion, to which Napo-

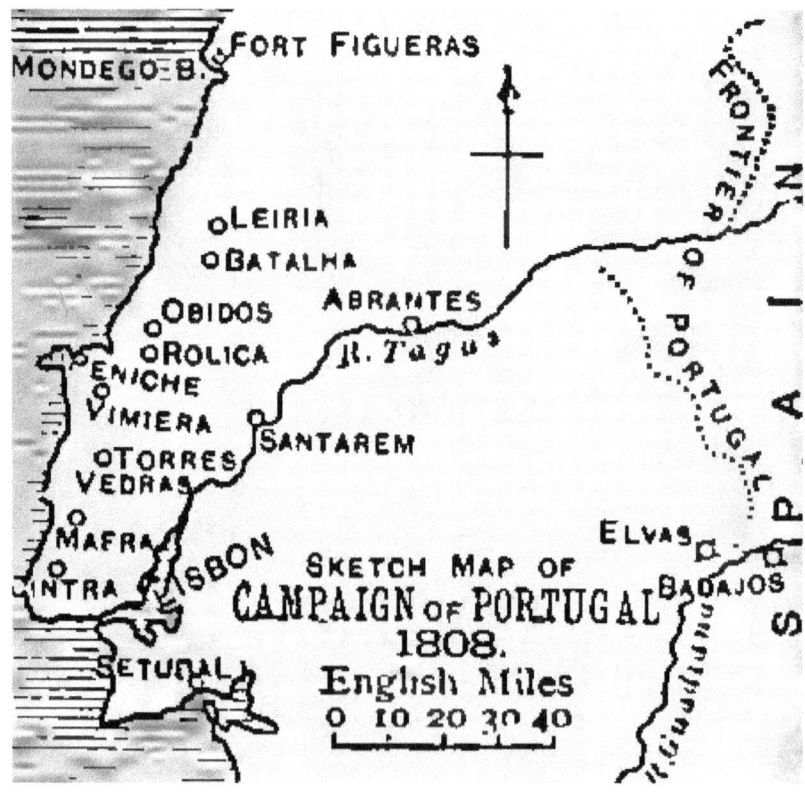

leon found it necessary to resort, had to be applied to Portugal, whose ports had always been open to Great Britain. This advantage he determined that she should no longer enjoy, and this not only in order to carry out his Continental system, but because he was conscious that an attack on his frontier on the side of the Peninsula might receive much assistance from troops and stores brought by sea and poured in through the ports of Portugal.

In 1806 he had already assembled an army at Bayonne intended to subjugate Portugal, but his project was postponed because his troops were required for his wars with Prussia and Russia in that and the early part of the following year; but, after he had settled matters to his satisfaction at Tilsit and elsewhere, he resumed his designs on Portugal and, secretly, on Spain, calling on the former to close her ports against Great Britain and declare war against her; and not content with forcing the Prince Regent to adopt these measures, further required him to confiscate the property of British merchants. The Portuguese Government refused to comply. Napoleon thereupon announced that "the house of Braganza" had "ceased to reign." On 27th October, 1807, he entered into a treaty with Spain for the partition of Portugal, under the provisions of which Junot, at the head of 29,000 men, made his way by forced marches through Spain to Lisbon, which he reached at the end of November, and took possession of the country. The prince regent fled to Brazil, in a fleet got quickly ready by the aid of British seamen.

The Portuguese were then disarmed, the army disbanded—except a part, who were sent to France—and the country was plundered—officially through forced contributions, and privately by Junot and his officers. Following shortly on these measures. Napoleon, early in 1808, without any pretence of right, marched his armies into Spain, surprised and seized the principal frontier fortresses, and by the beginning of March had possessed himself of all the country north of the Ebro, the cession of which he demanded from the Spaniards. Thence Murat marched, in the same month, to Madrid; Dupont was directed on Cadiz, Duhesme on Catalonia, and Bessières held the north-east and the communications with France. Napoleon resolved to dethrone the Bourbons, and set one of his own brothers on the throne of Spain. In April he craftily induced the king and queen and their son Ferdinand to come to Bayonne to discuss their differences and the affairs of their county with him, and compelled the renunciation of their throne; after which they were removed to Valençay and there remained.

The Spanish authorities of Madrid, and 150 notables assembled at Bayonne, were prevailed upon to elect Joseph Bonaparte king of Spain, and he proceeded to Madrid to take up the government.

The removal of the royal family caused an insurrection in Madrid, which broke out on the 2nd May, and was suppressed by Murat with great barbarity.

The news of this spreading through Spain, a general insurrection broke out all through the country. The Spanish regular army had been weakened by drafts sent to join the French troops in Germany, so numbered only 70,000 men; but by the middle of June 150,000 men enrolled themselves to support the regular army, and the French forces were attacked on all sides with varying success. Saragossa succeeded in repelling Lefèvre, and other towns in Catalonia were equally successful. Moncey was compelled to retreat from Valencia, and the French retained nothing in Catalonia but Barcelona and Figueras. Bessières obtained a great victory over Cuesta at Rio Seco, but the Spaniards struck a resounding blow against Dupont, who, with 20,000 men, surrendered as prisoners of war on the 19th July, at Baylen, in Andalusia.

The effect of this last victory was prodigious, for it destroyed the reputation for invincibility which had attached itself to the French troops all over Europe, and the more so because the victorious army was principally composed of untrained levies. It forced King Joseph to abandon Madrid and retire to Burgos, and Castaños, the successful general, entered Madrid in triumph.

The news of the revolt of the Spaniards was received with great satisfaction in England, which was increased by a deputation from the Asturias to solicit help. With the hearty approval of all parties, it was determined to aid the movement in every practicable way.

Portugal had not been behindhand in following the example of Spain, and had risen against her conquerors, largely under the guidance of the Bishop of Oporto.

It was determined to send an expedition to co-operate with and reinforce the popular movements in both countries. A suitable force was ready to hand when the determination was come to. A corps of 10,000 men, after assembling in the Downs, had been brought together at Cork, with a view to operations in South America; and here the force lay in transports for about six weeks, during which time most of them were not allowed to disembark, the delay being due, probably, to the change of circumstances which suggested a change in their destination.

Sir Arthur Wellesley was put in charge of this little army. He was the junior lieutenant-general on the list, and was not designated for the chief command of the expedition. This position was given to Sir Hugh Dalrymple, with Sir Harry Burrard as second in command.

This force sailed on the 12th July, with sealed orders. Sir Arthur went on in advance, to settle the point of disembarkation. He had an interview with the Spanish authorities at Corunna, but they were not anxious that the British force should disembark near their strong post of Ferrol, and encouraged him to land in Portugal, which, indeed, was the most desirable course, for it enabled them to support and connect the operations of the Spanish armies of the north and south from behind the curtain which the Portuguese mountains afforded.

Sir Arthur, after consulting Admiral Cotton at Lisbon, decided that it would not be prudent to disembark near that city, where the French were in force. He therefore directed the transports on Mondego Bay, which is about 110 miles north of Lisbon, and commanded only by Port Figueras, which was held by some English marines.

Here, then, they arrived, after a propitious voyage, on the 30th July, and heard the encouraging news of the surrender of Baylen.

This brief sketch is necessary for the understanding of the position of affairs in the Peninsula when our army landed in Mondego Bay to commence the war which lasted six years, with momentous results to our own country and to Europe. It is now necessary to give some description of the country, with a view to the proper understanding of the plan of campaign.

The Peninsula may be roughly described as being a square of about 500 miles north and south, and approximately the same distance east and west, surrounded by the sea on all sides excepting where it joins on to France on the eastern portion of its northern side, the boundary between the two countries being formed by the Pyrenees. A mountain chain, continuous with the Pyrenees, runs parallel with the northern coast, and cuts off the narrow provinces of the Asturias and Biscay.

Portugal, on the west, is not cut off from Spain by a similar continuous mountain chain, for the large Rivers Douro, Tagus, and Guadiana, which rise towards the eastern side, run a generally east and west course through the whole of Spain and Portugal, and are separated by mountain chains; but the spurs of the separating mountain chains interlace so completely at the lower part of the courses of, those rivers that they practically constitute a continuous rocky boundary, enclosing a width of a little more than 100 miles from the Atlantic seaboard,

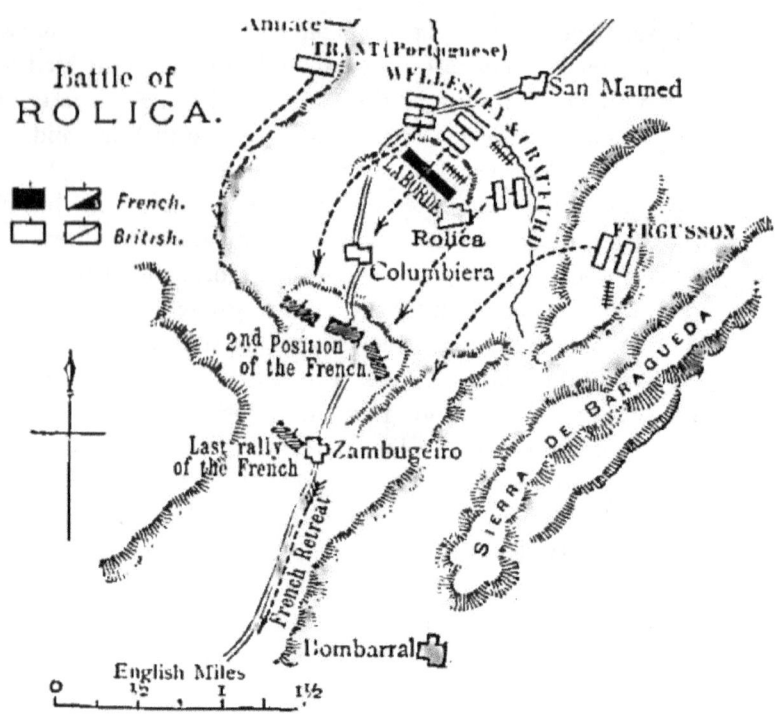

which constitutes the kingdom of Portugal. The mountains thus form such an effective obstacle as to have enabled that kingdom always successfully to resist forcible annexation by Spain.

To a country which had command of the sea, as Great Britain had, Portugal afforded a most favourable position to act against an enemy in Spain and France; for its ports afforded many secure landing-places for troops and munitions of war, which could be transferred by sea from one part to the other of the theatre of war, to issue from behind the rocky screen which the mountains afforded, and attack the enemy on the north, or south, as might be desired.

The first object, then, was to obtain possession of this country and its ports, or, in other words, to turn the French armies out of it. The operations by which this object was attained afford a very remarkable illustration of the advantage gained by the power of free movement by sea. secure from any interruption by the enemy, and they are given in some detail in order to show how the sea-coast of Portugal formed one prolonged base of operations, at any point of which reinforcements, victuals, and stores for the army could safely be delivered.

Junot was more or less isolated by the effect of the insurrection in Spain; he was further hampered by the insurrection in Portugal, and by the presence, as part of his force, of a contingent of Spanish troops. Those under his immediate command in Lisbon he disarmed and placed in hulks in the Tagus, but those who were in Oporto took the French general prisoner and marched for Galicia. Junot then took measures to concentrate his army at Abrantes, on the Tagus, holding the frontier fort of Elvas, which ensured his line of retreat to Spain by the basin of the Guadiana, and guarded him against attack on that side, and Almeida, which served the same office in the north in the basin of the Douro. He also kept possession of the forts of Setubal and Peniche, on the coast. The total force he held at his disposal numbered, on 26th July, 26,000 men.

He detached Laborde with 5,000 men, of whom 500 were cavalry, and six guns, north-ward, to suppress the insurrection—-in which he was not successful—to cover the concentration of the French troops, and also to watch and check the English Army, of whose anticipated arrival Junot had heard. Loison, with 7,000 foot and 1,200 horse, was operating against the insurgents in the south, and had gained a victory over them at Evora, when he was directed to join Laborde and concentrate against the new enemy. This they intended to do at Leiria, but were forestalled, as will be seen; and the two divisions were therefore separated by a mountainous and difficult country.

The army above referred to as having sailed from Cork, under Sir Arthur Wellesley, formed only a part of that which was destined to operate in the Peninsula. Five thousand men, under Generals Anstruther and Acland, sailed to join Wellesley—the former from Ramsgate, the latter from Harwich.

General Spencer had brought 5,000 men from Egypt to Sicily and thence to Gibraltar: it had been proposed to employ them at Cadiz, but, as their assistance was refused at that point, they were ordered to join Sir Arthur Wellesley's force, and disembarked at Mondego Bay.

A force of 12,000 men, under Sir John Moore, was recalled from Sweden and directed to join the British army in Portugal. The total British force, therefore, considerably outnumbered that which was at Junot's disposal, without taking into account any assistance the Portuguese could supply; but it was at first very deficient in cavalry, having only one squadron of the 20th Light Dragoons.

The disembarkation commenced on the 1st August by the landing of the Rifles, and was not completed until the 8th. The shores of Mondego Bay are open and shelving, and when there is any wind a heavy surf is formed, just enough to make disembarkation difficult.

Several boats were upset, and the cavalry found the advantage of the orders which had been given them, to stand upright in the boats with bridle in hand, ready to leap into the saddle.

On the 9th, Sir A. Wellesley moved off with 12,300 men and 18 guns, carrying eighteen days' provisions—three in haversacks and the rest on mules. On that day and the 11th the army, assembled at Leiria, on the main road from Lisbon to Oporto, forestalling and preventing the junction at that point which Laborde and Loison had arranged. Here the baggage and tents of the army were left. They followed the high road for some days, marching in burning sun and hot sand, and bivouacking in the open. On the 13th they were at Batalha, where Laborde had spent the 11th and 12th looking for a defensive position, but, finding it too extensive, had fallen back on Obidos.

It was observed that the Portuguese did not help the British very heartily. They had only 6,000 men, and refused to co-operate unless they were supplied with food, money, and arms from the English stores, so that no more than 1,400 joined under Colonel Trant, and about 300 cavalry came in by four and five at a time, with a few officers. They were well equipped and mounted, and some had belonged to the Lisbon police. On the 15th, the army first felt the French at Brilhos, in front of Obidos, and a few men fell in a skirmish, among them Lieutenant Bunbury, of the Rifles, who was shot in the head and died immediately—the first English officer killed in the Peninsular War.

On the 17th August the army, comprising 14,000 men and 18 guns, left Obidos. Sir Arthur reconnoitred Laborde's position from a steep rock about two miles west of the Roliça road, and found him, with 5,000 men and six guns, occupying isolated ground of moderate elevation near the village of Roliça, which closes in the valley three miles south of Obidos. Laborde's great care was to hold on to the mountains on his right, in the hope of Loison joining him with his 6,000 men. The British, on the other hand, wished to keep them separate, and to drive Laborde back before Loison could come up. Sir Arthur, therefore, formed his force in three parts. The centre, consisting of 9,000 infantry with twelve guns, he himself commanded, having Craufurd under him. On his left he sent Fergusson, with a division and six guns, to make a movement through the mountains by which he could turn Laborde's right. On the right he sent Trant's Portuguese to turn the French left. The cavalry were not engaged, but disposed so as to look more formidable than they really were.

General Foy, who was present with the French army, notices the fine appearance presented by the English, who marched slowly, regaining at once their compact order whenever it was broken by the obstacles of the ground, and ever converging towards the narrow position of the French. This, he observes, would much strike the imagination of the young French soldiers, who had hitherto only had to deal with bandits and irregulars.

As the movements were developed, Laborde found it prudent to retire to the heights of Zambugeiro, about a mile in rear, where the two mountain spurs join. The British general, who now further reinforced his left wing, continued the same tactics as before—namely, a centre attack, assisted by turning movements on both flanks, which his greatly superior numbers made possible—but Fergusson's force, instead of marching round the French right so as to take them in rear, inclined towards their own right, and thus came upon and attacked them in front, crowding the centre. The centre also attacked before the Portuguese, on their right, were in a position to give much assistance.

The whole British force was, therefore, crowded into a space of less than a mile of very broken and craggy ground—so broken that the different bodies of troops were unable to keep up effective connection. The advantage of numbers was therefore entirely lost, while the French retained the advantage of a very strong position. The right wing of the 29th Regiment, now taking a wrong direction, came upon a point in Laborde's line to which he was drawing in the troops from his left. The regiment was therefore taken in flank while it was attacking in front, and its right wing was almost annihilated, losing its colonel—Lake—and a major and some men prisoners; but General Hill (afterwards Lord Hill) galloped up, rallied them on their left wing, and on the 9th joining them, put himself at their head and charged the enemy, who resisted strongly, and Colonel Stewart of the 9th fell fighting with great vehemence. The French had possession of two small buildings on the hill, from which they annoyed the skirmishers of the 95th Rifles very much. They became angry, and one of them, jumping up, rushed forward crying "Over, boys, over!" to which the whole line responded "Over, over!" and dashed in, fixing bayonets as they ran. The French turned tail and evacuated the buildings, in which were some wine butts. These being pierced by bullets, the wine ran out and mingled with the blood of the wounded men lying there while they were being tended by the surgeons. A man of the 95th Rifle Brigade named Harris, who relates this incident, describes the French soldiers as wearing long white frock coats and bearing the imperial eagle in front of their caps. Laborde now found himself strongly attacked in front and both his flanks being turned, cutting off his line of communication with Loison. Retreat was therefore absolutely necessary, and this movement he carried out steadily, attacking his enemy three times with half his force and with cavalry charges, so as to enable the other half to retire. At the village of Columbiera, where the ridge of hill widened out, but was protected by ravines on the flanks, he made another stand, but finally was forced to retreat into the mountains, ultimately reaching Torres Vedras. The British bivouacked at and round Zambugeiro. In this action Laborde was wounded, and lost 600 men killed and wounded; the British loss was 500.

The high road towards Lisbon was now clear, and it was the intention of Sir A. Wellesley to march for Torres Vedras, and so cut off Loison and Laborde from that capital; but in the night he heard of the arrival of a fleet off the coast with reinforcements, so, relinquishing the high road, he moved by one nearer the coast, so that he might cover their disembarkation. On the 18th August, therefore, he marched to Lourinha, and on the 19th to Vimiera, a small village on the Maceira, nine miles from Torres Vedras, and two or three miles from Porto Novo at its mouth, where the troops brought by General Acland were to disembark, which they did on the night of the 20th. General Anstruther's troops disembarked on the 19th at Payo Mayor, at the mouth of the river which runs by Lourinha. They landed without camp kettles, and apparently with little baggage; for Captain Dobbs, of the 52nd, says:

"We used to wash our shirts in the nearest stream and sit by watching till they were dry; but the men had great joy, for they were relieved from hair-tying, which was an operation grievous to be borne."

Among the officers who landed with Anstruther's brigade was Colin Campbell—afterwards Lord Clyde—who says in his diary, "Lay out that night for the first time in my life." On the day of the battle his captain thought it well to commence his instruction, so, being in a rear company, he took him out and walked him about under fire, which he says was "the greatest kindness that could have been shown me, and through life I have been grateful for it."

Junot, meanwhile, marched from Lisbon, with Loison, to join Laborde at Torres Vedras, where he assembled a force of 14,000 men, including 1,300 cavalry under Margaron. Hearing that large reinforcements for the British were off the coast, he desired to attack them before the disparity in numbers became too great. The British force

now amounted to 16,000 men, and while Junot designed to march on the night of the 20th, in order to attack the British on the 21st, Sir Arthur Wellesley intended to march at 5 a.m. on the 21st round his flank, avoiding Torres Vedras and marching on Mafra, thirteen miles nearer to Lisbon than Torres Vedras. By this movement he would cut the French off from the capital. But at this juncture Sir Harry Burrard arrived off the port, in company with Clinton, the adjutant-general, and Murray, the quartermaster-general. Sir Arthur had an interview with him on board the *Brazen*, in which he communicated his proposed march. Sir Harry Burrard disapproved the project. Sir Arthur therefore issued the order on the 20th: "The army will halt tomorrow, the men to sleep accoutred tonight in readiness to move out, and to be under arms at three o'clock in the morning."

Sir Arthur's project was, perhaps, risky. The road he would have to follow was narrow and rocky, the troops would have to move on a single line with the French on their flank, and there was no good fighting-position available. Sir H. Burrard therefore observed, with some reason, that it would be more prudent to await the arrival of Sir John Moore and his large force, by which he would much outnumber the enemy. The position the army now occupied was not taken up with a view to a defensive battle, as Sir Arthur had not intended to stop there. Near the village of Vimiera the little River Maceira breaks through a chain of hills, the southern portion of which runs about east and west, and joins the sea above Porto Novo; the northern part runs almost parallel with the coast—or, say, north-east and south-west—and has an intermediate ridge between it and the sea. In front of these, and in front, too, of the little village of Vimiera, is a lower and isolated hill, which covers the opening in the chain of hills and the plain through which the Maceira runs. The bulk of the army—six. brigades, commanded by Generals Hill, Nightingale, Bowes, Craufurd, Fergusson, and Acland—besides artillery, was placed on the southern hill, which formed the right of the position, with advanced posts on the Mafra road. The lower hill in front was occupied by two brigades—Fane's on the left, and Anstruther's on the right—with six guns. The northern hill, forming the left, was protected by a difficult or impassable ravine in its front, and being without water, besides being out of the direct line of an enemy's attack, it was occupied only by Trant's Portuguese and some of the Rifles. The commissariat stores were posted on the plain behind the central hill, and here the cavalry were stationed, facing south, to protect the level opening between the centre and right.

The advance of Junot's army was detected during the night by a cavalry patrol posted about two miles south of Vimiera, who heard from an innkeeper in a village in front that his young man had that day come from Lisbon, and had passed the French army in full march. This news was shortly confirmed by the noise of horses and guns passing a wooden bridge in front of the village, and the patrol took back the information to Sir Arthur, who was found with his staff sitting back to back on a table in the hall of his house, "swinging their legs." Sir Arthur took the necessary precautions, though he did not quite believe the report, and this incredulity was confirmed by the continued failure of the French to appear, for indeed they did not advance that night beyond the village near which they had been heard. About seven o'clock in the morning clouds of dust disclosed the approach of the French: drums and bugles sounded, and the troops took up their positions. In an hour the French cavalry crowned the hill eastward of the English position, and, as no advance was made against the hill forming the English right, it became apparent that Junot intended to attack them on the left. He had, in fact, reconnoitred their right, which was the more direct point of approach, quite up to the mouth of the river, and having found them strongly posted on that side, he had decided to leave it entirely alone and to assail the centre of the position, at the same time marching round them to capture the hill on the left, which, as has already been described, was very scantily furnished with troops. If he got possession of this hill he would take in reverse all who were on the right of the position, as well as those who were in the centre, who were posted on the little hill in front of the village.

As soon as Sir Arthur Wellesley perceived this movement, and that no attack was to be made on his right, he withdrew all the troops on that hill except three regiments under General Hill, which he retained there as a reserve for the centre, and marched them across the valley, concealed by the ground from the French, to take position on the hill on the left, which they believed to be unoccupied. Trant's Portuguese, and one brigade of British under Craufurd, were posted on the ridge intermediate between that hill and the sea. Fergusson commanded on the extreme left. Bowes and Acland, with five regiments, were posted to form a column on the hill overlooking Vimiera, so as to be a reserve to Fergusson. General Laborde was directed, with 6,000 men, to attack the centre hill, supported by Loison. Each division was in column, with two brigades in front and artillery in the intervals. Laborde led at the head of the 86th French, which crossed bayonets during the action with the 50th English. Brennier, with a brigade, was at the same time sent directly at the hill forming the English left. Kellerman with his grenadiers was held in reserve.

The morning was bright and sunny, tipping the bayonets of the advancing French and of the steady British line, with the colours floating over them and the dark cannon on the rising ground. About eight o'clock a cloud of light troops, followed by a strong column of the enemy, entered a pine wood in front of our position, in which some Rifles were posted on picket, and drove them in on the 97th, who were in support. In this fight three brothers of the name of Hort, in the 95th Rifles, pressed on the French with such daring intrepidity that Lieut. Molloy, who himself was never far from his opponents in action, had to rebuke them repeatedly. "D—n you," cried he, "get back and get under cover. Do you think you are fighting with your fists that you run into the teeth of the French?"

The line, seeing the Rifles retiring, cried out, "D—n them: charge!" but General Fane interfered. "Don't be too eager, men—not yet. Well done, 95th! Well done, 43rd and 52nd!" As soon as the riflemen had cleared the 97th, passing by their right flank to the rear, the latter regiment poured a steady fire upon the advancing column and held it in check, while the 52nd took it in flank and drove it back in confusion.

With this attack began the battle of Vimiera. There was so little wind that the smoke from the rifles hung about and prevented the men from aiming. Anstruther then detached the 43rd to take up its position in a little churchyard on the edge of the declivity on Fane's left, in order to meet Kellerman's grenadiers, who were reinforcing the attack on that side.

This battle was remarkable for another innovation besides the absence of pigtails—*viz*. that shrapnel shell were first used there by the battery under Colonel Robe. Foy remarks on the shot first knocking over the leading files of French and then bursting among those in the rear. General Fane, on the left centre, soon made use of a discretionary

power which had been given him, and increased the artillery force on the hill by ordering up the reserve, and the French, on coming within a hundred yards of the summit, were met by the converging fire of six regiments. The artillery tore lanes through the advancing columns, and each time the English soldiers shouted; but the French closed up and marched steadily on. All the horses of the French artillery were killed, two colonels wounded, and two pelotons of grenadiers disappeared—being, in fact, wiped out. Soon they had to contend with the fire of another battery of artillery—for Acland, whose brigade was ascending the left-hand ridge when the battle began, halted his guns, unlimbered, and poured their fire into their right flank; and, again, of two English battalions who moved forward to meet them, and poured in a murderous volley on their reaching the summit of the hill; they were besides charged in flank by the 50th, who were wheeled to their left by Colonel Walker. They were also charged by the 43rd in mass, and driven back with strenuous fighting, in which the regiment lost 120 men. The French then turned and fled down the hill, with the loss of many prisoners and seven guns.

The moment had now arrived for making use of the small force of cavalry. General Fane therefore directed the 20th Light Dragoons to advance and charge the retreating troops. "Go at them, lads," he said, " and let them see what you're made of." The cavalry, therefore, went threes about and swept round the elbow of the hill, forming into half-squadrons on the way—the 20th in the centre, the Portuguese on the flanks. "Now, 20th—now" shouted Sir Arthur Wellesley, and his staff clapped their hands and gave them a cheer, on which the whole force put their horses to speed. The Portuguese, however, soon pulled up right and left, and no more was seen of them till the 20th returned, when they were found still standing where they had been left. The 20th are said by Foy to have made two officers prisoners and to have taken some guns, and that the charge reached the Duke of Abrantes, who was with the reserve. He says, too, that they were charged in their turn by the general's guard—the 26th Chasseurs, led by Prince Salm-Salm, and the 4th and 5th Dragoons, a formidable force against the small English body.

The charge is thus described in a letter written from Belem, on 28th Sept., by Lieut. Du Cane, of the 20th Light Dragoons. It differs curiously from the account given by the historians:

"I rather suspect my information will be more correct than the despatches, for they describe our being overpowered by the enemy's cavalry. Certainly they were strong enough to have cut us up if they'd known what they were about, but not one of them, although within fifty yards of us, ever attempted to come amongst us; and a few of our men, thinking they were Portuguese, by being so quiet nor offering to molest us, went in amongst them, by which they got either killed or taken. Otherwise, they were the only men we lost by the French dragoons, the rest being shot by the infantry. Poor Colonel Taylor was shot by them by pressing the broken infantry too far, without support. Captain Eustace was taken in the same manner by following them up too far, and was severely wounded in the thigh, but is getting a little better since he got out of the hands of the French. I thought it was a toss-up whether we were not all taken or destroyed; for we charged too far amongst them, and never was there a more unequal contest, on account of the ground. We first of all charged through a vineyard and got into a wood, which was intersected from the vineyard by immense large dykes, in which several horses fell, unable to extricate themselves."

Our infantry on the hill seemed disposed to follow the 20th to repair its check, but Sir Arthur forbade them to leave their position without his order, and the cavalry returned with their white leather breeches, hands, and arms all besmeared with blood. Lieut. Du Cane's letter proceeds:—

"When Eustace, my captain, was taken—which is the second time now—he was taken to General Junot, who appeared exceedingly pleased to see him, gave him refreshments out of his own canteen, and, after paying him several compliments, declared to him that he had seen a good deal of service, but that he never was a witness before of a detachment like ours of dragoons doing their duty so well. He gave us wonderful praise, and certainly not undeservedly."

While this attack on the English centre was going on—to end in a complete repulse——Brennier, who was trying to force his way to the hill which formed the English left, was faring very badly, for want of knowledge of the ground. The attack was directed on an impassable ravine, and his force for a long time produced no effect. Junot, perceiving this, sent Solignac with a column of all arms to make a wider sweep, so as to turn the ravine, and come upon the English left more on a level. Having effected this movement, he expected to find himself on the flank of the English, but instead of that he found himself opposed by a front, three lines deep, consisting of Fergusson's, Nightingale's, and Bowes's Brigades, which faced across the ridge, with skirmishers on their flank, relying for protection on one flank on the steep rocky ravine which had baffled Brennier, and on the other on a force of Portuguese, who, with one brigade of English under Craufurd, were so posted as to be able to cut him off if he advanced, and place him between two fires. As Solignac approached, Fergusson met him with a determined and impetuous bayonet-charge, which drove the French down the hill and destroyed the whole front line of one regiment. Solignac was wounded and his force cut off from their line of retreat, with the loss of six guns, of which the 71st and 82nd took charge. But at this moment Brennier, who had found an accessible place in the ravine, worked his way up to the ridge behind Fergusson, beat back the above regiments, and recaptured the guns. The English troops, however, rallied, charged, and broke the French, making Brennier a prisoner. Craufurd's brigade arrived and attacked them on their right.

The English had now gained a complete victory on all parts of the field, and their trumpets and bugles sounded all along the line. The French left had been completely driven back, leaving only Margaron's cavalry and half Kellerman's grenadiers unbroken. Solignac was cut off, and on the verge of having to lay down his arms. Brennier's brigade was completely broken. When that general was taken prisoner he anxiously inquired whether the reserve had attacked. Sir Arthur Wellesley heard him make the inquiry, and questioned the other prisoners on the subject, who declared that it had. Knowing then that the French were beaten and exhausted, while he had still a large force, fresh and available for further operations, and that owing to the movement of the French to his left, which was the side furthest from Torres Vedras and from Lisbon, the troops which formed his right were some two miles nearer to those towns than the French, he planned a combined movement which should finish the campaign at a stroke.

Solignac's division was, as has been related, on the point of laying down its arms. Sir Arthur proposed to assail the weakened French troops on his front, and drive them into the mountains away from Lisbon, and at the same time to detach the fresh troops from his right and centre, under General Hill, to march on Torres Vedras, and so effectually to bar the French from the capital. Unfortunately, at this time Sir Harry Burrard thought fit to assume the direction of affairs. He had landed about 9 o'clock, and finding the army engaged, considered it right not to interfere, but to allow Sir Arthur Wellesley to complete the operations he had commenced; but now he sent orders to Fergusson to halt, and thus allowed Solignac's force, of which Junot's chief-of-the-staff, General Thiebault, had been sent to take command, to escape and rejoin the main body; nor would he sanction the operations which Sir Arthur had designed. This decision is thus referred to in the letter from which a quotation has already been given, which exemplifies the feeling in the British army.

"There is not the smallest doubt but if the enemy had been pursued by us—for but a half of our force were in action, and all the French nearly—for an hour, they would have surrendered at our discretion, and which was Sir Arthur's intention; but he was ordered not by Sir Harry Burrard, to whom much blame is attached, as well as Sir Hugh Dalrymple, for making terms. As it was, we certainly gained a very signal victory over the common enemy, and never had the English so fine an opportunity of gaining one of the most

decisive victories ever known, as that on the 21st August: they would have made no less than 20,000 men prisoners of war." The justice of this view is confirmed by General Foy, who says that by 12 o'clock, though the action had lasted but two and a half hours, all the French army had fought, and had lost 1,800 killed, wounded, and taken; the English reserve infantry had not fought, and their artillery was intact. There was nothing for it, however, but to halt. Junot quickly recovered his position between our army and Torres Vedras, and the opportunity of ending the campaign was lost. The unfortunate wounded had still to be attended to. Two long tables were arranged end to end in the churchyard, and on these were placed the men whose legs were to be amputated. Private Harris relates how he saw as many as twenty legs lying on the ground, many of them still having on the long black gaiters then worn by the infantry. Less tragical was the loss suffered by Major Travers, commanding the 95th Rifles, who was seen riding about the field, calling: "A guinea to the man who will find my wig."

On the 22nd of August Junot assembled a council of war, and in conformity with its decision, Kellerman was sent to treat for terms. By this time another remarkable change had taken place in the British side. Sir Harry Burrard, who had superseded Sir Arthur Wellesley, was himself superseded by Sir Hugh Dalrymple. Sir Harry Burrard's action in this campaign seems to have been confined to forbidding the fine strategic movements which Sir Arthur Wellesley planned. Two instances of this have already been related, but another had previously occurred. On reaching Mondego Bay he found letters from Sir Arthur Wellesley recommending that Sir John Moore's division should, on its arrival, be directed on Santarem. where he would close the French line of retreat from Lisbon, while Sir Arthur attacked him with superior forces in front, thus ensuring their surrender. Sir Harry Burrard would not, however, accede to this, and directed Sir John Moore to proceed to Maceira Bay, though he afterwards gave him the option of marching on Santarem. Ultimately this force landed at Maceira after the 21st.

Sir Hugh Dalrymple, who commanded at Gibraltar, had been given general directions of the operations in Portugal and the south of Spain, with the option to act personally, where he thought most advisable, but with a special recommendation of Sir Arthur Wellesley to his confidence, which probably was meant as a hint not to interfere with him. He thought fit, however, to set off on the 13th August for the scene of operations in the *Phoebe*, and hearing at Lisbon from Admiral Sir A. Cotton that the army had landed at Mondego Bay, he made for that point, intending to join the reinforcements expected with Sir H. Burrard, but on the 21st they descried the fleet of transports in Maceira Bay and heard of the victory. On the 22nd Sir Hugh Dalrymple landed and saw Sir H. Burrard. Sir A. Wellesley soon after arrived, and expressed much anxiety that the army should advance. Sir Hugh acceded to this. It was determined that they should march next day, but between 1 and 2 p.m. the enemy seemed to be again advancing, and Sir Arthur was directed to take up his position as before. It turned out to be Kellerman with a flag of truce. Kellerman was a keen observer, and he at once concluded, from the defensive attitude so quickly taken up by the English army, that their chiefs did not feel the confidence and security of victory. He observed also that Sir Hugh Dalrymple was hardly able to conceal his satisfaction that the French were ready to treat, and further, he noted the conversation aside of the British generals, who did not reckon on his understanding English. They expressed their fear that Sir John Moore's army might not be very near—possibly might not be able to land on such a bad coast—that bad weather might prevent the armies from receiving . provisions from the ships, and that nothing was to be hoped for from the Portuguese. All these imprudent revelations suggested to him to hold high language, and to extol the energy of the French and the help they could get from the Russians. A suspension of arms was finally agreed upon, and an agreement come to for a convention, on the basis of the French giving up Lisbon and all the strong places in Portugal, the French army to be transported in English ships to France, and the Russian fleet to be taken to England. This convention was signed at Lisbon on the 30th August, and confirmed by Sir Hugh Dalrymple on the 31st at Torres Vedras; but, having been transmitted to Lord Castlereagh on the 3rd September from the headquarters at Cintra, has always been called the Convention of Cintra. This triumphant result of the operations, by which Portugal was freed and became available as a fortified base for further operations against the French in Spain, was, nevertheless, most unfavourably received in England, as it seemed to compare disadvantageously with the Spanish success at Baylen; and the sensationalists of that day would gladly have seen a Marshal of France and 20,000 French troops arrive as prisoners in England.

A commission of inquiry was therefore held, on which Napoleon remarked that he was about to send Junot before a council of war, but that the British got the start of him by sending their generals to one. To him, indeed, the result was in disastrous comparison with his successes elsewhere. Of 29,000 troops sent to Portugal, 3,000 had perished, either from fatigue or in hospital, or assassinated; 2,000 fell in battle or were made prisoners; 2,000 who were embarked never returned, having been either wrecked or, being Swiss, taken service with the English; 22,000 only returned to France. The English, however, were not satisfied. All the principal officers concerned were summoned home to give evidence on the subject, leaving Sir John Moore in command of the British forces. This general commenced in December the operations in Spain which ended at Corunna, and closed that chapter of the Peninsular War.

June 21-22, 1809
The Battle of Aspern-Essling

D. H. Parry

With Austria's gigantic preparations for war, presuming upon the absence of the bulk of Napoleon's veteran troops in Spain; with Napoleon's wild gallop from Valladolid to Paris, during which he is said at one time to have accomplished seventy-five miles in five hours and a half; with the complicated political considerations; the masterly activity of the French emperor; the short campaign, opened by Austria, that laid her capital at Napoleon's feet in a month— we have little to do in the scope of this article. Our mission is to describe the battle named from the two little villages of Aspern and Essling, in and about which a series of sanguinary combats was waged during two nights and two days, resulting in a severe check to the *Grande Armée*, which check had a wide influence among German-speaking peoples; a battle fought now in the blaze of the hot May noon, now in the river-mists of early morning, and continued into the dark hours by the light of burning houses and the silver moonshine—all the while under a cannonade that strewed the growing corn with countless slain!

After the French victories of Abensberg, Landshut, Eckmühl, and Ratisbon, there had been a race between Napoleon and the Austrian commander, Archduke Charles, with Vienna as the goal; Napoleon pressing along the southern—or right—bank of the Danube to take it, the archduke hastening from Bohemia on the other side to its defence.

Foolishly halting for three days at Budweis, the Austrians arrived to find the French in possession, with more than 80,000 troops about the city, consisting of Lannes with the 2nd Corps; Masséna with the 4th, the Imperial Guard, and Bessières' cavalry reserve; while Davout

BATTLE OF ASPERN OR ESSLING
21st & 22nd May 1809.

held St. Polten with the 3rd Corps; Vandamme, farther away at Enns, Ebersberg, and Lintz, only waited for Bernadotte to relieve him; and Prince Eugène was expected from Italy with 40,000 more.

It was not sufficient to have seized the Austrian capital, to dictate his despatches from the imperial palace of Schönbrunn, where twenty-three years later his then unborn son was destined to expire; a decisive battle was necessary for Napoleon's aims and projects, and the "god of war" set about without delay to cross the Danube and meet the enormous Austrian army on the opposite shore.

Rising in the Black Forest, and fed by a thousand tributaries, the

mighty Danube rushes through some of the grandest scenery in Europe until it enters the plain above Vienna, where, broken by innumerable islands, it flows down past the city.

Like all rivers that receive the melted snow of the mountains, it is subject to sudden risings; and it lay, with its myriad isles and channels, a formidable barrier between the two enemies.

At Nussdorf, a mile and a half above Vienna, were the remnants of a broken bridge, but the stream was very rapid there. A better spot suggested itself, in front of Kaiser-Ebersdorf, about six miles below the city, where the river flowed in four channels, its fury somewhat broken and divided, and having the large island of Lob-awe, or Lobau, in its centre, where the whole army could find shelter in the event of a reverse.

At first it was decided to make the passage at both places; but two battalions being taken by the enemy in an island near Nussdorf, the operations there were only conducted as a feint, to cover the real site in front of Ebersdorf, where Generals Bertrand and Pernetti began to construct a series of long and difficult bridges, with very imperfect material at their command.

It has been said that the great arsenal of Vienna furnished every means required, but, as a matter of fact, there was a dearth of cordage; and, having no anchors to moor the structure against the current, boxes of shot and huge boulders had to be utilised, with very imperfect results, as will be seen hereafter.

Long lines of waggons wound over the dusty roads to the bank of the river; grey-coated drivers of the *train des equipages* conducted their teams to where the blue pontoniers hammered and sawed at piles and

trestles; field forges glowed, and all was hum and bustle, for Napoleon himself rode hither and thither, with a keen eye to the smallest detail; and the scene was one of the most picturesque activity.

Sixty-eight large boats—some say eighty—were discovered sunk in the river, and these were hauled out and brought along-shore, with nine huge rafts.

Marshals, generals, *aides-de-camp,* smart light cavalry, and heavy *cuirassiers* covered the plain in all directions; the sun shining brightly on a multitude of uniforms and gigantic plumes, on the mighty blue Danube, the wooded islands that everywhere dotted its surface, and the myriad spires of that land of churches peeping above the tree-tops on every side. It was the second time the French army had spread itself about Vienna; the second time that Napoleon's escort of gay chasseurs had clanked their brass scabbards on the steps of the summer palace of the Austrian emperor. It was a remarkably ubiquitous army, finding itself in Berlin today, at Madrid tomorrow, visiting most of the capitals of Europe in turn, but, as even its most devoted admirers are obliged to admit, not greatly regretted by any of these cities when it had taken its departure.

The engineers found that no easy task awaited them, for first they had to encounter an arm of the river, five hundred yards wide, between the Ebersdorf shore and a small island, beyond which flowed the main channel, very swift and turbulent, and divided into two branches of three hundred and twenty and forty yards respectively; while beyond Lobau, again, was the last branch, a hundred and forty yards in width; and to cover the construction of this bridge, which was in reality a succession of four bridges, Molitor's troops were passed into Lobau in boats as soon as darkness fell on the 19th May. The Austrian sentries gave the alarm, but their post retired, and the French were in possession of the island, which was two miles and a half in length by a mile and three-quarters in breadth, well wooded and full of pheasants, the gamekeeper's lodge being the only habitation.

As boat after boat put off and steered straight for Lobau, Napoleon himself superintended the arrangements, saw that muskets were loaded, and spoke to many of the soldiers: it is even recorded that when reconnoitring on the bank. Marshal Lannes fell in, and the emperor sprang to his assistance, waist deep, and helped him out before the staff could get to them. Although the river was rough, the night was a glorious one, and Savary, who had been rowed over by two pontoniers, brought the good news that Lobau was occupied, without resistance.

On the morning of the 20th, intelligence came that the enemy had landed on the right bank at Nussdorf, above Vienna; and Savary was sent post-haste with a brigade of cuirassiers, to find that they had recrossed again.

The bridge was not finally completed until the 21st, but at four o'clock on the afternoon of the 20th the scarlet *flammes* of

the *escadron d'élite* of the 3rd Chasseurs passed over to the enemy's side to join Molitor's men; and as soon as their green jackets had penetrated into the undergrowth of briars that fringed the shore, the last bridge, made in three hours by Colonel Aubry with fifteen Austrian pontoons, parted, and the squadron bivouacked in the wood separated from the rest of Marulaz's division, which remained in Lobau until next morning.

That night Napoleon and Lannes slept in the gamekeeper's lodge, the staff camping on the turf outside in the brilliant moonlight, singing among things "*Partant pour la Syrie.*" Captain d'Albuquerque's fine voice rising in what was to prove in a few hours his "swan's song!"

The gurgling waves rolled unceasingly along the alder-fringed shore; the bridges from the right bank resounded all through the short night with the tramp of infantry and the clatter of the horses' hoofs as division after division poured into the island; and with the first faint gleam of morning, which came about two o'clock, they crossed the now repaired pontoons and debouched on to the battle-ground.

An English mile apart, and each about half that distance from the Danube's edge, were the villages of Gros-Aspern to the left, and Essling to the right, the land sloping gently up to them and merging into the level pastoral plain known as the Marchfeld.

The corn was growing green and very high in places, and instead of the circle of fires that all night had spread along the wooden Bisamberg, to the left beyond Aspern, nothing was seen of the foe but a few cavalry patrols dotted on the horizon. Lannes declared his conviction that only a curtain of ten thousand men lay before them; but wily Masséna, whose powers of vision were as marvellous as the

emperor's were defective, had been to the summit of Aspern steeple, and affirmed that the whole of the Austrian army would have to be faced, to which correct opinion the emperor also inclined.[1]

The first day's battle may be roughly summed up as a succession of attacks on the villages, the cavalry drawn up between the two, and cutting in to their comrades' relief time and again. Masséna held Aspern; Lannes was responsible for Essling, and Bessières, who commanded the cavalry, was placed under him, to Bessières's intense chagrin.

Aspern, a stone-built village with a walled churchyard overhung by fine trees, was rather nearer to the bridge than was Essling, which latter village had a large enclosure, a three-storeyed granary, and was more closely built than straggling Aspern; while connecting the two and running from Aspern into the river was a double ditch, cut for drainage. Molitor's division had occupied Aspern on the 20th, and was the first attacked; for about two o'clock in the afternoon of the 21st the Austrians appeared in five massive columns, supported by cavalry and the fire of 288 guns!

Hiller, Bellegarde, and Hohenzollern rushed on Aspern, Rosenberg made for Essling, and the fifth column, also under his command,

---

[1]. Some authorities say that it was Berthier who ascended the steeple, and, as he had himself injured Masséna's left eye out hunting not long before, there would seem to be some grounds for the statement.—D. H. P.

moved by a circuit round Essling to take Enzersdorf in rear of the French right flank.

To meet this force the French had between 30,000 and 50,000 men on the left bank during the first day's battle; for though the others were hurrying up with all speed and passing into Lobau, the bridges broke no less than three times; while the Austrian numbers were 80,000, with a magnificent artillery which played most of the time at musket range!

Exactly at one o'clock, with loud cheers and bursts of Turkish music, the archduke's army began its march under a hot sun that poured down fiercely on the plain dotted with white-walled hamlets and glistening spires, and an hour or so later smoke was rolling across

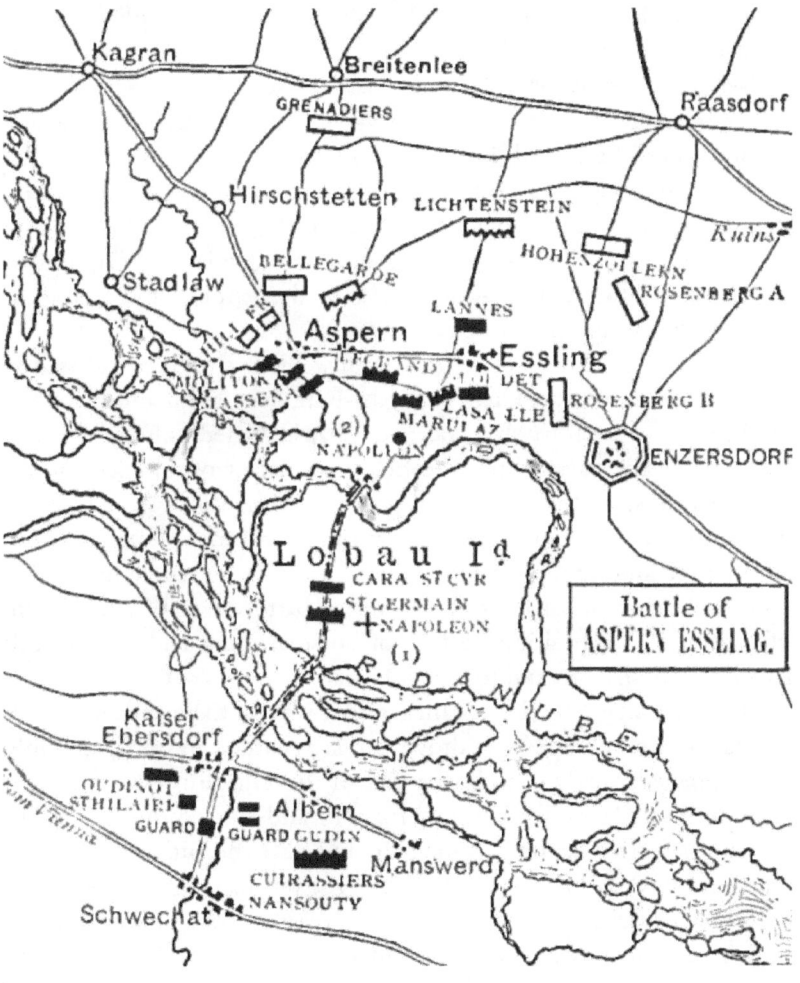

the marshy meadows as the guns opened, and tire skirmishers slowly retired. The archduke's plan of attack says:

"The principal object in view is to drive back the enemy entirely over the first arms of the Danube, destroy the bridges he had thrown over them, and occupy the bank of the Lobau, with a numerous artillery, especially howitzers."

Dust, shouts, and grape-shot drew closer and closer to Aspern, and when the bayonets crossed, which they soon did, the struggle became terrific.

Masséna, "cherished child of victory" as they called him, who combined the bravery of Ney with much of Napoleon's own skill, was seen everywhere, sword in hand. The heavy Austrian columns poured over the banks and hedges into the village street, and Molitor's weak regiments had their work cut out!

The trumpets of Marulaz's light cavalry sounded the charge, and the *chasseurs* spurred on the enemy with flashing sabres—again, again, a third time! The baron's horse fell under him in an Austrian square, but his men brought him off, and the same thing was repeated so often that the number of the charges has been lost!

Language has little power to render any adequate description of the carnage—the hand-to-hand *mêlée* in the gardens and houses at Aspern, all through that long day!

Leaves fell in showers over the combatants as shot tore incessantly through the trees; sword, bayonet, gun-butt, even teeth and fists were used for hours with barely a moment's pause, varied only by the sudden rush of the cavalry into the fields, an instant of mingled *shakoes* and bearskins, or the yellow *schapskas* of Meerveldt's *uhlans*, and a disordered return to their former position, riderless horses tearing madly back among the shattered squadrons, and the whole under that whistling storm of balls from the Austrian batteries, 18 of which were of brigade, 13 of position, and 11 of horse artillery, and which dealt havoc among friends and foes alike.

The first attack by the advance-guard was partially successful; but the gallant French linesmen drove Guylay's battalions out again, only to be pressed back to the lower end of the village by sheer weight and numbers. Again they rushed forward and cleared the streets, but the 2nd Austrian column joined in, and also the 3rd, while in the marshes on Masséna's left a stubborn fight was in progress among the woods and ditches, where the 16th of the Line strove to keep the enemy from a small island which commanded the pontoons.

Aspern caught fire, but they fought on in the flames; Massèna had orders to hold it at all costs, and anxious glances were cast to rearward for the reinforcements so long delayed by the breaking of the bridges.

Meanwhile, the 4th column, under Prince Rosenberg delayed its attack on Essling, to allow the 5th time to work round on Enzersdorf.

Enzersdorf fell an easy conquest to Stipsic's hussars, and the Wallacho-Illyrian Frontier Regiment, who found it partly evacuated and only took thirty prisoners, which done, both columns flung themselves on Essling, held by Boudet with the 3rd Light Infantry, some guns, and the 93rd and 56th of the Line, the attack taking place about five o'clock.

The defence of Essling was as gallant as that of Aspern, and the odds there were, if anything, greater. The *cuirassiers* of Nansouty and d'Espagne went in with a roar of shouting and a mighty whisk of horsetailed helmets against the *Czartorisky*, Archduke Louis, and Cobourg Regiments; but though they smote deep with their long swords, they were twice repulsed, and the wood behind the village being also cleared of the French by two battalions of the Bellegarde Regiment, the fighting there was concentrated immediately about Essling itself.

Napoleon's position was one of extreme peril: attacked with great fury at each extremity of his line, with nothing but cavalry to connect those extremities and cover the bridge, which was in so precarious a condition that it retarded the approach of succour from Lobau and the right bank, he had to maintain himself with three divisions of infantry and four of horse against the whole Austrian army, led by a man of whom the Duke of Wellington once said, when asked whom he considered the greatest general of that epoch:

"The Archduke Charles, until attacked by fits of epilepsy, which afterwards altogether changed his character and his fortunes."

The bridge-head, it is true, had been partially protected by entrenchments hastily thrown up, but the Danube rose and brought huge trees and other *débris* against the pontoons and piles that formed the bridge itself, and the enemy also floated out fireships and heavy baulks of timber for the current to dash against it.

Aspern was blazing fiercely, and the Austrians had carried the churchyard and part of the village; Boudet held Essling with difficulty, and the enemy began to advance his centre.

About this time a splendid charge was made by General Marulaz, by Nansouty's orders, and the general, who had entered the hussars thirty-one years before, led in with the 23rd Chasseurs, followed by the 3rd, 14th, 19th, and two German Regiments.

In the middle of the enemy his horse went down, Marulaz beneath it; but raising his powerful voice, he encouraged his men, who rallied and extricated him, and Lieutenant Carron of the 14th lending

him his own charger, the general killed two dragoons, wounded another, and upset a fourth, himself bareheaded, for his hat lay slashed to ribbons on the ground. When this, to English readers, little-known officer died at his *château* of Filain in 1842, his record was nineteen wounds and twenty-six horses killed under him!

Bessières, by Lannes's direction, poured his cavalry of the Guard, Lasalle's light horsemen, and the *cuirassiers* on the advancing columns, which had repeatedly to form square; and these charges across the water-ditches and through the tall corn, checked, although they could not wholly break, the enemy.

Essling, like Aspern, began to blaze as shells fell into it; but Boudet retained his post all night, and the flanking fire from the two villages arrested the general advance as evening approached.

About the time when the sun was slowly setting, Marshal Lannes sat in his saddle receiving reports from his *aides-de-camp*, who were ranged in a circle before him with their backs to the enemy, when a shot struck Captain d'Albuquerque—he who had sung Hortense's song so gaily the night before—and taking him in the loins, flung him over his horse's head, stone-dead at the marshal's feet, a shattered mass of crimson and gold and braided jacket!

"There is an end of the poor lad's romance," said Lannes, "but he has, at any rate, died nobly."

Almost immediately a second ball passed between the spine of another *aide-de-camp's* horse and the back of the saddle without touching either, but driving part of the saddle-tree into his thigh and inflicting a painful wound. Marbot, another of Lannes's aides, who tells the story, left for assistance to remove La Bourdonnaye, when, a messenger from the brave Boudet taking his place, a third ball carried off his head, and the marshal rode away to a place of greater safety.

The Austrians had practically taken Aspern, from which dense columns of smoke rolled over the trampled plain. Boudet was forced into Essling, and held his ground, and, seeing a disposition on the part of the enemy to retire their left, Lannes sent to Bessières to charge with his cavalry again, a command that gave rise to a serious quarrel between the two marshals.

For years they had been unfriendly, and Lannes chose the present moment to inflict a decided snub upon the Duke of Istria.

"Tell him I order him to charge home!" he said to an *aide*; but on questioning the officer he found that he had softened down the message on his own responsibility, and consequently Lannes despatched another in his place, who also gave the command in gentler phrase.

Turning to Marbot, the marshal repeated the message, laying stress upon the words *order* and *home*; and Marbot rode off, hoping, as he tells us, that a shot might bowl his horse over, and so rid him of the unpleasant task. But it was to be. The message was given correctly. The Marshal Duke of Istria stormed in his saddle, vented his wrath on Captain Marbot, and launched his squadrons on the enemy. They charged home with a vengeance, Lasalle's *chasseurs* and hussars, under Bruyère and Piré, and the splendid cavalry of General D'Espagne's division, the 4th, 6th, 7th, and 8th Cuirassiers, against the Austrian cuirassiers of Kroyker, Klary, and Siegenthal.

Dressed in white, with black breastplates, on the Austrian side, the French wearing the familiar uniform of their army, which hardly changed during the whole of the empire, the heavy horse met together with a terrific shock in the mellow glow of evening.

Guns there were in the corn, and the French claim to have taken fourteen. However that may be, they lost the brave D'Espagne, and many more beside him, for the Blankenstein and Riesch Regiments attacked their flank; and they had to retire after inflicting heavy loss upon the foe.

It was growing dark, to the relief of both sides. Masséna had recovered Aspern with the exception of the churchyard, Molitor's shattered regiments having been put in reserve about eight o'clock, and their place taken by the 1st Division; Boudet was still in Essling, but the gardens were full of corpses: if anything, the advantage was with the Austrians—certainly Napoleon had gained nothing up to that time.

Sleep there was little that night; for though the battle ceased about ten, as if by mutual consent, the firing was continued at intervals, especially at Aspern. Men lay down among the dead, and the wail of pain was blended with the murmur of the river, hidden in the mist.

Napoleon bivouacked in the sand; and Lannes, going over to the left, found the angry Bessières pouring out his tale to Masséna.

Lannes—who once, when enraged with Napoleon himself, deliberately slashed a glass chandelier to atoms—strode forward, and there was a violent scene. "When did you ever find me neglect to charge home?" demanded Bessières, both marshals drawing their swords, and restrained by Masséna with great difficulty from using them! There were only a few short hours of darkness at that season, and the pontoons creaked and trembled as the remainder of the Guard, together with Lannes's corps, came out of Lobau and marched up the left bank; but even then another delay occurred, as the bridge broke again at midnight, and the river was rising. Archduke Charles, on his side, ordered up the Grenadier Division to Breitenlee, and the

red glow from burning Aspern faded away as dawn came. Creeping stealthily up with the first pale breath of morning, before the sun rose, the Austrians burst into Essling with bayonets fixed at the same moment that Masséna rushed the churchyard of Aspern with St. Cyr's division and four guns. The second day's battle had begun by simultaneous action on each side, and, strangely enough, for the moment each attack was crowned with success.

The white-coats swarmed through the yards and alleys of Essling, driving Boudet into the granary for shelter; while Cara St. Cyr's brass drums kept up a dull roll as Vacquant was pursued out of Aspern into the meadows. This, however, did not last long. Napoleon, reinforced by the Guard, Lannes's corps, and Oudinot's men, had something like 80,000 troops in hand on the 22nd, and was, in consequence, superior in numbers to his adversary, whose losses had been heavy.

St. Hilaire, to whom the French applied Bayard's sobriquet of "*sans peur et sans reproche*," rode up with his infantry, among them the renowned 57th, known as "the terrible," and the 105th (who afterwards lost an Eagle at Waterloo), and Essling was retaken, remaining in Lannes's hands until almost the climax.

Heavy fog hung about the bridge and the river, as Napoleon inspected the battalions ranged in waiting there; the soldiers raising a shout of "*Vive l'Empereur!*" heard far over the plain above the musketry, and drawing the fire of the Austrian batteries, a shot from one of which killed General Monthion, who was riding in Napoleon's suite.

The fire was terrible, and did shocking execution, being con-

centrated for two days on so small a space, crowded with men and horses; but those men stood firm, waiting their turn, and it soon came when the emperor assumed the offensive a little after seven in the morning.

Essling, we have said, had been recaptured by St. Hilaire, but Aspern was still the theatre of a continued struggle.

Scarcely had St. Cyr bayoneted Vacquant out than the regiment of Klebeck forced its way among the burning houses and held its ground for an hour; and when Klebeck had been disposed of, Benjovsky took his place, seizing the ghastly graveyard, which without exaggeration was covered with dead in every attitude of agony just as they had

passed away, writhing on the steel or stricken down by the balls that lay everywhere, thick as apples on a windy day.

Orders were given by the Austrian general Hiller to throw down the walls and burn the church and parsonage, and Bianchi supporting, the head of the village was held for some time.

To follow the varied fortunes of each brigade, division, and column would be tedious and difficult; but a new phase of the battle was commencing—a grand advance by Lannes to break the enemy's centre, which Napoleon saw was too much extended.

Between the commands of Rosenberg and Hohenzollern was the weakest spot, and forming in echelon the French army advanced, Lannes's corps leading on the right, Oudinot a moment later, followed by the *cuirassiers*, the Imperial Guard in reserve, and the whole preceded by the crash of 200 cannon!

It seemed at first that the tide had turned in Napoleon's favour: Lannes broke through the enemy, took five guns, a colour, and captured a battalion. The Austrians at that point slowly retired, in good order at the outset, but afterwards in disorderly fashion, their officers being distinctly seen using their canes to keep the men together.

St. Hilaire, Tharreau, Claparède, were marching proudly on, dealing destruction right and left, and opening a path for the *cuirassiers*, who had yesterday's scores to repay.

The French cavalry even penetrated as far as Breitenlee, a good four miles off, where the Sous-Lieutenant Bertin was taken prisoner with his *peloton* of the 23rd Chasseurs, and the heavy horsemen raged round the enemy's squares as they afterwards did about our own at Waterloo.

The Austrians had adopted a novel formation for the first time— the chequer of squares, of which Archduke Charles had read in Jomini only a few weeks before. Marulaz—who, hardened *sabreur* as he was, had wept the previous night at the death of Adjutant-Commandant Ransonnet—charged with Lasalle under Aspern, and then sat exposed to a fearful fire for three hours. Aspern was still contested, but Masséna had the best of it; Boudet remained in the granary of Essling, and the Austrian rear was crumbling.

Victory was within the French grasp, but the tables were to be turned again for the last time, and Lannes received orders from Napoleon to retire and take up a position between the two villages. *The bridge behind them had broken again*, the best part of Davout's corps was still across the river on the other bank, and, what was of vital significance, ammunition began to run short.

The advance became a retirement—masterly, as were all Lannes's movements in the field, but a retirement notwithstanding—of which the enemy made good use. The archduke rallied his reserves and the fugitives that had been carrying panic to the rear, seized the standard of Zach's regiment, and surrounded by a brilliant throng of officers, brandishing their swords, led it back against the French, waving the folds above his head.

A perfect hurricane of white dragoons, their helmets surmounted by nodding plumes, swept upon St. Hilaire's division, the most advanced of all; and as Marbot reined up with a message from Lannes, a discharge of grape-shot hissed into the staff, felling them in all directions, brave St. Hilaire among them, who died afterwards under amputation.

The marshal galloped to the division and withdrew it, under a fearful fire, often facing round when Lichtenstein's troopers came too close; and about the same time, when the French cuirassiers and cavalry were vainly slashing among the chequered squares, Hohenzollern espied a flaw in the enemy's front on the right near Essling, and penetrating with Frölich's regiment, maintained himself until the grenadiers of the reserve arrived to his assistance.

Matters were growing very serious. Never had Austria fought better. The magic spell that had hung about the very name of the *Grande Armée* seemed to have lost its power, and the "*Kaiserlicks*" were pressing it closer and closer to the river.

Masséna's hold over Aspern was now relaxing. The remains of Molitor's division protected the island that commanded the pontoons, warding off the logs and dangerous masses sent down on the current by the Austrian engineers; but their loss alone had been 79 officers, 2,107 *sous-officiers* and men, and not a regiment or a squadron but had its bleeding quota under the trodden crops, mangled by the battery wheels or charred and smoking in some corner of the burning villages.

At half-past eight Napoleon had learnt of the disaster that had befallen the bridge across the main arm of the Danube. Boats full of stones, fireships, everything that ingenuity could suggest, had come whisking against the piles; the river foamed angrily and had risen; in spite of the ceaseless efforts of the pontoniers the largest section of the bridge was destroyed, and the army cut off from the right bank!

A whisper reached the enemy that all was not well with Napoleon: his troops were retiring, and the attack upon them was redoubled.

Fifteen hundred is the number of slain given in it for those two days of carnage. As a matter of fact, 7,000 were buried on the field alone, and 29,773 wounded were conveyed to the hospitals of Vienna! Of the Austrians, 87 superior officers and 4,200 privates were killed, and 16,300 wounded.

Although the archduke did not succeed in capturing Lobau, Napoleon was decidedly beaten, and, passing into the island, his army remained there six weeks, binding its wounds and filling up its gaps until the July day when it issued forth to write Wagram on its standards.

NOVEMBER 1808 - JANUARY 1809
The Retreat of Corunna

D. H. Parry

East of the kingdom of Portugal lie the great plains of Leon, bordered north and south by mighty mountain ranges; and in the short December days of 1808, when wintry winds swept howling through the passes and across the level land, and the red roofs of Salamanca were covered with snow, a small British army, some 23,000 strong, was preparing to assist Spain against Napoleon.

Led by the gallant Lieutenant-General Sir John Moore, and wearing the red cockade out of compliment to the nation, we had been received with great enthusiasm, and were given to understand that the country burned with patriotic zeal and had large forces, perfectly equipped; but this was soon found to be untrue, for, while the Spaniards were ready for any amount of castanet playing and looking-on, the English were expected to do their fighting for them.

Their magnificent army dwindled upon investigation to half its supposed numbers, and, with a few honourable exceptions, proved itself one of the wretchedest collections of ragamuffins if which history bears any record, so that Sir John Moore found himself in as awkward a position as ever fell to the lot of a British general. Nevertheless, in spite of the severity of the weather, the impertinent meddling of Mr. Frere, the English Minister at Madrid, the poor equipment of our troops and the absence of Spanish aid, we marched boldly out of Salamanca on the 11th December to attack Soult in the north, and afterwards succour the capital if that should be practicable.

It was a brave little army, and its doings are deeply carved on the pillar of British fame. There were five cavalry regiments, all Hussars,

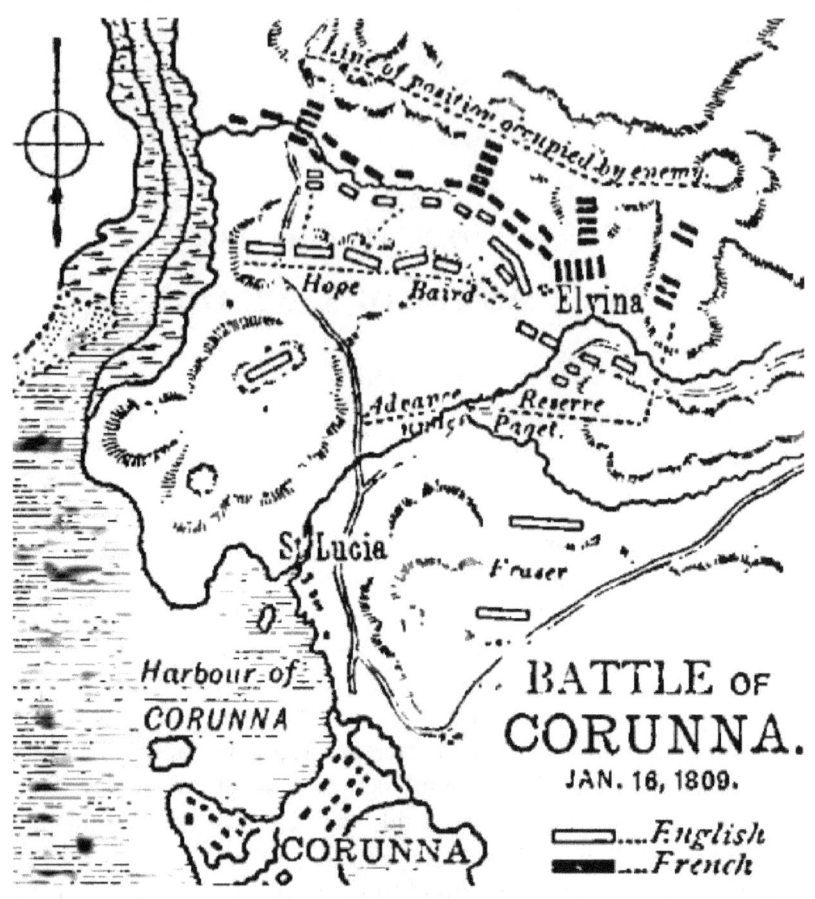

dashing fellows in braided pelisses, and mounted on active nagtailed horses: *viz.*, the 7th, 10th, 15th, and 18th, with the 3rd of the King's German Legion.

Artillery, engineers, waggon train, and a detachment of the scarlet-coated staff corps filed out across the plain, white and monotonous under a gloomy sky.

Two battalions of the 1st Guards and thirty-two of the Line completed our force, including amongst others such splendid regiments as the Royal Scots, the 4th, 5th, and the 9th, nicknamed the "Holy Boys," because they afterwards sold their Bibles for wine; the Welsh Fusiliers and 28th "Slashers," the Black Watch, the Fighting 43rd, the 71st Glasgow Highland Light Infantry. now the strictest regiment in the service, the Cameron Highlanders, and the green 95th Rifles.

*****

General Baird was hastening from Corunna to join us, and we had already advanced several marches towards the enemy, when a blustering French *aide-de-camp* got himself murdered in a village; his papers were purchased for twenty dollars, and Sir John Moore learned for the first time the true extent of the overwhelming odds, against him.

Madrid, which was to have made such a brave defence, had held out *one* day; the shops were open and the people tranquil; Toledo, Ocaña, and the whole of La Manche were in the hands of the French; a strong force was about to march on Badajoz, and the Emperor Napoleon was reviewing 60,000 veteran troops, including part of his famous Imperial Guard, at the capital.

Two hundred and fifty-five thousand men were mustering to oppose us; their cavalry alone exceeded our entire army by 12,000, and to linger on the plains with such a horde closing round us would have been absolute madness. There was nothing for it but to show a bold front to Soult, and gain the sea with as much honour as possible before the others could come up; and though the word "retreat" has an unpleasant sound to English ears, when it is attended with as great a display of heroism as upon that unfortunate occasion, it becomes a page in British annals which we could ill afford to spare.

******

The Reserve, on whom, with the cavalry, most of the fighting devolved until the army reached Corunna, was formed of the 20th and 52nd, and the 28th, 91st, and 95th, under Generals Anstruther and Disney. First blood was drawn at Rueda, where the 18th Hussars took fifty prisoners, and the same evening the band of the 7th Hussars played the Reserve into Toro, on the Douro.

Paget, afterwards Marquis of Anglesea, whose brother. Lord Edward, was in command of the Reserve, marched the 10th and 15th Hussars on a bitter and intensely dark night to Sahagun, arriving in the grey dawn to find the place full of French cavalry. Without a moment's hesitation the 15th charged and overthrew them, taking thirteen officers and a hundred and fifty-four men in twenty minutes.

The 15th was the Duke of Cumberland's regiment, and one of the most expensive in the army.

Napoleon heard of our advance on the same day that Sahagun was fought, and, leaving 10,000 men to overawe Madrid, marched with 50,000 to cross the Guadarama range.

Pushing on in the depth of winter—the Spaniards forced to cut

roads through the snow for them—they reached the passes, and toiled up for twelve hours without the advance guard being able to gain the summit; but so tremendous was the wind that the emperor had to dismount and struggle forward on foot, holding on to the arms of Marshals Lannes and Duroc, the staff following linked together, with heads bent before the driving snow.

Halfway up they stopped, the generals exhausted in their heavy jack-boots, and bestriding some brass guns, Napoleon and his officers in that manner arrived at the top, seeing through the whirling flakes the plains of Leon far below them.

Scrambling down, he hurried the jaded troops ten and twelve leagues a day until he came within three miles of the River Esla—only to find that we had already crossed it, and had had two days' rest at Benevente.

Furious at our escape, he sent his favourite *Chasseurs-à-Cheval* of the Guard in hot pursuit, with a support of infantry; but without waiting for the foot-soldiers, the gallant Charles Lefebvre Desnouettes splashed through the fords with his horsemen into the open fields full of camp-followers, and drove our pickets back towards the town.

Six hundred of those splendid troopers, in green jackets and red *pelisses*, careered magnificently over the trampled snow; but behind some straggling houses Paget was waiting with the 10th Hussars, until they should have got sufficiently forward.

Then a line of blue and silver, and curving sabres and brown busbies, tore out of the concealment, gathered up the retiring pickets, and rushed upon the chasseurs. There was slashing and shouting and riding down, and the French squadrons returned through the fords again at full gallop, leaving fifty-five killed and wounded, and seventy prisoners.

They re-formed on their own side, and for a moment it was thought they would charge us, but a couple of guns put them to the right-about, and their leader remained in our hands.

Private Levi Grisdale, of the 10th, saw him riding for the river, in a green frock, with a hat and feather, and, spurring after him, dodged a pistol-ball and cut him over the left cheek.

Grisdale was promoted, although the 3rd Germans claimed that a private of theirs, named Bergmann, had taken the general; but the uniforms of the two regiments were very similar then, both being in blue with yellow facings and white braid, and it is difficult to distinguish things accurately in the hurry of a combat.

Desnouettes lived at Malvern and Cheltenham, where he made many friends, until May, 1812, when, breaking his parole, he escaped to France, only to be taken again at Waterloo, where Grisdale also fought as a sergeant, and the unlucky general was eventually drowned off the Irish coast in 1822.

At Benevente the 3rd Hussars alone lost forty-six men and twenty-two horses, with forty-seven more wounded; but we had checked the Guard and shown our teeth; and when the night winds were howling among the porcelain friezes and broken porphyry columns of the old castle on the hill, we withdrew cautiously in a thick fog and continued our retreat.

Captain Darby and seventeen privates of the 10th died of fatigue during the march to Bembibre, and they shot sixty horses that could go no farther.

Deep snow lay on the ground, rutted and trampled by the passage of the guns and bullock carts; this had frozen like iron, and then been concealed by another snowstorm, so that men and horses stumbled and lamed themselves at every stride. One officer lost a boot among the ruts on Christmas morning, and marched all day without it! Every regiment had received a new blanket per man and a hundred and fifty new soles and heels, but the execrable roads quickly wore out the leather.

Astorga was found to be full of miserable Spanish soldiers, who had eaten up most of the stores, and whose condition was summed up in their own words: "Very hungry—very sick—very dry!"

A number of women and children followed the army, and their sufferings were truly terrible. Soldiers began to fall out, unable to keep up with the columns, and the rear-guard passed scores of poor wretches frozen to death in the snow, while at Bembibre, where there

were large wine-vaults, discipline began to relax its hold, and shameful drunkenness stained the hitherto excellent record of the troops.

Meanwhile, Napoleon made the most strenuous efforts to overtake us. He insisted on marching from Benevente to Astorga in one short winter day, a distance of thirty odd miles, under an icy rain, the infantry being obliged to strip five or six times and scramble through the streams, holding their clothing and ammunition above the water.

So exhausted was his army that three veteran grenadiers of the Old Guard blew out their brains, unable to go on, and knowing that the sullen peasants in their sheepskin *capas* would murder them if they lagged behind.

Napoleon was much affected, but he still pushed forward, and late at night, drenched to the skin, and attended only by Lannes, the staff, and a hundred *chasseurs*, he dashed into Astorga.

Had Paget, who was only six miles off, learned this, he might have swooped down with the Hussars and changed the future fate of Europe by capturing the emperor himself. Napoleon had marched two hundred miles in ten days with 50,000 troops in the depth of winter, but for all his haste, we had eluded him and gained the mountains, and at Astorga the emperor handed the reins to Soult, reviewed his legions, and returned to Valladolid, leaving the Marshal Duke of Dalmatia to drive us into the sea.

The features of the retreat now underwent a change: our columns began to ascend into a wild and dreary region, the road winding along the mountain sides halfway between the summits and the rushing water in the valleys below.

Here and there a solitary cottage showed its slate roof; at intervals the weary leagues were marked on stone pillars by the way; the droning hum of the axles of the bullock carts could be heard for a great distance, and slanting rain beat on the tired stragglers, whose numbers were by this time terribly increased.

Bembibre, when the Reserve entered it on New Year's Day, was full of drunken soldiers from Baird's divisions; officers and men grew careless, and thought only of themselves, and it was found necessary to flog and hang to restore some semblance of order, with an active enemy on our very heels.

The light troops had marched for Vigo, whither Sir John Moore intended to follow, but at Orense a message overtook them, bidding them send the transports round to Corunna, and Captain Heisse, after a hard gallop through the snow, was just in time to despatch the vessels before an unfavourable wind set dead into the harbour mouth.

At Calcabellos, while Lord Edward Paget was haranguing the Reserve on the subject of the growing insubordination, two plunderers were caught in the act. The troops were instantly formed in hollow square round a tree to witness their execution, when a hussar dashed in with news that the enemy were upon us.

"I don't care if the entire French cavalry are here," roared the general; "I'll hang these scoundrels!"

They were lifted in the arms of the provost-marshal's men, the ropes were adjusted, and in another moment they would have dangled in mid-air, when a second hussar came up, and carbine shots rang out from the 3rd Germans at the bridge.

"Soldiers," cried Lord Edward, "if I pardon these men will you promise better behaviour for the future?"

"Yes," was the unanimous reply.

"Say it again!"

"Yes, yes!" from a thousand throats.

"A third time!"

It was done with a cheer, the men were released, and the troops went off at the double towards the firing.

Colbert attacked us there with a large body of cavalry, and our Rifles, posted in a vineyard, emptied a score of saddles as the French dragoons and light horse tore up the road to the bridgehead. Colbert was not only a splendid soldier, but a good man, in an army, where, unfortunately, virtue was at a low ebb, and two days before, at the review, Napoleon had said to him, "General, you have proved in Egypt, Italy, and Germany that you are one of my bravest warriors: you shall soon receive the reward due to your brilliant successes."

"Make haste, sire," replied Colbert, "for, while I am not yet thirty, I feel that I am already old."

At Calcabellos, an Irishman of the 95th, named Tom Plunkett, ran out and threw himself on his back in the snow. Passing the sling of his rifle over his foot, he sighted and fired, and Colbert fell from his horse. Jumping up Plunkett cast about and reloaded, firing again and killing the *aide-de-camp* who had rushed to his general's assistance, after which the lucky marksman rejoined his comrades in safety (only to be discharged some years afterwards, without promotion, a victim to drink, that curse of our Peninsular armies).

Wherever the danger was pressing, Sir John Moore was to be found—nothing could exceed his personal exertions on the retreat.

At Villa Franca, romantically situated in a deep valley, with the pointed turrets of a Dominican convent rising against a background of bare hills, and where the ferocious Duke of Alva once had a castle, the army committed great disorders, and Sir John had a man shot in the market-place as a warning to the others. Although we checked the enemy wherever the rear-guard faced about, the march had not been resumed long when their horsemen were again riding among the stragglers, cutting them down without mercy—man, woman, and child!

The 28th, with its brown calfskin knapsacks, taken from the French stores in Egypt, toiled over the snow, and the handsomest man of the grenadier company, named McGee, fell lame and dropped behind, his comrades carrying his pack and musket for him, but two French troopers came up, and, unarmed as he was, slashed him to pieces almost in sight of his company.

Misery and disorder increased; the cavalry were sent on ahead, with the exception of a part of the 3rd Hussars, and the rear-guard fought every yard of the way until they reached Lugo, where Sir John drew up in order of battle, and discipline was again restored.

All day, in the drenching rain, we waited for the French to attack, but Soult was too wary; and at night, leaving the fires burning, the army continued its retreat, gaining several hours' start before the enemy became aware of it. The pay-waggons, heavily laden with silver dollars, were abandoned, as the oxen were quite used up, and Lieutenant Bennet stood with a drawn pistol and orders to shoot any soldier who lingered there. Hugo, of the 3rd Hussars, gave an equal proportion to each man of his detachment, and it was carried in their corn-sacks to Corunna and delivered to the commissariat; but the rest—£25,000 worth—was pitched over into the valley, the barrels breaking on the rocks and sending a silver cascade far down beyond the reach of the marching army.

The stragglers crowded round and fought for the money spilled on the road, one woman—wife of Sergeant Maloney, of the 52nd—making her fortune for life; but, stepping from the boat on to a transport at Corunna, she slipped, and the weight of the stolen treasure took her to the bottom of the harbour, never to rise again!

While the miserable wretches were scrambling in the snow, the enemy came up and slaughtered without mercy, stopping in their turn to gather up the spoil, and giving us a little breathing-time.

Farther on we met some Spanish troops discharging their muskets briskly, as though skirmishing, and it was feared that the French had intercepted us, but on getting closer we were told that the contemptible riff-raff were "*only firing to warm their hands!*"

At Lugo Sir John Moore had issued an order in which he said:

"It is evident that the enemy will not fight this army, notwithstanding the superiority of his numbers, but will endeavour to harass and tease it on its march . . . . The army has now eleven leagues to march; the soldiers must make an exertion to complete them. The rear-guard cannot stop, and those that fall behind must take their fate!"

Many of the troops were now barefooted, and all were more or less in rags. Far too many camp-followers had been allowed to accompany us, and all were starving in a wild and sterile country, where a yellow fowl was often the only result of a plundered cottage. The 28th found nothing at Villa Franca but one piece of salt pork, which Major Browne tied to his holsters—to lose it in the night-march to Herrerias.

The same officer, on embarking, exchanged his horse for a pig, but in the confusion the major was shipped on board one transport and the pig on to another!

Small wonder that the "Slashers," on finding some Spaniards frozen to death among the *débris* of two bread-waggons, moved the corpses to hunt ravenously for the crusts among which they were lying!

At length it was the custom to stop all stragglers and take from them a proportion of the food they carried, and by that means they collected sufficient to serve out a ration to every man of the rear-guard!

At Nogales—where the country reminds one of Glencoe—a private who had been sent on ahead found a quantity of potatoes, which he boiled, and as the 28th filed past the house he distributed three or four to officer and man alike, without distinction; and at the same place some officers of the "Slashers" went into a cottage where there was a fire, and where they stripped to dry their clothes.

A Spanish general was sleeping snugly in an inner room, well wrapped in furs, and his two *aides-de-camp* were standing by the fire.

One of the "Slashers" laid his valuable watch down, and, returning from the door, where he had been directing some stragglers, found that one of the *aides-de-camp* had walked off with it!

"I cannot be held responsible for all the people about me," was the grumpy remark of the Spanish general. What could be expected from an army whose officers were thieves?

The last halt was made at Betanzos, and while the rear-guard covered the partial destruction of .the bridge there, the army marched in column to Corunna, only to find the Atlantic roaring on the rocks, but not a sail in sight!

The French were in great force at Betanzos, and furious at our continued escape. One sergeant charged alone in advance of his squadron, to the centre of the bridge, but a private of the 28th, named Thomas Savage, stepped out and shot him, securing his cloak before the others came up.

The engineers bungled the bridge, and blew up one of their officers with it, while we had to fall back on Corunna before it was properly destroyed. Fine weather now dried our rags. On the 11th January the Guards were quartered in the town, the Reserve near St. Lucia, and the other regiments posted in strong positions. Vast stores were meanwhile destroyed in Corunna and two hundred and ninety horses of the German Legion shot in the arsenal square at St. Lucia, amid the tears of the brave troopers.

The 12th proved damp and foggy, and no trace of the fleet could be seen. The French still held back, our officers exchanging potshots with them until Paget put a stop to it; and on the 13th a terrific explosion from 4.000 powder-barrels caused something very like a panic in both armies. Corunna was shaken, its windows smashed, and a rain of white ashes fell for a considerable time.

At last, on the afternoon of the 14th, the transports hove in sight, and as soon as they were anchored we began to embark the wounded and the guns, the cavalry being ordered to ship thirty horses per regiment and shoot the rest as there was not time to get them on board with a heavy sea running. The 15th Hussars brought four hundred to Corunna, and landed in England with thirty-one! The 10th—the Prince of Wales's particular regiment, and the first in our service to wear the showy Hungarian dress, which its hussar troop had adopted in 1803 and the entire corps two years later—began the campaign with six hundred handsome chargers and took thirty home again.

The greatest confusion took place among the camp-followers, but by degrees the embarkation proceeded, our gallant tars going in some cases two days without food in their noble efforts to help us.

There was a little skirmishing, but no very decided movement, until the 16th—in fact, French officers were seen picking up shells on the sands at low water within range of our muskets—but at last the infantry alone remained on shore, and the 28th, among others, was ordered to fall in at two o'clock on the 16th to march down to the boats.

Scarcely had they mustered when, a violent cannonade being opened upon us, and a forward movement being observed, they went off at the double towards the enemy again. They had done eighty miles in the last twelve days, standing several nights under arms in the snow; they had repulsed the French seven times, and the 28th alone had lost more than two hundred men; yet, when the Battle of Corunna began, the Reserve had fewer men missing than any other division!

Some of the generals wished Moore to come to terms with Soult, but nothing was farther from the brave Scotchman's thoughts.

Circumstances had compelled us to retreat, but it was no part of a British soldier's training to shirk a battle at the last moment; consequently, the low hills behind Elvina were soon echoing to the rattle of musketry as our black-gaitered infantry opened fire on the French columns.

There was little or no manoeuvring during the engagement: Soult advanced in three masses, driving our pickets out of the village of Elvina. Baird, of Seringapatam fame, held the right of our line, Sir John Hope formed the centre and left with his division, while Paget and Eraser were in reserve before Corunna: 14,500 men in all, facing 20,000.

Sir John Moore sent the 50th and 42nd to retake Elvina, which was rendered formidable by sunken lanes and stone walls, but after a brave scrimmage which lasted half an hour, the French were driven out and the Guards advanced to take up the position originally occupied by the two regiments.

The Black Watch having exhausted their cartridges fell back, thinking the Guards were marching to support them, and the enemy returned in force and entered the village again.

Sir John rode up to the 42nd, and learning that their ammunition was expended, said, "You have still your bayonets, my brave Highlanders—remember Egypt!" and with a yell the Black Watch rushed forward once more.

While Sir John Moore was watching the struggle, a round shot struck him on left breast and dashed him out of the saddle; but without a groan, he sat up, resting on his arm and for a moment gazed intently at the Highlanders driving the French steadily back.

Then, as a happy look came into his handsome face, the staff crowded round him and saw the shocking state of his wound. The shoulder was completely shattered, and the left arm hung by a piece of skin; the ribs over the heart were broken and bared of flesh, while the

muscles of the breast were torn into shreds and strips, among which the hilt of his sword had got entangled.

"I had rather it should go out of the field with me," said the dying hero, as Hardinge made an attempt to disengage it.

Men of the 42nd and Guards carried him tenderly in a blanket, taking an hour to reach Corunna, the general frequently making them halt and turn him round.

Like Wolfe at Quebec, his anxiety was for the success of the army, and like Wolfe his last moments were cheered by the knowledge that we had beaten the French.

Soult had fallen back, General Baird was badly wounded, and Hope carried out Sir John's original plans for the embarkation.

"I hope the people of England will be satisfied," said the dying man.

"I hope my dear country will do me justice. Oh, Anderson!" he whispered to his friend, "you will see my friends at home; tell them everything—my mother—" then he broke down.

He was believed to be devotedly attached to Lady Hester Stanhope, eldest daughter of the third Earl Stanhope, famous alike for his eccentricity and his study of the electric fluid; and Moore's last recorded words were in remembrance of her, addressed to her brother, his *aide-de-camp*. He passed away very quietly in his forty-eighth year, and England lost one of her most chivalrous soldiers. His burial, in the citadel at night by some men of the 9th, has been described in a poem which does immortal honour to the Irish clergyman who penned it, and the gallant enemy flew the tricolour half-mast high on the citadel and fired a salute over his grave, Marshal Soult afterwards erecting a tomb to his memory. Our loss at Corunna was 800, the French, from their own accounts. 3,000.

Six cannon, 3-pounders, sent on without Sir John's orders, had been abandoned during the retreat, and nearly 4,000 men left their bones to whiten the plains of Leon and the rugged roads of Gallicia; but the retreat won praise from Wellington and Napoleon alike, and not a regimental colour remained in the enemy's hands. The 95th was the last regiment to enter Corunna, the 23rd the last to leave it.

Great confusion existed on board the vessels, and an attempt to transfer the men to their respective ships was prevented by the enemy opening fire from St. Lucia. The cables were cut, and the three hundred transports put to sea on the 17th, convoyed by several men-of-war, the old *Victory* amongst them, and after cruising about in the offing for two days, they put helm up for England, where the army landed in a wretched condition.

All the clothing of the Rifles was burned behind Hythe barracks, in a state that spoke volumes for the misery undergone.

The *Smallbridge* went ashore near Ushant, and over two hundred of the German Legion were drowned. Then the newspapers began to raise a disgraceful outcry against the whole expedition, and the good name of Sir John Moore was placed under a cloud by men whose information was false, and whose opinion was of no more value than a spent cartridge.

We have learned the true state of things since then, and ample justice has been rendered to Moore's noble character in the subsequent histories of that glorious period.

The last survivor of Corunna, Thomas Palmer, of the 23rd, died at the great age of a *hundred*, and was buried at Weston-super-Mare, with full military honours, in April, 1889—*eighty years* after his chief was laid to rest "with his martial cloak around him."

May 10-11-12, 1809

The Passage of the Douro

Lieut.-Col. Newnham Davis

Lisbon shone with light on the night of the 22nd April, 1809, for a deliverer had come; and when the news of the landing of Sir Arthur Wellesley, the young general with the glory of Roliça and Vimiero still fresh upon him, spread through Portugal, every city not held by the invading French was illuminated for three successive nights.

Never was there a deadlier hate than the Portuguese, townsmen and peasants, had for the soldiers of Napoleon's armies. No Red Indians ever dreamed of more fiendish tortures than those that a straggler from the line of march, a wounded man left in the whirl of a skirmish, or a forgotten sick man, suffered at the hands of the Portuguese before he met his death; and for hate, hate was returned with interest. The olive trees were cut down, the ripe crops trampled, the farm animals and domestic pets slain and cut or torn limb from limb in wantonness; the blackening corpse of many a priest swung from a tree hard by the deserted village where he ministered and wherever the fierce peasants stood; and the might of the trained legions of France crushed their savage resistance, the cavalry killed and killed in the pursuit so long as horse could gallop and sword arm be raised to strike.

And now this stern young English general was come as a deliverer, and the Portuguese, ever variable as a weathercock, went mad with joy at his advent. It was to a despairing country that he had come.

Up in the north, Soult, charged by Napoleon to hunt the English leopard into the sea, had swept like a whirlwind after Moore, to be mauled when the hunted turned and stood before Corunna; and now, rearmed and equipped from captured British and Spanish maga-

zines, had swooped down on Oporto, captured and held the town. The shrieks of the dying wretches on that day of storm, of murder and rapine, when the flying Portuguese cavalry trampled a red way through the streets of the town glutted with frightened women and children, and the great gap in the bridge of boats was filled with the heaped corpses of drowned, pushed on to their fate by the maddened crowd behind, when forty thousand Portuguese perished by sword or fire or drowning, still rang in the country's ears.

On the eastern frontier Victor had been joined by Lapisse, and their joint armies, distant only some eighteen marches from the Portuguese capital, were being weakly watched by the rickety old Spaniard Cuesta, that strange mixture of tenacity, faithlessness, pride, incapacity, who, clothed in a mediaeval uniform, looking like the spectre of Don Quixote, held upon his horse by two pages, or commanding his army from the heaped pillows in his coach drawn by eight mules, ever defeated, often the leader of the runaways, yet held a power no other Spaniard of the day had, and, however sorely buffeted, always appeared again with a fresh army, ready to run anew. On the 28th of March at Medellin his wavering line, advancing over the edge of the ridge, had been pulverised by Victor, three-fifths of his men had been slain, and Latour-Maubourg's and Lasalle's dragoons wore, many of them, their sword arms in slings for days afterwards, so strained were they with the smiting of the flying Spaniards.

Sir Arthur, however, entered on the campaign under circumstances that at least promised a chance of success.

Beresford, fiery, impulsive, full of energy, by his genius and a stiffening of British officers, had shaken the Portuguese uniformed rabble—those desperate partisans whose fierceness went waste through feeble leadership, and who always shrieked "Treason!" as they fled, pausing only to murder their generals—into troops who with each day gained confidence in their officers and discipline, and, with their eyes turned north, longed to cross bayonets again with Soult's Frenchmen.

Craddock—a badly treated man, who had kept his head, though hustled by the impulsive Beresford, plucked by the sleeve by Frere, our representative with the Spaniards, and by the Portuguese regency, threatened by the rabble of Lisbon, and now superseded by a younger man—handed over to his successor a British army as ready for campaigning as the circumstances would allow, with magazines ready stocked to supply the needs of a march north or east.

The reinforcements Sir Arthur had asked for had been given him. The confidence of the ministry at home, who had at last made up their minds to hold to Portugal, was his. The rank of marshal in the Portuguese service had been bestowed on him, in acknowledging which he wrote "a very fine letter;" and, above all, there was the Genius of the man, a Genius waited on by her handmaid Luck.

For luck was with the taciturn young general.

As he slept in his cabin aboard the *Surveillant* frigate his first night out from Portsmouth—to which town he was not to return until in 1814 he landed there as Duke of Wellington, Sir George Collier came down to him and awakened him, telling him that the ship, then off St. Catherine's Head, had missed stays several times and must go ashore, and advised him to hold to the ship until she went to pieces; but as Sir Arthur came on deck a sudden slant of wind from the shore bellied the sails, and the great vessel tore away in the darkness to carry him to safety and glory. And now in Soult's camp treachery was fighting for him, for Argenton, Soult's adjutant-major, of old days his *aide-de-camp*, had been to Beresford, and was strong on a plan for seizing Soult and carrying him back into France.

Sir Arthur, a little doubtful whether he had chosen the wiser course, left Mackenzie and a tolerable force to hinder Victor should he march on Lisbon, hoping something also from Cuesta should this come to pass, and himself, with Beresford always edging forward on the east of him, set forth against that noble adversary, Soult.

A few words as to the country in which the fighting had to be done, and as to the troops who had to do it.

EXPLANATORY SKETCH
OF THE
PASSAGE OF THE RIVER DOURO
BY
SIR ARTHUR WELLESLEY,
May 12, 1809;

AND OF THE STORMING OF OPORTO
BY
MARSHAL SOULT,
March, 1809.

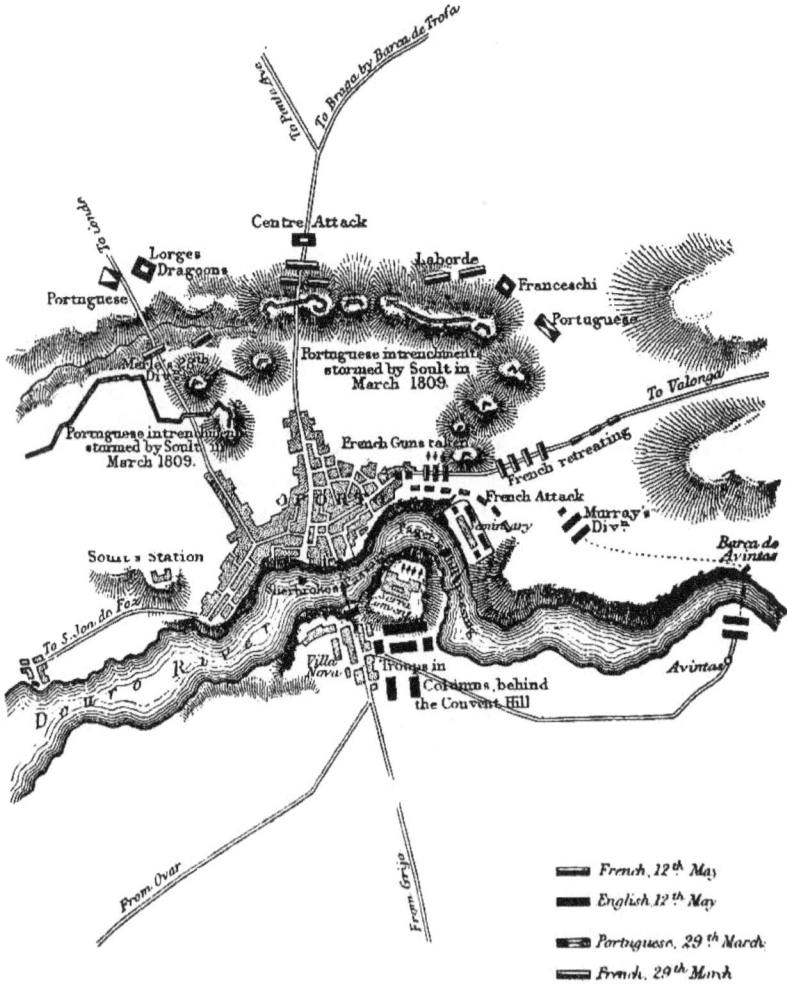

The rivers in Portugal, speaking in general terms, run from northeast to south-west, with mountainous country in between them. Four rivers only are of importance in connection with the fighting I am going to write of: the Tagus, the most southerly of them; the Mondego next, south of which Sir John Craddock had been gathering troops and stores; the Vouga next, the right bank of which was held by the French outposts; and the most northerly, the Douro, near the mouth of which is Oporto.

The troops with which Sir Arthur moved against Soult were a division of horse under General Payne, two divisions of infantry under Lieutenant-Generals Edward Paget and Sherbrooke, the German Legion, and twenty-four guns—sixteen thousand combatants in all, of whom fifteen hundred were horsemen. Beresford, who was to cut off Soult's retreat to the east, the only road by which he could take his train and artillery, had six thousand Portuguese, two British battalions, and some heavy cavalry.

Sir Arthur wasted no time in setting to work. Six days he stayed in Lisbon to get a firm hand on the strings that set the puppets dancing, and then rode up the north road, through villages where he was hailed already as a conqueror, to Coimbra, south of the Mondego, where the ladies showered rose-leaves and confetti down on him from the balconies.

On the 6th of May Sir Arthur reviewed his forces on a sandy plain some two miles from Coimbra, and his staff scanned anxiously enough the appearance of the men who had to meet Soult's veterans. It was by no means the *beau ideal* of an army. The Guards and the German Legion were all that any general could desire, but the ranks of the infantry of the line had been filled by drafts from militia regiments, and there were as many knapsacks with the names of counties on them as with the numbers of regiments. The Portuguese, four regiments of whom had been added to the force, were considered by lenient critics to present a "sombre" appearance, their dark complexions and single-breasted blue coats showing unfavourably alongside the fresh-coloured faces and red uniforms of their British brothers-in-arms; but Sir Arthur wrote to Beresford in stronger terms than that, telling him that his men made a bad figure at the review, that the battalions were weak, the body of men very bad, and the officers worse than anything he had seen. He spoke in kindlier terms of them when the three days' fighting which ended in the capture of Oporto were over.

In the early morning of the 10th May the two forces first came

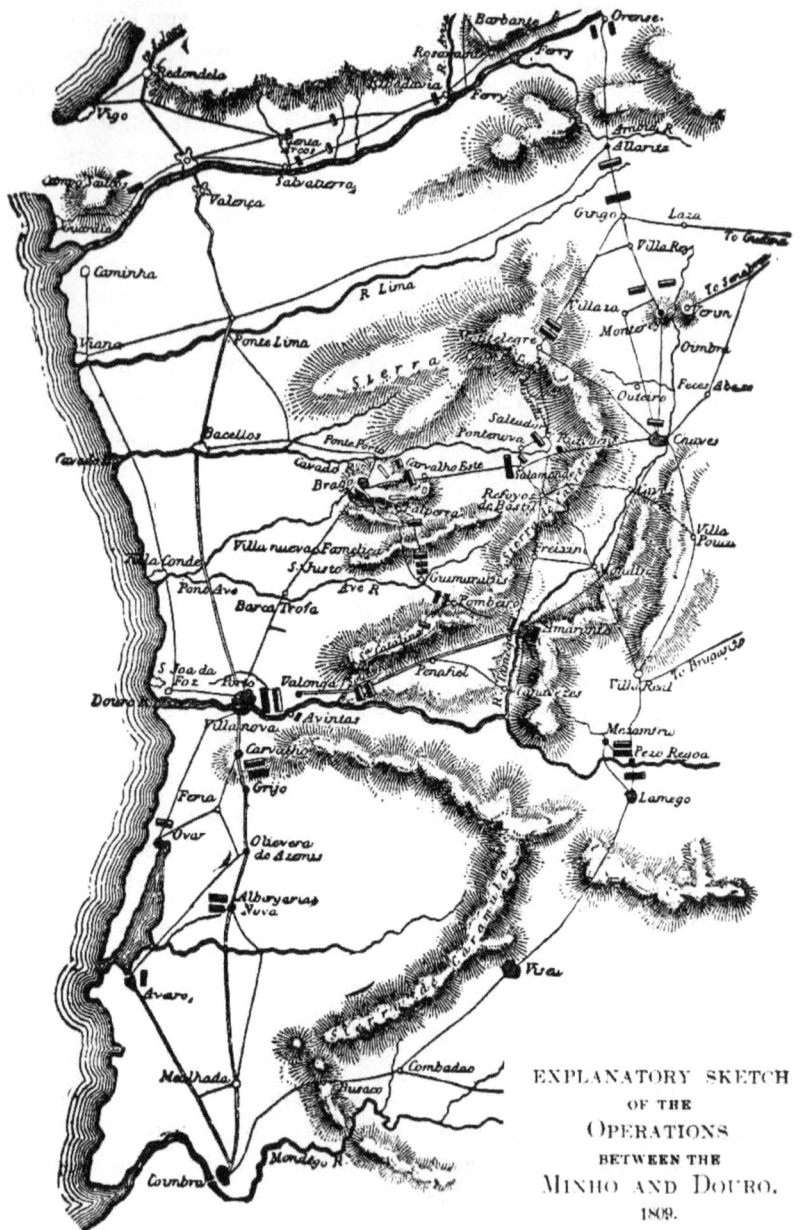

EXPLANATORY SKETCH OF THE OPERATIONS BETWEEN THE MINHO AND DOURO, 1809.

into contact. The country folk were with us and against the French—all their movements were known to us; ours were concealed from them. We were, guided by the peasants, to have surprised Franceschi, the French cavalry general, whose quarters were some eight miles to the north of the Vouga at Albergaria Nova, while Mermet with a division of infantry was a march further north at Grijon. Hill had been ferried across the lake of Ovar, and was in rear of Franceschi. Cotton with the light cavalry was to attack in the grey of the morning, thrust Franceschi back on to Mermet, and when the defeated troops made for Oporto, Hill with his fresh troops was to keep up with them and seize the bridge of boats.

The lake of Ovar lies on the sea-coast, and its northern end was well behind the French outposts. That it was not guarded by the French was discovered by an officer who went by night to meet Argenton, the traitor in Soult's camp, halfway across the lake. In the darkness their boats missed each other, and the British officer found himself unchallenged behind the French picquets.

Hill, aided in every way by the Portuguese boatmen, landed at Ovar at sunrise, but Cotton's men failed in their attempt—most of them were young fighters, a night march is always difficult, and the Portuguese guides were desperately afraid of falling into the hands of the French. The neighing of the horses of the Portuguese cavalry put Franceschi's *vedettes* on the alert, the 16th Light Dragoons lost their way, and when Cotton came on Franceschi in broad daylight, the Frenchman was quite ready for him. There was a volley from the advanced French troopers, a charge on the English side, which the young officers compared in its harmless effect to a field-day manoeuvre, and then Cotton found Franceschi waiting for him flanked by a wood that swarmed with the *tirailleurs* of the infantry regiment that Mermet had lent him.

Cotton dared not risk the charge. Sir Arthur himself brought up Paget's division, and drove the enemy from the wood, and Franceschi, always showing his teeth, retired in good order upon Mermet, seeing Hill's troops, whom he thought had been landed at Ovar from the British fleet, on his way.

Soult learnt that night that the British were advancing upon him in force. He also learnt that he had treason in his camp; for Argenton had confided in Lefebvre, and the marshal heard from that general for the first time of the pit that had been dug under his feet.

On the 10th, too, though neither Soult nor Sir Arthur was to hear of it till after the Battle of Oporto had been fought, Beresford had driven back *Maneta* ("the one-handed"), Loison, the most hated Frenchman in Portugal, and held the only bridge by which Soult could retreat to the eastward.

At Grijon the next day Mermet fought a rear-guard action. He held a ridge covered with olive and fir woods, and held it so stoutly that Sir Arthur had to send the 29th British to support the 16th Portuguese, who were skirmishing in the woods. The French were so strong, indeed, that they pushed a column down the road through the village of Grijon, and the young officers on the staff heard for the first time the calm distinct order from Sir Arthur's lips to close on them with the bayonet. It was not needed, for the German Legion had already turned the French left, and Mermet retired to stand again on the heights of Carvalho, where two squadrons of the 16th, forcing their way out of a deeply-wooded ravine lined by the French skirmishers, charged and broke the *47ème de ligne*, who stood in line to receive the cavalry.

Fighting and retreating, Mermet wore out the day, and under cover of dark retired across the Douro into Oporto.

Sir Arthur halted at dark; his men slept on their arms. During the night Hill's brigade was startled by a distant roar and the shaking of the earth like an earthquake. Soult in Oporto had destroyed the bridge of boats, and was getting rid of his spare powder.

At the grey of dawn on the misty morning of the 12th as the troops stood to their arms, a little hairdresser, a refugee from Oporto, was brought before Sir Arthur by Colonel Waters, of the Adjutant-General's department; and as the force slipped away into the grey mist, a ghostly army of silent battalions and squadrons, the little trembling man told his story. And he had reason to fear should Wellington fail; for just outside the headquarter camp there swung in the cold morning wind nine shrivelled things that had once been Portuguese peasants.

Sir Arthur, stern and silent as ever, muffled in that white cloak that served him through his Spanish campaigns, listened. Soult had destroyed the bridge—he expected that; but, what was worse news, all the boats on the river had been secured, were moored under the fire of French sentries, and the only boat on the near side was the little skiff in which the barber had rowed himself over during the night, and which, half filled with water, was hidden in some reeds. That boat was to be found, and it was that frail little bark that lost Soult the day.

The discovery of the conspiracy had shaken Soult for a moment only. He assured himself that the men immediately about him were

faithful, and then turned his mind to the preparations for delaying Sir Arthur's passage of the Douro. He knew that he could not hold on to Oporto for long, and intended to retire at his ease to the eastern frontier of the country. During the night of the 11th-12th he had personally super- intended the breaking up of the boat-bridge, and did not leave the quay to take rest until 4 a.m.

His quarters were on the seaward side of the town, and he believed that the next day he would see at the river's mouth the white sails of that fleet—of Franceschi's imagination—that had landed the troops at Ovar, and that with the fleet's help Sir Arthur would try to force a passage below the town. He intended to hold Oporto during the 12th, and then to retire leisurely with Franceschi as his rear-guard.

The mist had thinned and lifted, and the morning sunshine of a fine spring day was pouring on a landscape beautiful, except where the smoke still hung above the villages burnt by the retiring French, as Sir Arthur mounted, and, with the staff clattering behind, rode after his troops.

At 8 a.m. he was at Villa Nova, the suburb on the south side of the river from which the boat-bridge had stretched across to Oporto, and found its narrow streets choked with his troops. Sherbrooke and Paget were both there waiting.

Sir Arthur rode at a walk through the crowded streets, and, turning to his right, set his horse at the hill on which the Serra convent stands, and round the rocky cliffs of which the broad rapid stream of the Douro makes a bend. Walking through the convent garden, the staff and monks following a dozen paces behind, he stood on the highest point and looked across the river to where the terraced town clustered round its granite cathedral. It was almost as if it had been a city of the dead. His quick eye caught the boats moored on the far shore, the sleepy sentinels mechanically pacing their beats, the leisurely patrols, the silent squares, the deserted streets, the houses where no trace of life was seen. No Portuguese dared show at the windows, and the Frenchmen were waiting in their billets for the call that was to send them marching towards the river's mouth to beat back the English.

Sir Arthur's eye rested on an unfinished building, a long brick palace for the bishop, three storeys high at one part, which stood on high ground across the river. On the water side it was reached by a zigzag path up the rocky cliff; on the other three sides it was enclosed by a stone wall, with one iron gate leading on to the *prado*, now a cemetery, on the side farthest from the river. The French had left this building unguarded, and as he looked a daring project formed itself in the great general's mind.

He saw the long column of dust rising from the baggage waggons that Soult was sending off eastwards; he feared for Beresford's safety, and until the river was passed he could give no aid to the fiery commander of the Portuguese. It was a time for a gambler's throw, and he was ready to risk it.

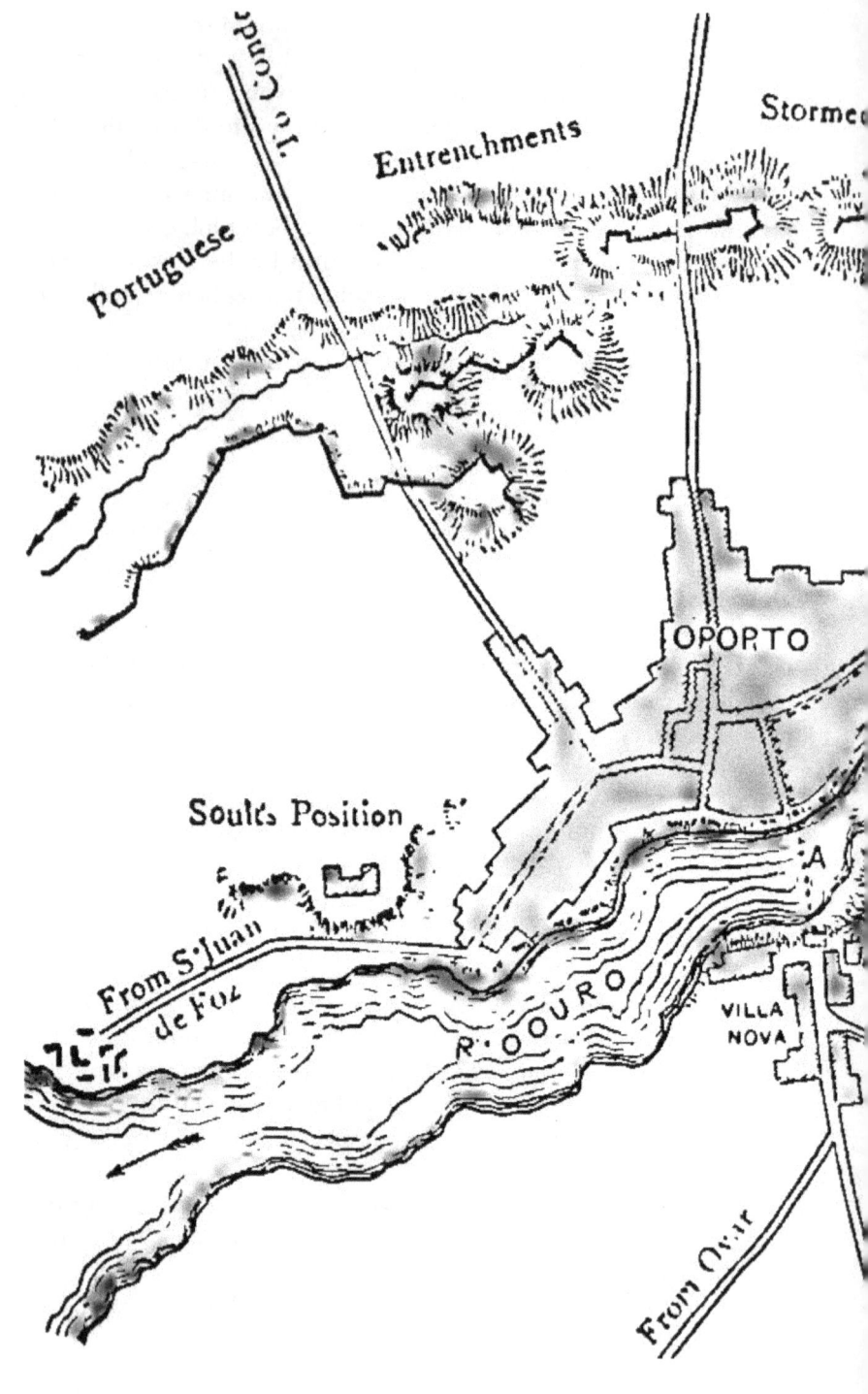

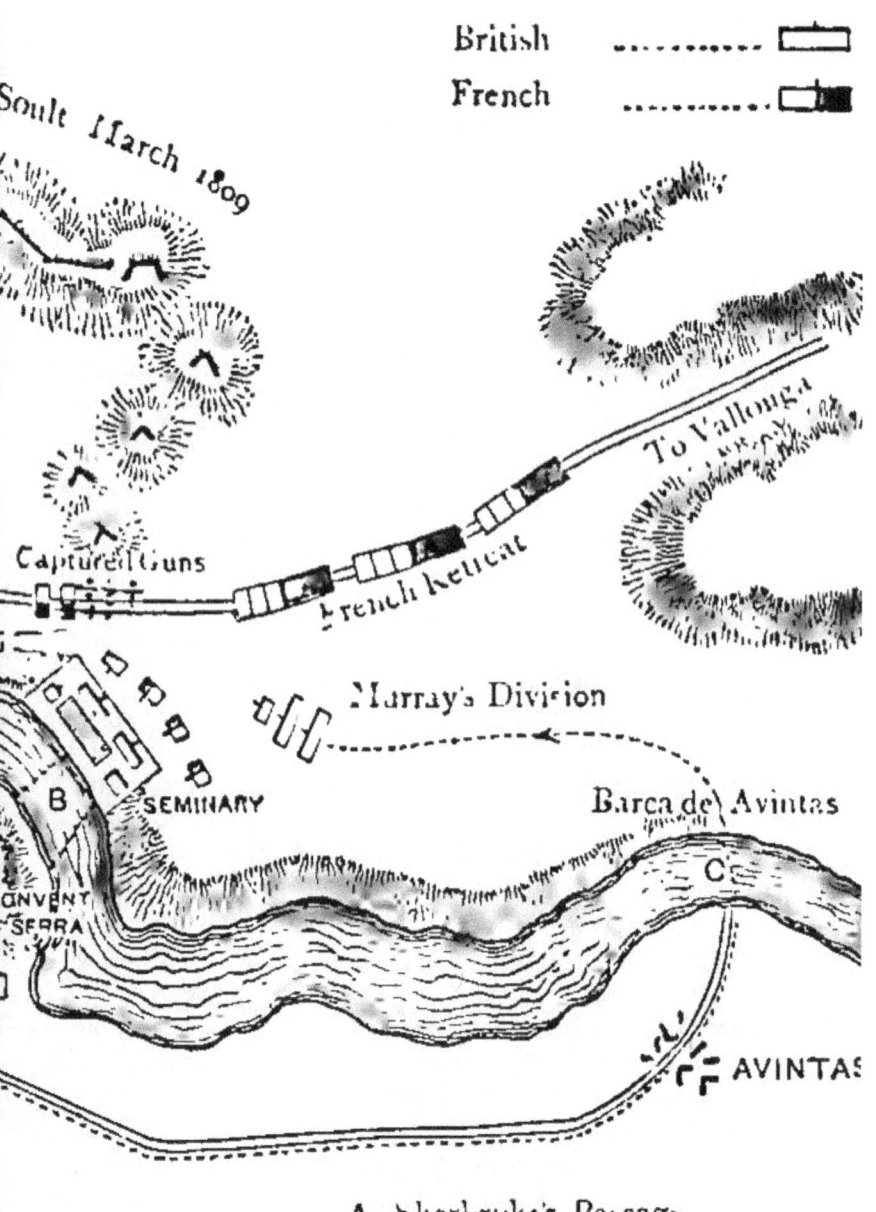

He ordered Waters to go with the barber, and a priest, the Prior of Amarante, who was anxious to help against the French, to find the little skiff and, crossing over, by some means to bring boats from the other side.

The strangely matched trio, with two peasants rowing them, passed over the rapid stream, and Sir Arthur made his dispositions. Murray, with the German Legion, the two squadrons of the 14th Dragoons, and two guns, was sent three miles up the river to attempt a crossing at the Barca de Avintas, should he find boats there; Paget massed behind the convent hill; Sherbrooke was ready in Villa Nova. The sun climbed up the heavens; the city across the swirling yellow river, which jostled the rising tide from the ocean, slept in false peace. Behind the solitary figure of the commander who stood and waited and watched there was the rumble of wheels as the gunners brought eighteen guns into position, screened by the fir-trees of the convent enclosure.

The bells of the Serra convent struck the hour of ten, and the bells of half a hundred churches across the river echoed them.

It was reported to Sir Arthur that some boats had been secured, and that one of them was already at the landing-place.

"Well, let the men pass," was the laconic order that he gave, and Paget with the Buffs, the first regiment of Hill's Brigade, went cautiously down the rocks to the water's edge.

Twenty-five men and an officer were passed over, and, reaching the further bank, went up the zigzag path and into the seminary—as the great unfinished building was called; and the enemy took no notice. A second boat passed, and then a third, which had Paget on board of it; and as the men from this toiled up the steep ascent, the drums beat the *générale* in the city, and Oporto woke to sudden life.

The crossing of the boats had not been unnoticed; a *chef de bataillon* had told his general that the English were crossing the river, and had been laughed at for his pains. Soult, himself, hearing that against his orders there were boats passing, had asked the French governor of the city for an explanation, and had been told that stragglers left on the far side when the bridge was destroyed were being ferried over; but it was not till Foy climbed a steep pointed hill that overlooked the seminary and saw the redcoats moving in the building that Sir Arthur's bold plan of thrusting a handful of Englishmen into the heart of the French army was discovered, and that, rushing in masses from the town and throwing forward *tirailleurs* as they advanced, Soult's men dashed at the building to drive the redcoats back again into the river

On the British side as well all was life. Hill's men crowded down to the river's bank waiting to pass, Sherbrooke's men showed themselves at Villa Nova, and the eighteen guns amongst the fir-trees spoke. The Portuguese, here and there waved an encouragement from the windows of the town.

The Kentish lads in the seminary held firm, though the 17th, led by Foy and supported by the 70th, with a fury of musketry and artillery fire attacked the building. The iron gate in the enclosure wall was where the storm of lead struck fastest. The French brought a gun up to it and through it to batter the building, but were charged and driven back.

The odds were tremendous, though as each minute passed the English grew stronger. All the Buffs were across, and the 48th and 66th and a Portuguese battalion were crossing; but it was more than doubtful whether the men in the seminary could hold out against the fierce attack, and anxious eyes were directed up the river in the direction whence Murray, who had found boats at Barca de Avintas, should come.

Paget had been deeply wounded while directing the defence from the roof of the seminary, and Hill took his place. Sir Arthur, feeling how critical the moment was, would have crossed himself, but his staff were urgent that he should not, and, knowing that Hill, in whom he had the firmest confidence, was commanding on the other side, he forbore.

Sharper and closer grew the conflict as attackers and attacked increased in numbers; when, moving along the river bank, his files opened out to make as much of a show as possible, Murray appeared, and at the same time a great burst of cheering and a waving of handkerchiefs from the windows told that the French had evacuated the lower town, and the inhabitants, rushing down to the quays, rowed their boats over to Sherbrooke.

It was an impressive sight. The tide was up and the river full; the boats laden with Guardsmen and men of the 29th covered the broad stream; from every window facing the water handkerchiefs were waved; the cheering was continuous; and on the left bank amidst the clustering troops a great white banner bearing the sign of the cross was hoisted and flapped lazily in the breeze blowing up from the sea.

Hill advanced his men from the building to the stone wall of the enclosure, and rained bullets on the stream of fugitives that poured out of the town; for Sherbrooke was hunting them through the nar-

row streets, and 10.000 men were flying for their lives in full rout. The army of Soult was beaten and retreating.

Five guns caught between two fires were taken, and when the stream of fugitives swept past Murray, giving him an opportunity which "might have tempted a blind man," his cavalry, fretting under his inaction, charged with Charles Stuart at their head, unhorsed Laborde, wounded Foy, and took two hundred prisoners.

That night in the Carrancas Sir Arthur sat down to the banquet that had been cooked for Soult; the town was illuminated as for a great public' holiday, though the streets were strewn with the bodies of dead horses and men; and in the darkness beyond the savage peasants prowled like wolves, stripping the corpses and murdering the wounded men.

The sequel is soon told:—Sir Arthur halted at Oporto the night of the 12th and during the 13th to bring up his guns and baggage.

Soult, moving eastwards and reorganising his forces as he went, heard on the 13th that Loison had been beaten back by Beresford, and that the only line of retreat by which he could take his guns and waggons was in the hands of his adversaries.

"The weather was boisterous, the army, worn with fatigue, was dismayed, and voices were heard calling for a capitulation. But in that terrible crisis the Marshal Duke justified fortune for having raised him to such dignity. He had accidentally fallen from his horse, and his hip, formerly broken by a shot at the siege of Genoa, was severely injured; but neither pain, nor weakness of body, nor peril could shake the firmness of his soul."

With a fierce will he silenced the traitors, he destroyed his guns and baggage and military chest, put his sick men and ammunition on the mules, ordered Loison and some outlying cavalry to join him, and took to the mountain paths.

On the morning of the 15th he drew up his troops, now 20,000 strong, in battle array on the field of Braga, where, two months before, he had scattered the Portuguese, and then, with Sir Arthur and Beresford at his heels, continued his retreat. Sir Arthur, when he heard that Soult had destroyed his guns and baggage, knew that Beresford must have succeeded, and pressed the pursuit, while Beresford, anticipating orders, joined the chase.

Through torrents of rain, along paths on the mountain side where the waterfalls came streaming down to the thundering torrent in the abyss below, Soult forced his men, starving and shoeless; and the peas-

Montserrat Convent, Oporto.

ants from the heights swept down whole files to death by rolling stones, and murdered every straggler and sick man left on the march. Behind, the British cavalry pressed hard, and the guns opening on the massed Frenchmen crowding to cross the Ponte Nova— where Sir Arthur stayed the pursuit—heaped the bed of the torrent with corpses.

Sir Arthur, with a pardonable touch of pride that Moore had been avenged, wrote that "in everything, even weather," Soult's retreat was a pendant of that to Corunna, and then with the characteristic wish as to his own men—"I hope this army will not lose their heads"—turned his thoughts towards Victor.

Soult, with his men bowed with fatigue, without shoes, many without accoutrements or muskets, his artillery, baggage, and military chest destroyed, with a loss of 6,000 good soldiers out of the 25,000 he had led into Portugal, reached Ney in the north.

"He had entered Portugal with fifty-eight pieces of artillery, he returned without a gun: yet his reputation as a stout and able soldier was nowise diminished."

July 27-28, 1809
Talavera

D. H. Parry

Dense woods drooped under the burning heat of a Spanish July afternoon; the grass of the plain was scorched to a dull brown, and white dust lay thick on the roads that led to Talavera. The one-storied, red-tiled houses of the squalid town on the banks of the Tagus were reflected in the broad river, but the habitual siesta of its inhabitants was for once interrupted as, from the shadow of the ancient ramparts, they watched a British army drawn up in line of battle—a line stretching, with here and there a gap, until it rested on a steep hill, two miles away, beyond which again a chain of blue mountains rose against a cloudless sky.

It was a tattered line—patched, torn, and campaign-stained, and the dust of the roads had sullied it, dimming the scarlet of its coats. It was, moreover, a hungry, half-starved line, having lived for many days on a handful of raw wheat and a draught of water, or a species of field-pea called *corovanzen*, by way of rations. There were rough detachments and undrilled lads among its regiments, some still wearing militia badges on their appointments, as many of our men did afterwards at Waterloo; but nevertheless they were waiting for the French, who were somewhere across a little river hidden by the woods in their front, beyond the Casa de Salinas, where Sir Arthur Wellesley lay with the outposts, 10,000 Spaniards under Cuesta being strongly posted on the skirt of the forest, nearer to the town itself.

The plain that stretched before the line was level, and well grown with olives and handsome cork-trees; and on the 27th July, 1809, it was baked and dry, the passage of a single horseman being sufficient to raise a great cloud as the sun beat fiercely down.

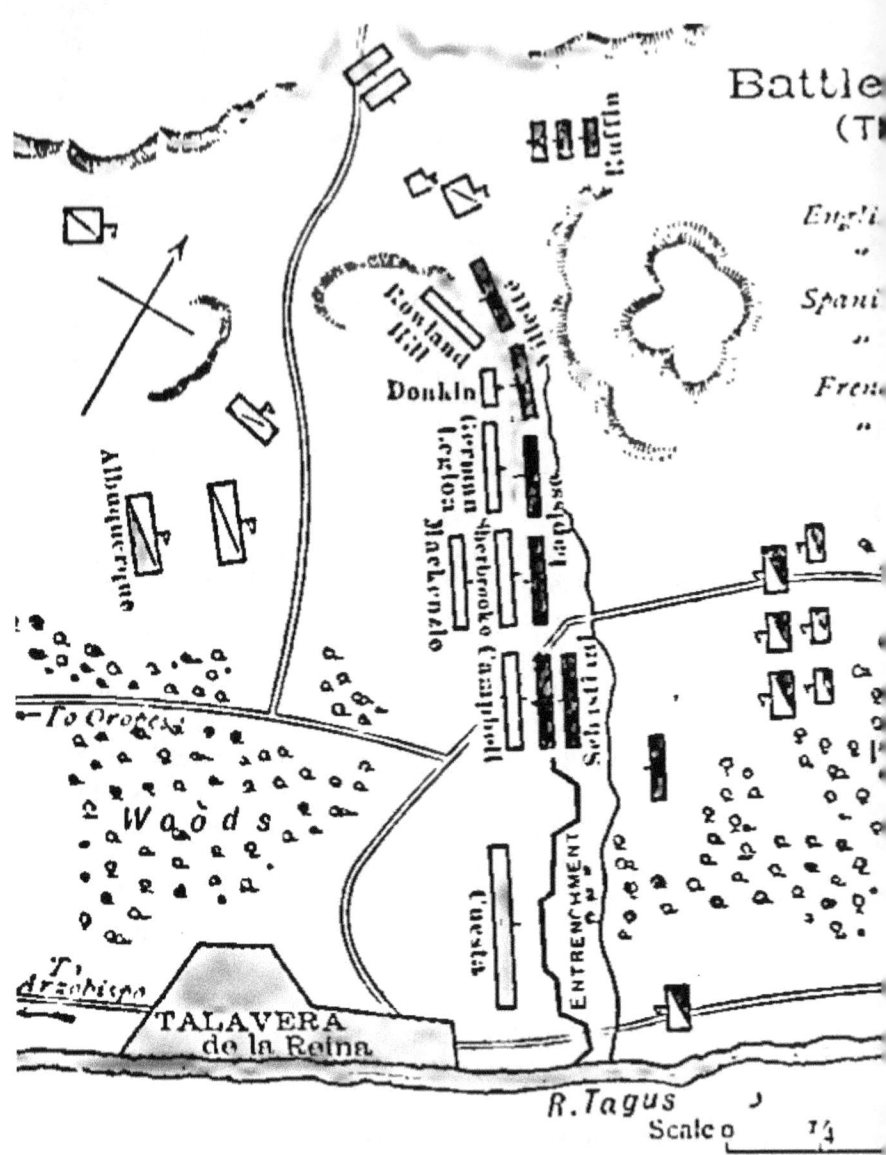

King Joseph Bonaparte, brother of the great emperor, was marching to oppose our further progress into Spain, and when the clocks of Talavera were striking three the divisions of Ruffin and Lapisse, having forded the Alberche, came through the forest, with their cartouche-belts and red epaulettes worn outside long white linen overcoats, and debouched so suddenly that our leader was nearly captured in the *Casa*, and the outpost was thrown into momentary confusion.

The young, untrained troops lost their heads, fired on each other, and were driven into the open, the gallant "Old Stubborns"—as the 45th were nicknamed—and the 5th Battalion of the both Regiment alone remaining firm, and receiving the French with a heavy fire from the well-known "Brown Bess" and the Baker rifle.

After 400 of our men had fallen, and a goodly number of the enemy, the French paused, and our two brigades retired step by step, under cover of our light dragoons, to take up their position in the main line, which had eagerly listened to the rattle of the musketry and watched the smoke drifting slowly away above the tree-tops.

With drums beating, and the sun pouring on them until the brass eagles on their *shacko*-plates glowed like gold—with the bold assurance of men whose colours bore the magic names of a score of battles won beyond the Rhine against Germany, Austria, and Russia—the veteran soldiery of the empire came proudly on, their artillery unlimbering to open a cannonade against our left wing, while their green *chasseurs* trotted forward to discover the position of the Spaniards.

Sir Arthur Wellesley had taken great precautions in posting our allies, who were placed behind mud walls and high banks between our right and the town, screened still further by the cork woods and barriers of felled timber and the buildings of a large convent, whose musical chime went unheeded amid the strife; but he had no confidence in them, and events proved him to be right.

The character of their leader is well indicated in a perfectly true incident which happened some time before Talavera was fought. Sir Arthur, wishing to give battle on one occasion, sent to tell Cuesta and to desire his support. The ancient tyrant, thinking the enemy would make a stand, replied that, the day being Sunday, his conscience would not allow him to fight; but, hearing directly after that the French were retreating, his religious scruples vanished and he intimated his readiness to engage! No pen can picture the wretch in his true infamy, and his villainous countenance was a fit index to the craven soul within.

The *chasseurs* soon discovered the Spaniards through the screen of leaves, and, cocking their carbines and pistols, sent some balls whistling among them.

For a moment there was a returning fire, but the next instant, without warning, *ten thousand* able-bodied cowards turned tail and fled helter-skelter to the rear, carrying with them artillery, stores, and baggage-waggons, Cuesta himself being driven hurriedly off in a lumbering coach-and-six, amid a crowd of grenadiers in white and linesmen in brown, tumbling over each other in their frantic fear, and spreading the report that we were beaten and all was over!

A few remained, and after a while a few more returned, driving off the enemy, who fell back in confusion; but six thousand of the scamps had melted into air—a fair sample of the Spanish valour of Peninsular days and the difficulties our general had to encounter.

We meanwhile were emptying many a saddle, and more than one bold chasseur was dragged away dangling to his stirrup iron in that encounter, which was the first of the three pre- cursors of the sanguinary hand-to-hand battle of Talavera.

Close to a large field redoubt the Oporto road bisected our position, and Brigadier-General Campbell's division stood there in two lines, on their left being Sherbrooke's division—the 1st Battalion of the Coldstreams and 3rd Guards with Mackenzie's men behind them, panting from their recent skirmish at the *Casa*.

To the left of the Guards were the King's German Legion, their artillery posted on the slope of the height that bounded our line, and which was also occupied by Rowland Hill's 2nd Division, with our cavalry in their rear—10,846 men only on whom we could depend, to oppose 50,000 veterans under Marshals Jourdan and Victor, with such well-known generals as Villatte, Lapisse, Ruffin, Sebastiani, Latour-Maubourg, and Milhaud to execute their commands.

******

The last gleam of the setting sun was fading from the spires of the town, and twilight had already begun to shroud the two hostile armies, when they came at us again, making a desperate attempt to seize the hill, Ruffin's division rushing forward with great rolling of drums on Colonel Donkin's brigade posted there.

Luckily, two regiments lost their way in a ravine, and the 9th arrived alone, thus giving us time to bring up reinforcements before Villatte and Lapisse reached our line; but as it was, some of the bold fellows got round in the dusk and climbed the height, from which they fired down on to Donkin's men, who were taken in front and rear.

Rowland Hill was ordering on the 48th when bullets began to rain round him, and thinking that some of our lads were aiming in the wrong direction, he rode up the rising ground with his brigade-major, Fordyce, to find himself instantly surrounded by the enemy.

A grenadier wounded his horse and grabbed at the bridle, but the

general spurred so violently that he broke away, and, leaving Fordyce dead, galloped down again to meet the 29th, which he led back at the charge.

The Worcestershires, with bayonets lowered, made short work of the daring 9th, and pitched them over into the valley; but red flashes came from the darkness as two other French columns advanced. The whole of our line stood to arms, cartridges were bitten and ranks dressed, while the brass drums kept up their dull roar, amid cries of "*En avant!*" "Steady there!" "Make ready, present, fire!" and all the jumble of sounds and shouting that told of a deadly combat.

Villatte—who, to his immortal honour, refused in after years to sit in judgment on Marshal Ney—urged his horse forward and brandished his sword in vain; in vain the gallant Lapisse—formerly colonel of the famous 57th Demi-brigade—pushed his men on against the German Legion until his feint attack became a real one. The British kept their ground, cheering as they reloaded, and closing up the ranks as man after man sank bleeding on the withered herbage, until Victor drew off and silence fell over the plain. The wounded crawled towards their own lines, where bright bivouac fires were soon blazing; but 1,000 Frenchmen and 800 of the allies lay stark and stiff in the starlight.

During the short summer night there were several alarms that kept us on the alert, though they arose principally from our Spanish friends, who suddenly began tiring at nothing at all, with no object whatever; but with the dawn of the 28th the serious business of war recommenced. The French beat the *pas-de-charge*—known as "old trousers" by our men—and Ruffin again advanced to turn the coveted hill, followed by Villatte, and heralded by a cannonade that mowed us down by sections.

From the openness of the plain in front of our position—for the Spaniards had all the cover to themselves—we could see the enemy's masses and the French officers flying from one division to another. They, on the other hand, had a precipitous hill before them, dotted here and there with patches of dingy red above which the grey smoke floated—dangerous patches which resolved themselves into companies and battalions as they approached them at a quick step. There is something grim and soldierly in the clean-shaven faces of our Peninsular infantry, with the little tufts of side-whisker then in vogue as we see them in the prints of the time; and grim they must have looked to the enemy on that Talavera morning, with the sunrise lighting up their bayonets and the pikes of the sergeants, as they awaited the attack unflinching under the fire of the guns.

As the grenadiers and light infantry neared our position, the cannoniers turned their pieces on the centre and right of the British, leaving the hill to the stormers, who approached at a run on two sides, shouting loudly. Rocks and ridges, grassy dips and hollows, broke the compact columns as they got within arm's length, and the attack became a series of little struggles where all formation was lost, and each man fought for himself.

Kentish Buffs clubbed their muskets and hewed at the moustached veterans of Jéna and Austerlitz; the Connaught Ranger and the *enfant de Paris* grappled with each other and rolled down the slope strewn with ammunition-paper and cartridge-cases.

The vicious little curved *briquet* of the French officer flashed in the sunlight and met the regulation sword of our subaltern, generally in favour of the former; for we were behind them in the use of small arms, as in many other things. Some of their men mounted the height, and were dislodged with difficulty. Hill was wounded, and many of our best and bravest met a soldier's death with the hurrahs of their comrades ringing in their ears. But inch by inch we forced them back, and after a fiendish forty minutes they retired in disorder, with the loss of no less than *fifteen hundred*, to the shelter of their batteries.

Sir Arthur sent to Cuesta for artillery, but the cowardly Spaniard only responded with two guns, though the Duke of Albuquerque came up on his own account with a fine brigade of Spanish horse, disgusted at the conduct of the old tyrant, who after the battle began to shoot his runaways for following an example he had himself set them on many occasions.

King Joseph now reconnoitred our line with a glittering staff, and held a council of war at which Jourdan and Victor violently opposed each other in a way that seriously embarrassed poor Joseph, at heart an amiable, good-natured fellow, but a mere cat's-paw in the hands of his ambitious brother.

Marshal Jourdan, who had been so frequently beaten in battle that the soldiers christened him "the anvil," was in favour of taking up a position and waiting for Soult to arrive; but Victor, smarting 'under his three repulses, urged the king to reopen the conflict, promising to carry the hill if they would attack along our whole line simultaneously. The greatest indecision prevailed, but the king eventually gave in to Victor against his own better judgment, afraid lest Napoleon should rebuke

him for neglecting an opportunity. Sir Arthur Wellesley sat on the summit of the hill, calm and cool under a fearful weight of responsibility, and when Albuquerque sent to tell him that Cuesta was about to betray him, he listened to the news without turning his head and observed quietly to the officer: "Very well; you may return to your brigade."

Our "General of *Sepoys*," as he was contemptuously called in some quarters, had full confidence in his own powers, and continued to gaze across the plain, where our thirsty men mingled with the enemy at the stream, forgetting for a time their mutual animosity.

This may seem a strange statement, but the history of that war is full of generous instances on the part of both armies. Many courtesies were exchanged between brave fellows who, perhaps, next day met in mortal combat; sentries would often chat, and obtain a light for their pipes from each other, or the French bands give concerts for the benefit of our men.

The British cavalry, which had gone some distance to water their horses, had now returned and drew up behind the hill. Several hundred infantry came back from their duty of bearing the wounded to a place of safety, and were mistaken by the enemy for Sir Robert Wilson's corps; and now the drums and bugles recalled each army to its ranks, as the French eagles were uncased about half-past one.

The day was intensely hot; a blue sky stretched in unclouded brilliancy overhead, and every feature of the landscape showed with great distinctness, except where the dust rose round the mustering men, whose accoutrements and flashing bayonets scintillated in the glare.

Eighty pieces of cannon stood ominously silent, waiting the touch of the dark-blue uniformed artillerymen to vomit death among us. Three strong brigades of infantry with mounted officers were drawn up in columns, the silk tri-colours drooping in the breathless air, each ensign flanked by two *sergents-porte-aigles*, chosen from the most valiant in the ranks who could neither read nor write, and hence could not hope for promotion, and whose honourable duty it was to guard the eagle with their lives, carrying a formidable halbert and a brace of pistols for that purpose.

Behind the infantry were long lines of horsemen, the tall yellow-and-black plumes of the 5th French Chasseurs—whose first colonel, D'Andigeau, was a romantic Spanish *brigand* far back in the seventeenth century— and the crimson facings of the 10th, lending a touch of bright colour to the array, further increased by the brass helmets of the 1st and 4th Dragoons, with gay scarlet revers to their green coats.

In rear of Villatte a bunch of red-and-white pennons showed where the Polish lancers stood, stern troopers from the Vistula with light yellow plastrons and blue uniforms, and a great cloud of the ubiquitous dust betrayed King Joseph's Guards marching up in reserve.

The people of Talavera, once more on the ramparts, saw a movement agitate the four French columns; eighty tongues of flame darted from the cannon behind them; eighty puffs of white smoke mingled into a dense pall which threw its shadow along the plain, followed by a mighty crash that set the horses rearing and made the Spaniards tremble in their security. Marshal Victor had given the signal, the enemy sprang forward, and the battle proper, to which the other affairs had been merely preludes, began.

The 4th Corps was the first to reach us, the active little *fantassins* scouring over the ground and flinging themselves upon *our* 4th Division, only to be impaled on the bayonets of the 7th Fusiliers and the "Old Five-and-Threepennies," which was the cant name of the 53rd Shropshire; while the 5th Battalion of the 60th, in whose ranks were many Germans, emptied their rifles into them again and again. The universal practice of Napoleon's armies was to send a cloud of light infantry against the enemy, preceded by a cannonade and followed by the line. It was the light infantry that Campbell's regiments had repulsed, and as the column behind came through the dust General Mackenzie's men and some Spaniards stepped out to help the 4th Division, reserving their fire until they came to close quarters.

Sir Arthur watched the combat from the hill, and seeing Ruffin creeping round to turn our left, and Villatte advancing at the double in front, he sent orders to Anson's cavalry to charge down the valley which lay between the mountains and our friendly eminence.

"Squadrons, march!" rang the trumpets, and two gallant corps—the 1st King's German Legion Hussars and our 23rd Light Dragoons—moved off and trotted towards Villatte.

The 23rd, in blue with crimson facings and huge bearskin crests surmounting their helmets, rode on the right of the Hussars, whose yellow-braided *pelisses* and scarlet busby bags floated gracefully out when they got under way and the trot merged into a canter.

Villatte threw his men into three squares and began firing; steel scabbard and black sabretache clashed and jingled as the canter became a hand-gallop and the trumpets sounded "Charge!"—Hill's division cheering lustily as they thundered past the height.

Within thirty yards of the squares there lay a hidden gully, quite concealed by the long grass until you came close on to it, and which history has exalted into alarming proportions, like the very much overrated "sunken road of Ohain;" but, although it was only eight feet deep by from twelve to eighteen in width at its worst part, it was still an obstacle bound to disorder a charging squadron, and the watchers on the hill saw the Germans rein up, as Arentschild pulled his horse on to the crupper and cried, "Halt! I will not kill my young mens!"

Some of the Hussars, nevertheless, jumped it and continued their way, and the 23rd, who arrived at a spot where the hollow was broader but much more shallow, dipped into it at full speed, lost their forma-

tion as some of the horses fell, and scrambled up the opposite bank in twos and threes, having lost their impetus and order, but not their hearts, for they rode right through the intervals of the squares before them, and laid about them gallantly with their half-moon sabres on the green *chasseurs*.

Their triumph was short. Colonel Seymour was hurt, and Major Frederick Ponsonby led, gallantly as was his wont; but down came the Polish lancers and the Westphalian Chevaux-Légers; the 23rd were outnumbered, cut down, and ridden over; and although a few got back, amid the redoubled cheering of our infantry, 207 lay under their horses, the loss of the 1st Hussars being also heavy—37 men and 64 mounts.

While this incident was enacted, Campbell and Mackenzie had closed with the main body of the 4th Corps, under the brave Corsican general. Count Porta Horace Sebastiani, and a furious struggle took place, the carnage on both sides being horrible.

At Talavera French and English fought hand to hand, the French having the advantage of length in their musket-barrels, although our Brown Bess bayonets were longer than theirs. We were half-starved into the bargain, but we possessed that historic characteristic of never knowing when we were beaten.

The huge silk colours were riddled with balls; writhing groups of mutilated wounded screamed piteously as they were trampled underfoot. It was more like a *mêlée* of the Middle Ages than a nineteenth-century battle; for men got at each other and hit hard, the blood spurting right and left until the musket-butts, and the trodden grass, and every bayonet in the division was red with it, while the cannon-balls came *whang-*

ing and tearing into the throng, and we smashed and smote blindly through the smoke and sand.

"Forward, forward!" was the cry, and with tremendous cheering we sent Sebastiani's veterans back and captured ten guns, a regiment of Spanish horse cutting in as they tried to rally, and driving the 4th Corps to the rear. Sir Arthur thanked the 2nd Battalion of the Fusiliers; but Lapisse's drums turned all eyes on the hill again, and the German Legion, who were assailed with fury in their turn.

Magnificent as the Hanoverians always proved themselves while they were in our service—equal, and in some points superior even, to our troops, whose uniform they wore—the impetuosity of this attack shook them. Sherbrooke's Guards were shattered at the same moment by the French artillery, and the very centre of our line was broken.

The Guards charged valiantly, and were for an instant successful, but they advanced too far and there was great confusion. Von Rettberg's battery pounded steadily, and Bombardier Dierking won the notice of Sir Arthur Wellesley, who exclaimed, "Very well, my boy!" clapping him on the back as shot after shot fell into the middle of the enemy; but the situation was most critical.

Our leader ordered Stapleton Cotton up with his cavalry, sending to Colonel Donellan to bring the 48th from the hill; and soon the broad buff regimental banner was seen approaching side by side with the king's colour, as the Northamptons marched proudly into the disorder, wheeling back by companies to let the retiring jumble through and then resuming their steady line, shoulder to shoulder.

Gallant Lapisse lay dying on the grass, his life-blood welling out over the general's gold aiguillette; but his column, hot with victory, had penetrated our centre, and were making the most of a triumph destined to be short.

The sun had got behind us, for it was afternoon, and the band of purple shadow that preceded the scarlet line of the 48th was ominous of the disaster about to fall on the Frenchmen.

Taking the column on its right, the Northamptonshire poured a tremendous volley into it and closed with the bayonet.

Colonel Donellan fell mortally wounded near the gruesome masses of dead guardsmen, 600 of whom were slaughtered there; but even in his agony the line old man remembered his regiment, and raising his three-cornered Nivernois hat—the last seen in our service—he desired Major Middlemore to take command, sinking back with dimmed eyes as the stout fellows faded from his sight for ever.

Like an avalanche the 48th fell on the column and checked its progress, giving the Guards and the Germans time to rally; then another hand- to-hand struggle began, fiercer if possible than the last, for we were fighting desperately to recover lost ground, and two of the bravest nations in the world strove for mastery, loud and long.

Those who could not get to the front held aloof, and fired shot after shot wherever they saw an enemy: men wrestled and rolled over, clutching at each other; fists were used when weapons were broken; bearded *sapeurs* in bearskin caps and white leather aprons hewed with their axes as though our men had been the walls of a fortress; officers in topboots shouted themselves hoarse; and Dermoncourt's 1st Dragoons slashed and pointed in the most frantic attempt to break us; but our order was restored by the example of the Northamptonshire, and our cavalry came up at a trot with sabres in hand.

Nearly all the staff were either unhorsed or wounded, and Sir Arthur was hit on the shoulder, but not seriously. Ruffin hesitated beyond the valley, and was lost; Lapisse lay dead, and Sebastiani was in disorder. King Joseph's reserves and his Guard had not been engaged, but the French *morale* was shaken and we began to cheer—a pretty usual sign that we were conquering.

The artillery still continued; but little by little the enemy retreated to their own side of the plain, and about six o'clock the battle was over.

Towards the end, while the shot was plunging around Von Rettberg's battery, a distinguished act of heroism was performed by Sergeant Bostelmann, who was bringing ammunition up from the waggons in the rear. The dry grass caught fire, scorching the wounded and burning some of them to death, and it threatened the powder as the flames ran rapidly across the heath.

With four brave gunners named Luttermann, Zingreve, Warnecke, and Lind, the sergeant dragged each waggon, four in all, to a place of safety behind a trench, heedless of the fact that they might all be blown to atoms in an instant should one of the tempest of balls strike their dangerous charge; and after superhuman efforts all the waggons were saved and galloped down the road beyond, when the limber teams arrived, Bostelmann being publicly thanked, and afterwards receiving a commission. Fearful was the slaughter when men found time to look around them.

Generals Mackenzie and Von Langwerth of the Legion were killed, and 31 other officers, with 767 rank and file; 3 generals, 192 officers, 3,718 sergeants and men wounded, and 652 of all ranks missing; or a total on our side of 6,268 during the two days. Of these the 7th Fusiliers lost 65, and the German Legion nearly 1,500 and 88 horses; while other corps counted their casualties in varying proportion.

One strange incident reaches us from the private journal of an English officer to whose friend it occurred: the enemy, seeing him to be badly wounded and in great pain, requested his permission *to put him out of his misery*. Needless to say, he declined with thanks!

The French are reported to have lost 10,000 men, 2 generals, and 17 guns, the prudent Napier giving the number at between 7,000 and 8,000. Truly an awful feast of blood and woe!

Again the bivouac fires flared up in the darkness, and the surgeons were busy on each side. We were too weary and too weakened to press in pursuit, and both armies remained all night within range of each other, ours suffering in addition from hunger—the commissariat, as usual, unequal to its duties, and death threatening any who attempted to plunder.

Bread had not been issued since the 22nd; men were pale with exhaustion and sick for want of food, but there was no grumbling; although in Talavera alone there was enough corn concealed by the unspeakable Spaniards to have lasted our army a whole month!

In the morning the search parties of the German Legion discovered three blue standard-poles among their dead, and after a ghastly hunt Captain von Düring, of the 5th Battalion, found the brass eagles belonging to them.

A burst of military music rose unexpectedly, and shading their eyes from the sun which again beat down on the now corpse-covered plain, our army saw Craufurd's light division march proudly in, too late to take part in the battle, although their efforts to arrive in time have made their march historic. The iron warrior, whose stern discipline rivalled that of Martinet, the celebrated colonel of the *Regiment du Roi* under

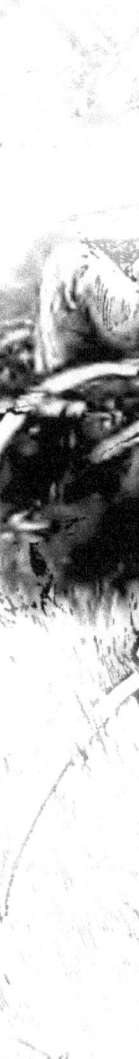

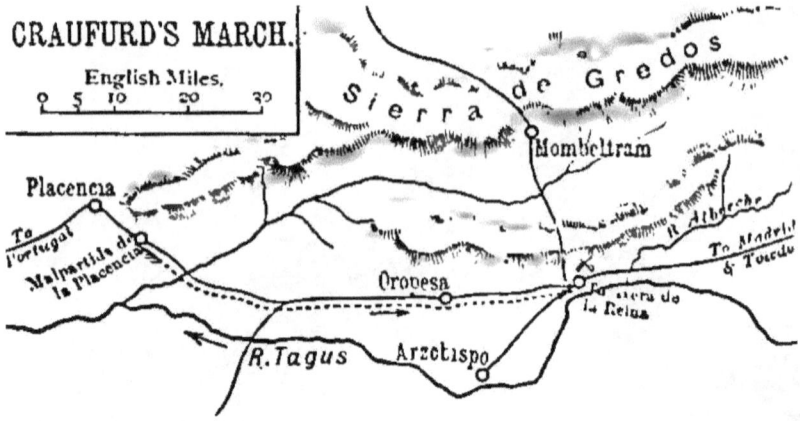

Louis XIV., had halted his men, after a twenty-mile tramp, near Malpartida de Placencia, and they were cooking their meagre rations when Spanish fugitives hurried up with a report of our defeat.

"Buglers, sound the 'fall in!'" cried Craufurd, buckling on his sword-belt; and there and then, after selecting fifty of the weakest to remain behind, he marched off with his three regiments—the 43rd, 52nd, and 95th Light Infantry—covering *sixty-two* English miles in twenty-six hours, every man carrying sixty pounds on his shoulders.

Although it was the hottest season of the year, only seventeen stragglers dropped behind a glorious record of British endurance and eagerness for the fray, the division taking over the outpost duty immediately on its arrival. Before this, however, with the first gleam of daylight, the French army left its gory bivouac.

For the last time the dust floated along the edge of the forest, and whitened the foliage of the cork trees; regiment after regiment, squadron after squadron, gazed with sullen anger at the tattered British line, now sadly thinned, which had maintained its position in spite of them, and which still stood to arms in the pearly haze of the morning. The dull tap of the drums grew fainter; the rumble of caissons, and waggons heavy with the wounded, died away; the lancers wheeled in a cloud and followed, and the sunshine burned in a dazzling blaze on the brass helmets of the vanquished dragoons. Then the woods hid them; the crows and the vultures settled undisturbed as the dust subsided—the French army was gone!

April–August, 1809

The Liberation of Tyrol and Three Captures of Innsbruck

A. J. Butler

Five hundred and thirty years ago the land of lofty mountains and deep valleys called Tyrol was made over by its last Countess to the Duke of Austria; and from that day to this the people have owned no sovereign but the head of the House of Hapsburg. Above all, they have resisted every effort to incorporate them with Bavaria. Of the same blood and speech, customs and religion, it might have been expected that the two countries would have long ago united; but the old rivalry between the Austrian and Bavarian houses seems to have extended itself to the peoples, between whom there has always been more or less feud. In 1703 the Elector Max Emanuel, in alliance with: France against the House of Austria, attempted to pass through Tyrol to join Marshal Vendome coming up from Italy. The historian of Bavaria says:

"But in Tyrol there dwells a breed of men loyal to their old customs and to their prince. Moreover, this people is rough and valiant, and proud of its mountains, which, with poverty, guarantee freedom and security against the might of foreign foes."

And so Max Emanuel found. He reached Innsbruck, pushed on to the Brenner, and sent a small detachment round by the Inn valley to look for the expected Frenchmen. They got as far as the bridge of Pontlatz, above Landeck. At this point the valley contracts to a gorge, and at the narrowest point the Inn, here a turbulent torrent forty or fifty yards wide, has to be crossed. The Bavarians found the bridge broken down. On the further side a breastwork had been erected. Not a single foe could be seen. Presently shot after shot cracked from the mountain side; tree-stems and rocks rolled down crushing men and horses, and cutting off all retreat, and in a few minutes such of the unlucky Bavarians as were not shot down or drowned were prisoners in the hands of the Tyrolese. A few days later the whole country was up. The alarm bells rang from every church tower; every road towards Italy was barricaded; every mountain side was alive with sharpshooters, and nothing remained for the Elector but to cut his way through the swarming foes back to his own territories, with a heavy loss of officers (including his chamberlain, Count von Arco) and men. A worthy Tyrolese peasant of those days kept a short diary, which has been preserved. Here is an extract from it:—

"In 1703, on the eve of St. John Baptist (June 23) 20,000 enemies invaded Tyrol, did great damage, killed many of our people, but still more fell on their side, came as far as the Lower Meadow (a place at the south foot of the Brenner, of which we shall hear again), and after that were driven out by our marksmen and militia on St. Anne's Day (July 26)."

Tyrol was not troubled with a hostile invasion again till the last years of the century. In March, 1797, the French general, Joubert, attempted to cross the Brenner from Italy. Where the great eastern road through the Pusterthal falls into the Brenner road, and close to the point where the strong fortress of Franzensfeste now dominates the junction of the two railways, stands a little village called Spinges, lying in the angle between the roads, and about 1,000 feet above them. Here a peasant army awaited the French, and for some days the surrounding forests were the scene of desperate fighting. The peasants fell on with clubbed guns, and with a fury that nothing could withstand. One Prixa of Axams was found dead after the fight, with seven Frenchmen lying around him. Peter Haider brought down six with his rifle. He was then attacked by five at once. He shot one with his rifle, one with his pistol, and cut down a third before a shot laid him low. The two remaining opponents slashed him with their swords, leaving him for dead; but it took more than that to kill a Tyrolese of those days, and Haider survived. In these mountain villages the church and churchyard often form a natural citadel. Time after time did the French storm that of Spinges. A girl of twenty-two, Katharina Lanz, who lived to relate her exploit till 1854, led the defenders. With her hair floating in the wind and her skirts well tucked up, she plied a pitchfork with a goodwill and efficiency that

was too much for the French bayonets. Meanwhile the road back to Italy was blocked by an Austrian force, and General Joubert had to make the best of his way down the Pusterthal. By April 13th the enemy was out of the country.

The hostilities between France and Austria in 1805 affected Tyrol so far that Innsbruck received a visit from Marshal Ney; an honour which the Tyrolese had done their best to decline, by offering a stubborn resistance to his passage from Bavaria by way of Scharnitz. Their positions, however, were turned; but Ney was shrewd enough to see the benefit of exasperating so warlike a people as little as possible.

In December the war ended with the Peace of Presburg; and now for the first time what Tyrol had dreaded for centuries came to pass. The province was annexed to Bavaria, and the bond of over four centuries was snapped. No more brutal disregard of national wishes and national rights was ever shown, even by Napoleon. The Bavarian Government was probably sincerely anxious to act fairly by its unwilling subjects, but it went to work all in the wrong way. Into a land of well-to-do, independent, intensely religious peasants, who had never felt the pressure of external authority, but had gone on governing themselves for centuries on the old Germanic system the Bavarians tried to introduce all the pedantries of officialism. Compulsory enlistment was substituted for free volunteering; the local authorities were replaced by officials from Munich, who gave themselves airs;[1] the parish priests were removed, and the church organisation generally inter-

---

1. "The King is a nice gentleman enough," said a peasant with whom he had happened to speak when, passing through the country, "but his clerks are no use."

fered with to the point of persecution; the name "Tyro" disappeared under a new-fangled division into "Circles;" worst of all, the old castle of Tyrol, near Meran, the very heart of the land, was sold by auction.

Tyrol had never abandoned the hope of recovering its freedom under its former sovereign. Communications were maintained all

this time between the Archduke John, the most beloved member of the Imperial house, and certain men in Tyrol who enjoyed the special confidence of their countrymen. The most notable of these, Andrew Hofer, was an innkeeper and horse-dealer from the Passeir valley, which runs up into the mountains behind Meran. His humble inn, which still exists, stands by the wild torrent of the Passeir, where the bed widens into a little beach. From its situation, it is known as "On the Sand," and its owner was often spoken of in Tyrolese fashion as the "Sandwirth," or landlord of Sand. The position of Hofer's house is as central as any in Tyrol. From it Meran may be reached in four hours, while in the opposite direction a seven-hours' march brings you to Sterzing, halfway up the Brenner on the south side. It was, therefore, possible for Hofer with his force to attack the rear of an enemy crossing that pass in either direction. Hofer was a man of about forty, distinguished more for physical strength, kindly disposition and upright character, than for any special military talent or capacity for government. It is, indeed, a little difficult to explain the great influence which he undoubtedly exercised. Though there is no reason to doubt his courage, he showed none of the dash amounting to recklessness with which some of his subordinates exposed their lives; while his extreme good-nature, and unwillingness to distrust any man, led him especially towards the end of his career into pitiable vacillation. Nor had he any gift of eloquence, such as often has made men with no other qualification into popular leaders. Yet there can be no doubt that for five months he was the recognised chief in the grand stance which this little mountain-country offered, and offered for a time successfully, to the conqueror of Europe. Other leaders whose names should be mentioned were Martin Teimer, Joseph Speckbacher, and the Capuchin Joachim Haspinger. All these men had taken part in the fighting of recent years. Teimer, who was the youngest of them, being thirty years of age, had risen to the rank of major in the *landsturm*, or militia. He was probably the ablest of all the Tyrolese leaders, as he was no doubt the best educated; but he never inspired the same confidence. Joseph Speckbacher was ten years older. He was now an *employé* in the salt-works at Hall, near Innsbruck, and comfortably off. His youth had been very wild. As a boy of twelve he had taken to a poacher's life; and poaching among those mountains is a very different business from the rabbit-snaring and pheasant-netting which occasionally enlivens English coverts, and helps to fill English gaols. Even the most authorised chamois-hunting is fairly dangerous sport; and when the hunter is liable at any moment to become the hunted, and share with his game the sensation of a bullet in the ribs, unless his own wits can save him, it will be easily seen that no better training could be found for mountain warfare. Speckbacher was a man of undaunted courage, boundless resource, and a thorough knowledge of the country which was to be the chief field of operations. Father Joachim had served as an army chaplain, and had earned a medal for valour. Now he was to lead in many a fierce attack; but he made it a point of honour to carry no weapon save a great ebony crucifix, which, it was currently reported, became in his hands as formidable as the maces wielded by mediaeval bishops. "The Redbeard," as he was called, was perhaps the especial favourite of the people. He, too, survived into the second half of the century.

Thus when Austria, encouraged by Napoleon's growing difficulties in Spain, plucked up courage to declare war against him once more in March, 1809, the Tyrolese were all ready to bear their part. On April 9th, Teimer and Hofer issued a general order, making it clear to every district that its special task would be. Teimer then departed to take the command in the Inn valley above Innsbruck; Speckbacher being in charge of the district between the capital and the Bavarian frontier. Hofer disseminated the order through other innkeepers—the country inns in Tyrol being the natural centres of information—until every man knew precisely what he would have to do, and had merely to await the arrival of the little note bearing the words "It is time." Another signal was given by strewing sawdust in the streams, and sending planks bearing red flags down the rivers.

The men from Passeir and the neighbourhood of Meran assembled round the little inn "on the Sand." There were some thousands of them altogether, Hofer, with his broad shoulders and mighty black beard, conspicuous among them. All wore the dress of their valley—brown jacket with red facings, a red waistcoat with broad green braces over it, a broad leather belt on which were worked the owner's initials, leather breeches, bare knees, and red or white stockings. Each man carried his heavy rifle, with which he could make pretty sure of a chamois at 300 yards; and a Bavarian was a larger mark. It must be remembered that few regular troops of that day had anything but smooth-bore muskets. Hofer made a short speech:

"When you have carved a wooden figure, may you take it to Vienna and sell it? Is that liberty? You are Tyrolese—at least your fathers called themselves so; now you have to call yourselves Bavarians. And our old castle of Tyrol has been demolished. Does that content you? If you raise three ears of maize, they demand two from you. Do you call that prosperity? But there is a Providence, and it has been revealed to me that if we plan to take our revenge, we shall have help. Up then, and at the Bavarians! Tear your foes, ay, with your teeth, so long as they stand up; but when they kneel, pardon them!"

The first shot was fired not far from the place where Joubert had been overthrown eight years before. Colonel von Wrede (who in later days was to be a thorn in the side of the French) was in command of the garrison of Brixen. Intelligence reached him that an Austrian force under General Chasteler was approaching through the Pusterthal, and on April 10th he sent a detachment to destroy the bridge over the River Rienz at St. Lorenzen, near Bruneck. The peasants were up in a moment, the detachment was not suffered to approach the bridge, and when Wrede brought up his whole force in support, it was met with a hail of bullets from the mountain side. An attempt to get the guns into a position whence their fire might destroy the bridge was frustrated by a furious charge of the peasants, who, many of them armed only with cudgels and flails, dashed upon the troops, surrounded the guns, and hunted the gunners into the river. Wrede could do nothing but try to make his way to Sterzing, where he might unite with the garrison of that town. A force of 3,000 French under General Bisson, on its way from Italy, accompanied him a little below where the fortress of Franzensfeste now stands. The way from the Pusterthal to the great northern road passes through a narrow defile—the Brixener Klause, or Gorge of Brixen—and here the unlucky French and Bavarians

were, of course, at the mercy of their furious enemies. Pelted with rocks, tree-stems, and bullets by an invisible foe, in momentary fear of being overtaken by the Austrians, whose advance-guard actually appeared before they were well out of the defile, they made their way with heavy loss to the plain in which lies the little town of Sterzing.

Meanwhile Hofer and his men had dashed over the Jaufen Pass. Colonel Bärenklau (this looks like a mythical name, but appears to be correct), the commander of the Sterzing garrison, wisely decided to meet them in the open, where military discipline might tell. The steady fire of grape-shot and musketry checked the onward rush, and the peasant force retired into a hollow road to re-form, while girls and women from the town supplied refreshments. A second rush was similarly checked. Hofer, sitting, as one historian of these events remarks, like Moses on a hill above, and watching the fortunes of the fight, espied some loaded hay-waggons, doubtless bringing supplies for the garrison from the mountain hay-sheds. A brilliant idea struck him, or was suggested to him. If these could be brought up they would serve as cover for the sharpshooters, who could then dispose of the enemy's gunners. But at first no man ventured to bring them within range of the deadly grape. Then a girl stepped forward, swung herself on to the back of one or the oxen, and, regardless of the bullets, urged the team on with whip and voice, exhorting her countrymen at the same , time "not to be afraid of the Bavarian dumplings." The guns were now soon silenced; the Tyrolese fell on with the butt, and in a few: minutes the whole Bavarian force, or so much of it as remained, was disarmed, and before evening safely under lock and key in a neighbouring castle, under the guard, as often happened, of the women. All traces of the fight were carefully removed, the victors dispersed among the mountains, and when Bisson and Wrede arrived, on the following morning, April 12th, no garrison was to be found, no news of its fate could they extract, no enemy was to be seen. Puzzled, and still more alarmed, they pursued their march, or rather flight, harassed, as before, wherever a gorge or defile—of which there are many along this mountain road—gave an opportunity to the Tyrolese for their favourite tactics.

But a yet more terrible surprise awaited them. In the early dawn of the 13th, the weary, battered army, still numbering nearly 4.000, saw the domes of the Innsbruck churches below them, and hoped for a respite. A mounted officer was sent on to announce their approach to General Kinkel and Colonel Dittfurt, commanding the garrison of the capital. As he rode through the gate of the town he dropped from his horse, pierced with a bullet. To explain what had happened we must pass to the Inn valley. The village of Axams had incurred a fine for resistance to the conscription, and on the 11th a detachment had been sent to collect this. They fared little better than their comrades at St. Lorenzen, and retired, vowing vengeance. In the course of that day the whole of the valley above Innsbruck was astir, and ready to march upon the town. Meantime, Speckbacher had summoned the lower valley to arms. All night long beacon fires blazed on the mountains which look down into the streets of Innsbruck. The morning of the 12th had hardly dawned when he was at the gates of Hall, and no sooner had these been opened as usual by the unsuspecting garrison than the Tyrolese rushed in. The officers were seized in their beds, hardly a shot was fired, and in a few minutes, with a loss of two only of his men, Speckbacher had captured 400 Bavarian soldiers. These were marched off to Salzburg, again under the escort of women, for no men could be spared from the task of liberating the country. Hall is a short eight miles from Innsbruck, and long before noon Speckbacher was with the levies from the upper valley, who were attempting to storm the two bridges that here cross the Inn just outside the walls of Innsbruck. Up to this time they had made little progress, for want of leading; but when Speckbacher, waving his hat and shouting "Long live the Emperor Francis" placed himself at their head, they wavered no longer. The gunners fell under the terrible clubbed rifles, or were

thrown into the river; some young mathematical students from Innsbruck University slewed the guns round, and poured volleys into the troops who were hurrying up from the town; the peasants pressed forward, some with no weapons but their fists; an attempt to break through with cavalry was frustrated by the sharpshooters, who by this time had got into the houses, and were dealing death from every window. To complete the victory, at this moment appeared Major Teimer, with some more or less drilled battalions of *landsturm* from the upper valley. General Kinkel, thoroughly terrified, wished to capitulate,

The Liberation of TYRO[L]

English Miles.
0 5 10 20 30 40

Alps of North

To Bavaria & Munich
Scharnitz
Zirl
INNSBRUCK
Hall
Upper Inn Valley
Arzros Berg
Vatters
Amras
Landeck
Schönberg
Pontlatz
R. Inn
Steinach
BRENNER PASS
Oetzthal Alps
Tschoffs
Sterzing
JAUFEN PASS
Mauls
St. Leonhard
Am Sand
Mitter
Ober Au
SARNTHAL ALPS
Meran
Br[ixen]
R. Adige
Botzen
To Italy
Ortler Alps
Fa

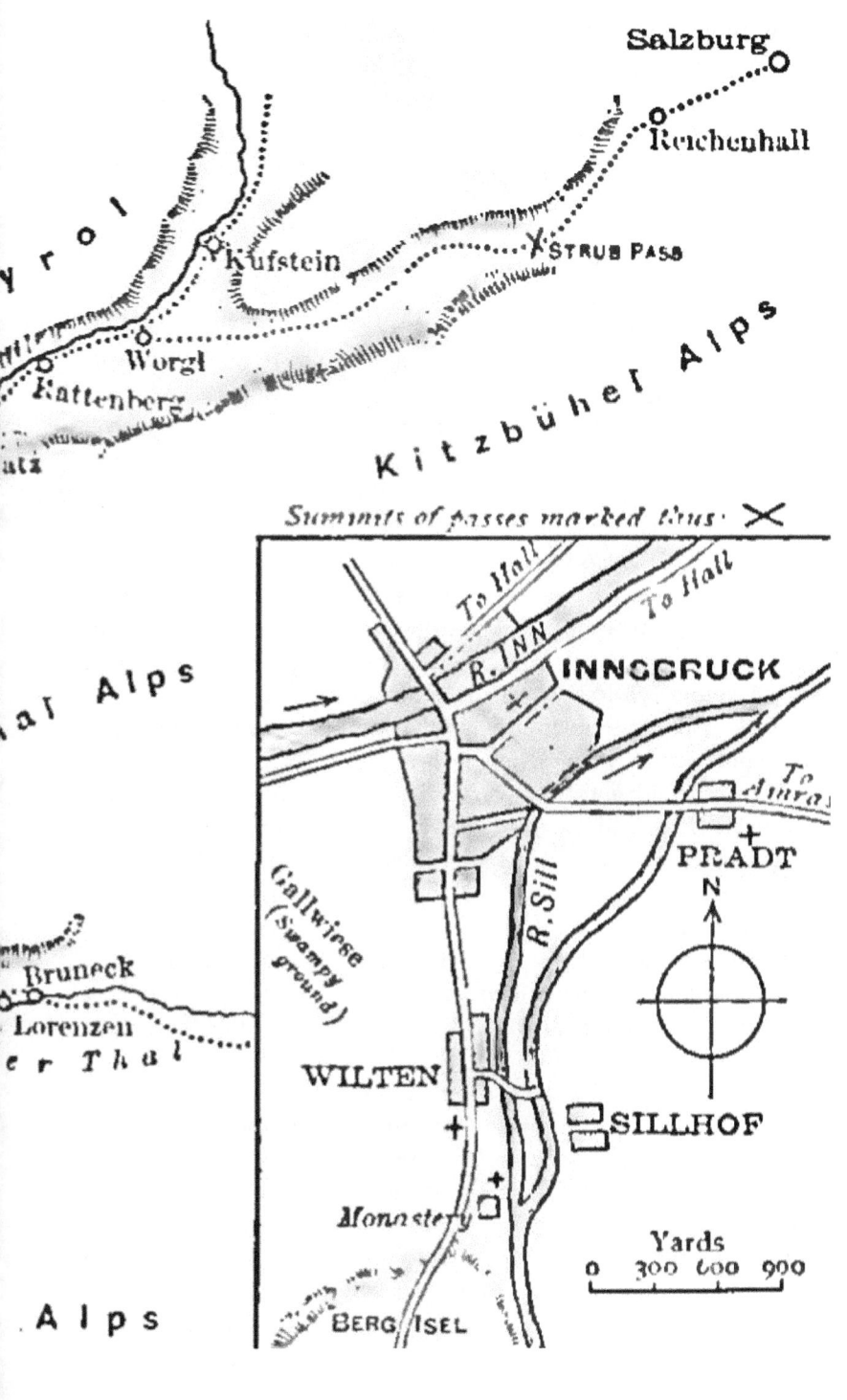

but his more energetic subordinate, Colonel Dittfurt, declared that he would sooner die than surrender to a rabble of peasants whom a couple of squadrons could keep in order, and made a last desperate effort to rally his men. As he was speaking two bullets struck him, and he fell from his horse. Struggling to his feet, he dashed with drawn sword on the advancing mass, to be again shot through the chest. Even then he made one more effort, aided by a few officers, to dislodge some of the enemy from a position which enabled them to keep up a galling fire; but a fourth bullet, in the head, stretched him senseless, and he was carried to the main guard. After his fall the surviving troops surrendered, and Innsbruck was in the hands of the Tyrolese. It was not yet eleven o'clock.

The remainder of that day was passed in rejoicing, and, it is to be feared, to some extent in pillage. Such of the *burghers* of Innsbruck as were thought to have been on too good terms with the hated *Boar* were regarded as fair objects for a little plunder. At the same time, many generous actions were done by individuals in saving the lives of the vanquished. A Bavarian official was on the point of being struck down by a furious mob when a girl flung her arms round him, and asserted, quite fictitiously, that he was her betrothed. He was spared at once. A young Tyrolese who had captured a French officer took him to an inn and gave him food. The officer, in gratitude, offered him a pair of gold earrings which he was wearing. "Do you think I did it for pay?" said the lad; and only with difficulty would he accept them as a keepsake. The old imperial eagles were hunted up, and rapturously greeted when found. "Your feathers are grown again, old tail," said a grey-haired man, as, with the tears flowing down his cheeks, he embraced the beloved symbol.

Men slept that night where they could—in streets or gardens. In the earliest dawn the alarm-bells rang, and the word went round that the French were upon them. As we know, this was the force under Bisson and Wrede; but those in the town knew nothing of the way in which they had fared on the other side of the mountains. The gates were barricaded, and all preparations made for a street fight. At five o'clock the head of the column appeared on Berg Isel; and by six they were drawn up in order of battle in the level, ground that lies between the south side of the town and the foot of the mountains: Bavarians on the left wing, French on the right. At the same time a strong force of Tyrolese had slipped round to the rear, and occupied Berg Isel. They were fairly entrapped. Teimer had meanwhile extracted from General

Kinkel an order bidding the Bavarian commander send someone into the town to see how matters stood; in compliance with which Wrede himself, and a French staff officer, came in, and the former was detained, while the latter was sent back to report. The sharpshooters had already opened fire. Teimer then came himself to meet General Bisson at the suburb of Wilten. The French commander asked for a free passage into Germany, and offered to take all the flints out of the muskets before moving; but Teimer would hear of nothing but capitulation. All this time the bullets of the sharpshooters were dropping into the dense ranks, adding to the general demoralisation, and enforcing the arguments of the Tyrolese leader. At length General Bisson yielded. The French and Bavarians laid down their arms. Two generals, 130 officers, and 6,000 men, with seven guns and 800 horses, surrendered to the Tyrolese.

Colonel Dittfurt, lying in the guardhouse, during one of the intervals of his delirium, had paused in his furious cursing, to ask: "Who led your forces yesterday?"

"No one," was the answer; "each man fought as he best could for Emperor and Fatherland."

"Not so," he said; "I saw him again and again: he was riding a white horse."

And the story went round that St. James, the patron saint, as it happens, of Innsbruck, had fought for his city, as of old he fought for Spain.

The Austrian troops, under General Chasteler, Arrived next day; but it was not expected that the Tyrolese would be left long in undisturbed possession of their conquests. Napoleon's fury when he heard how his troops had been served by a herd of undisciplined mountaineers knew no bounds. He issued on May 5th an order of the day, in which "a certain Chasteler, calling himself a general in the Austrian service," was accused of having caused an insurrection in Tyrol, and allowed some Bavarian conscripts to be massacred; and it was directed that the said Chasteler, whenever captured, was to be brought before a military commission and shot in twenty-four hours. To the Tyrolese, of course, this mattered little, but it undoubtedly shook Chasteler's nerve, and to some extent prevented the regular troops from giving efficient help.

On May 1st a strong force of Bavarians and French, under Wrede, now general, and Marshal Lefebvre, the Duke of Danzig, occupied Salzburg. The shortest route from that city to Innsbruck lies by Re-

ichenhall and through a narrow defile called the Strub Pass, entering the Inn valley at the little town of Wörgl. The Strub was held by Tyrolese and soldiers, 275 in all, with two guns. Wrede's entire division was sent on May 11th to force the pass, and succeeded in doing so after nine hours' hard fighting, in which the handful of defenders had four times repulsed the assailants. On the following day General Deroy, advancing by way of Inn valley, relieved the frontier fortress of Kufstein. which the Tyrolese were blockading, and on the 13th the two forces joined in the neighbourhood of Wörgl. The Bavarians had encountered a stubborn resistance all the way, and were infuriated: village after village was set on fire, property destroyed, women and children slaughtered. General Chasteler, with a force of 2,000 regular troops, having failed to prevent the junction of the Bavarians

with the French, was forced to accept battle at Wörgl and utterly routed, himself escaping only by the speed of his horse, and after the commission which was to carry out Napoleon's order had already been selected. On his way through Hall he was roughly handled by the salt-miners. The French and Bavarians marched upon Innsbruck, ravaging and burning, a task in which the former now seem to have taken the lead.

At any rate, it is recorded that Lefebvre, enraged at the sight of the Austrian eagle over the gate of the little town of Rattenberg, was only prevented from burning the place down by Wrede's strenuous opposition. Fifty-three peasants, taken with arms in their hands, also owed their lives to the firmness and humanity of the Bavarian general, who further issued a stringent order forbidding all ill-treatment of the inhabitants. On May 19th the Duke of Danzig entered Innsbruck. Two days later Napoleon was defeated by the Archduke Charles in the Battle of Aspern, or, as the French call it, Essling; but before the news of this could have reached them, Lefebvre and Wrede, believing all opposition was at an end, and wishing to cut off the Archduke John's retreat from Italy, had returned to Salzburg, leaving General Deroy's division to hold Innsbruck.

Marshal Lefebvre was so far right, that orders had been received by the Austrian commanders in Tyrol to withdraw their troops. But he reckoned without Speckbacher. That indefatigable man, on the day of the defeat at Wörgl, had been in Innsbruck collecting all the weapons and powder upon which he could lay his hands. Then he went to General Buol, who was at Völders, near Hall, preparing to retreat over the Brenner, and vainly tried to persuade him to make a stand. Finally, climbing one of the mountains whence all the country round Innsbruck could plainly be seen, he carefully estimated the strength of the enemy, and found that he had not more than 18,000 men to deal with. On May 23rd with two faithful companions, George Zoppel and Simon Lechner, he made a dash for the Brenner. Two more joined the party at Steinach, and the five, by spreading themselves about the mountain side, and changing their position at every shot, succeeded in putting to flight a cavalry patrol of several hundred men, which had been sent up to reconnoitre. General Buol was still holding the defile of Lueg, just north of the Brenner Pass, and Hofer with 6,000 men was also there. To them Speckbacher addressed himself, pointing out that the panic among the inhabitants of the Inn valley, caused by the events of the previous days, was over, and that they were quite ready to rise again. Buol was persuaded to put 1,200 men with 6 guns at the disposal of the Tyrolese leaders; and on May 25th, Hofer took up his position at Berg Isel, while Speckbacher, with the men from the lower Inn valley, held the right wing as far as Hall. The Tyrolese numbered some 18,000; Deroy had at most 12,000, but many of these were veterans. Some isolated fights ensued that day; more than once the Bavarians attempted to storm the position, and were repulsed. In the evening heavy rain came on (it rains most days at Innsbruck) and fighting was suspended. Owing, it is said, to the injunctions of an old man, who pointed out to Hofer that May 20th was a great church festival, Hofer fixed that day for the attack. This delay also gave time for Teimer, who was at Landeck, to bring his men down the valley. General Deroy, a kind-hearted old man, used the interval to issue a proclamation recommending submission, which, naturally, produced little effect, unless that of impressing the peasants with the idea that he was wavering.

On the morning of May 28th the Bavarian army was drawn up round the town of Innsbruck. The Tyrolese line extended in a great crescent to the south, its left on Zirl, ten miles above the town, its right on Völders, about as far in the other direction. The battle began on the wings. Speckbacher took the bridge of Völders and attacked Hall. On the left, Father Joachim Haspinger led the men from Meran, supported by two Austrian companies, by way of the villages of Mutters and Natters, into the marshy tract known as the Gallwiese, just above the town on the right bank of the river. He was soon at hand-grips with the enemy. A Bavarian soldier was delivering a thrust at him with his bayonet when a bullet laid the assailant low—fired over the Capuchin's shoulder, and so close that the famous red beard was singed. Only staying now and again to shrive a dying man, he pressed forward at the head of his peasants, who slowly but steadily drove the Bavarians before them. At a farmhouse called Rainerhof another gallant deed was done by a girl. With a small cask of wine on her head, and a glass in her hand, she was going about in the thick of the fight, dispensing drink to the weary men. A bullet went through the cask, and the wine began to pour out. In a moment she had it down from her head and her fingers in the holes. "I have only got two hands," she shouted; "if another bullet comes the wine will be lost. Put your mouths to all the holes, and drink while you can!" The fighting went on till noon with no definite results. An attempt of the Bavarians to storm Berg Isel, the centre of the Tyrolese position, was repulsed with the aid of Colonel Ertel's troops, though not till the right had nearly been turned by the foe. Hofer—surveying the whole field from the heights of Schonberg, where his headquarters were—cast anxious glances towards the left to see if any signs of Teimer were visible. At the head of his column, he appeared on the other side of the river; but they came up slowly, and ammunition was failing. To gain time, Hofer sent a flag of truce to the Bavarian commander, with proposals for a surrender. This was refused; but Deroy asked for a twenty-four hours' armistice, which Hofer equally declined. However, it was now too late in the day to resume the fighting, and under cover of the night General Deroy managed to evacuate the town unobserved, the wheels of the guns and the hoofs of the horses being all muffled, and to march away, never halting till the Bavarian frontier was reached. By seven o'clock next morning the Tyrolese were once more in Innsbruck.

The next month passed in tranquillity. After his defeat at Aspern Napoleon remained for several weeks on the island of Lobau, in the Danube, making his preparations to retrieve his. lost ground. For reasons which have never been satisfactorily explained, the Archduke took no steps to do more than watch his foe. On July 5th Napoleon again crossed the Danube, and on that and the following day inflicted on the Austrians the decisive defeat of Wagram. An armistice quickly followed, and again all Austrian troops were ordered to evacuate Tyrol. This time the persuasions of the Tyrolese leaders were of no avail, and General Buol could do nothing but withdraw, after issuing a proclamation in which the peasants' were exhorted to tranquillity and resignation. On July 30th the Duke of Danzig re-entered Innsbruck, and ordered that all weapons should be given up within forty-eight hours, and that the leaders should surrender at once. A force was sent over the Brenner, another up the valley of the Inn. Hofer, on his side, sent round a circular note calling all men to arms. On August 2nd, a body under Haspinger and others took up a position in the valley of the Eisach, a little higher up than the spot where Bisson and Wrede had been so roughly treated in April. They secured the Peisser bridge, where the road crosses the river between the hamlets of Oberau and Unterau—the Upper and Lower Meadow. Speckbacher, with the Pusterthal men, joined them, and all was made ready to receive the first enemy who should appear. General Rouyer's division had reached Sterzing on August 3rd. At 7 a.m. on the 4th the leading column—a Saxon regiment, over 2,000 strong—entered the narrow gorge below Mauls. A barricade brought them to a halt, during which they afforded a mark to Speckbacher's men. A torrent of stones also came on them. Still they moved forward as far as Mittewald, where artillery had to be used to clear the road. Fully 800 marksmen were in front and on both sides of them, and they were losing heavily. As they reached the bridge a voice rang out overhead:

"Stephen, shall I cut away?"

"Not yet," came the reply.

The column halted, and an orderly was sent to report the matter to General Rouyer. He ordered the advance to be continued, but, it is said, himself retired to the rear of the column. Then the voice was heard again:

"Now cut, John, in the name of the most Holy Trinity!"

With a roar like thunder the terrible "stone-battery" burst out. Rocks, larches, huge fragments of the mountain side, crashed down upon the luckless Saxons and Bavarians, overwhelming hundreds and

cutting the column in two. The losses of the force by the day's end amounted to 1,300. In the night Rouyer withdrew his rear to Sterling. The Saxons were surrounded, and after a gallant defence compelled to surrender. To this day the defile between Mittewald and Oberau is called the "*Sachsenklemme*." Hofer, meanwhile, had again crossed the Jaufen, and lay a couple of hours' march to the west of Sterzing, in a position where he could join hands with Haspinger on the right and on the left with Speckbacher, who, with his usual rapidity, had moved to the north of Sterzing, and now occupied a line of which the centre was the village of Tschöffs. At noon on August the 6th Marshal Lefebvre, with 7,000 men and 10 guns, entered Sterzing, and at 3 a.m. on the following day marched forward to Mauls, having taken the precaution of putting on the uniform of a private soldier. He also endeavoured to clear the heights with skirmishers. Haspinger gave way at first, probably only with the view of getting his enemy into greater difficulties. When the Tyrolese really advanced, Lefebvre was beaten back, escaping narrowly with his life, and the evening found him back at Sterzing, where he tried to rally his men. But the Tyrolese gave him no rest, and on the 10th he ordered a retreat.

The column which was trying to make its way round by Landeck had no better luck. At the ill-omened bridge of Pontlatz they fared just as their countrymen had fared 106 years before. The "stone-batteries" played so effectively on them that most had to surrender, and only a third of the whole number got back to Landeck. On the 10th they were again at Innsbruck, with a loss of 22 officers and over 1,000 men.

Lefebvre arrived on the following day, but he had not been allowed to reach the capital unmolested. "The finest hunt I ever had in my life," said Speckbacher, who led the pursuit, and stuck so close to the heels of the enemy that he himself dragged a Bavarian officer from his horse, and, like one of Homer's heroes, carried off his sword and spear as a trophy. Some of the German officers seem to have found a little consolation in the thought that the French had now had a taste of the Tyrolese.

Both sides rested on the 12th. The 13th was a Sunday. In the early morning Father Joachim said mass in the church of Schonberg. Hofer made one of his short speeches:

"Are you all here, Tyrolese? Then we will advance. You have heard mass, you have taken your dram. In the name of God, then."

The military service in the great abbey church of Wilten was not over when the first shots were fired. The numbers were about the same—some 20,000 on either side, the Bavarians, Saxons, and French having perhaps slightly the advantage. The tactics were very much as in May. Haspinger again led the left wing, Speckbacher the right. The marshal, however, in order to keep his retreat open, had detached a fore under Count Arco to hold Schwatz. The levies from the upper Inn valley were on the opposite side of the river, but they were unable to do much more than give employment to part of the enemy's force. At 2 p.m. the marshal ordered an advance. Covered by artillery fire,

two regiments stormed Berg Isel, while others attacked Ambras, on the further side of the river Sill. Every foot of ground was stubbornly contested. The men of Passeir were forced to give way. Speckbacher was driven from his positions. Only Haspinger, on the left, hurled the attacking columns back into the plain. The Bavarians began to set fire to the houses. It was the worst move they could have made, as it only served to infuriate the Tyrolese. Rallying under cover of the forests, they burst out again, and after one volley charged home with clubbed guns, the weapon which served them best. All the positions were recovered, and though Lefebvre ordered five more assaults, the assailants reeled back each time with broken heads.

The struggle only ended with daylight The Bavarians had lost 2,000 men. Count Arco had fallen, like his ancestor, to a Tyrolese bullet, but the way to Kufstein was still open; nor was Hofer desirous to drive the enemy to extremities. So long as the land was freed from his presence, it was enough. At 7 p.m. on the 14th the Marshal Duke of Danzig left Innsbruck with his whole force. That night he entrenched himself at Schwatz, but soon found that the neighbourhood of Haspinger and Speckbacher made the position undesirable, and on the 19th he proceeded to Salzburg. For the third time in four months Tyrol was freed.

It is beside our present purpose to trace the course of events further. It may be said that for some weeks Hofer governed Tyrol from Innsbruck, with about as much success as could be expected from a peasant suddenly raised to such a position. His upright nature prevented him from making so many blunders as his want of education and experience might have been expected to lead him into. On October 4th, the emperor's "nameday," a great festival was held, and Hofer was presented with a medal, sent by the emperor himself. On the same day the treaty of Schönbrunn was signed, and Tyrol was finally handed back to Bavaria, and overwhelming forces were sent to enforce submission. Speckbacher was defeated on the Salzburg frontier on October 16th, and barely escaped capture. A few days after, Hofer left Innsbruck, and took up his quarters at Schonberg. Once again, on the 27th, the Tyrolese turned to bay, and inflicted some loss on the Bavarians; but on November 1st General Wrede succeeded in surprising their position on Berg Isel at a time when they were celebrating the festival of All Saints in the neighbouring churches, and inflicted a heavy defeat. Once more victory was propitious to Hofer, when, after three days' hard fighting at St. Leonhard, close to his own home, he compelled 1,200 Frenchmen, who had crossed the Jaufen in pursuit of him, to lay down their arms. But this was the last gleam of success. Hofer's mind seemed failing; he was no longer master of himself. A price was set on his head, and on December 2nd he fled into the mountains, and took refuge in a remote spot known only to himself and a few trusty friends. The secret was, however, betrayed, and at the end of January a force of

600 Frenchmen was sent to take him. He was brought to Mantua, and tried by a military commission. The majority were in favour of some penalty short of death; but Napoleon was not likely to spare the man who had baffled his generals so long, and a peremptory message commanded that he should be shot forthwith. He underwent the sentence with heroic fortitude on February 20th, 1810.

On the fall of Napoleon, Tyrol again came under its old counts.

MARCH 5, 1811
The Battle of Barrosa

Archibald Forbes

An almost unique example of steadfast perseverance, crowned at length by success after long years of disappointment, presents itself in the career of the brave old fighting-man whose prompt resolution and ready daring won the battle of Barrosa against desperate odds. Thomas Graham of Balgowan, a Perthshire laird of old family, was born in 1748. In youth he was passionately fond of horses and dogs, but gave no indication of a liking for the career of a soldier. While he was an undergraduate at Oxford in 1766 his father died, leaving the young laird in possession of a handsome and unencumbered rent-roll. According to the custom of those days he made the grand tour, remaining for several years on the Continent, where he acquired a thorough knowledge of the French and German languages. In 1774 he married a daughter of Lord Cathcart and for nearly twenty years afterwards lived the life of a country gentleman, shooting and farming in his own county, hunting in Leicestershire, travelling and yachting with his wife until her death on board ship in the Mediterranean in July, 1792. Striving to dispel the melancholy caused by his bereavement, Graham accepted the position of volunteer *aide-de-camp* to Lord Mulgrave, who had arrived at Toulon in September, 1793, to take command of the troops employed in the defence of that fortified city. In this service he distinguished himself so highly and displayed a military capacity so marked, that Lord Mulgrave urged him to become a professional soldier and to raise a regiment which should serve under his command.

Returning to London in the spring of 1794, Graham obtained

from the commander-in-chief a letter of service to raise a regiment at his own expense, with the temporary rank of colonel during its continuance on the establishment. So successful was Colonel Graham's effort that within four months he was in command of the 90th Regiment (Perthshire Volunteers) with the full number of 1,000 rank and file. Presently he was induced by his first success in recruiting to raise a second battalion of the same strength. But when he applied to be permitted to obtain permanent rank in the service, he was informed that it was the king's determination not to make permanent the temporary rank held by an officer who had not served regularly and for a stipulated time in the several ranks.

Most men would have been discouraged by this rebuff; but so keen for active service was Graham that he accepted the position of British military *attaché* to the headquarters of the Austrian army in Italy, where he saw a great deal of hard fighting against Napoleon and other French commanders. After a year's service with Beaulieu, Wurmser, and finally with the Archduke Charles, he returned to England in 1797. In the Mediterranean in 1799 he had much intercourse with Nelson, who sent him, with the rank of brigadier-general, to Malta, there to blockade the fortress of Valetta, held by a superior French garrison. With a much inferior force he carried on the blockade with steady perseverance until the arrival of Sir Ralph Abercromby in July, 1800, when Graham arranged the terms of surrender with the French commander. From Malta he hurried to Egypt, where his regiment had greatly distinguished itself in the battle of Alexandria, and he accompanied it home at the Peace of Amiens in March, 1802.

After the eminent services performed by Graham and the distinguished conduct of the regiment he had raised, the treatment which he had received and was still receiving at the hands of the commander-in-chief roused his long-suffering nature, and he determined that he would not give up the command of the 90th while it continued to exist. Now a man of fifty-four, he was as keen for soldiering as if he had been looking forward to his first campaign. When Sir John Moore in 1808 took command of the expedition destined to co-operate with the Swedish forces, Graham solicited and obtained permission to serve as a volunteer, and was appointed to act as *aide-de-camp* to the commander of the forces. Moore withdrew without delay from an impracticable service, and returned with his force to England accompanied by Graham, who retained his appointment near his friend during the disastrous Coruna campaign, at the close of which a life was lost so precious to his country. Sir John Moore, as he lay dying, felt sure that any recommendations from him would be given effect to by his Sovereign, and he charged Colonel Anderson with his latest breath to bring to the king's notice those officers whose services he deemed most worthy of reward. Among others whom their dying chief wished to honour was Colonel Graham, who on 4th March, 1809, received a letter from the Horse Guards which ended all his anxieties as to promotion and gave him a recognised position in the army. The commander-in-chief wrote:

"I have not failed to submit to the king the communication made to me by General Hope, at the dying request of the late Sir John Moore, regarding the eminent and important services performed by

you in Spain; and His Majesty, in testimony of the zeal you have upon several occasions manifested, has been graciously pleased to direct that the established custom of the army may be departed from by your being promoted to the rank of major-general. Your appointment as major-general in the army has accordingly taken place, and you stand among the major-generals in the situation you would have held had the lieutenant-colonelcy to which you were appointed in 1794 been a permanent commission."

For years Graham had known the hope deferred that maketh the heart sick. He bore a stout heart within his broad breast; but, and little wonder, there must have been many moments when his feelings were very bitter against a government which could promise freely, but, when the hour of danger was seemingly passed, had refused everything. Yet disappointments had not soured his fine nature. On the subject of his unexpected promotion, the veteran wrote:

"To have merited in so high a degree the approbation of so distin-

guished an officer as the late Sir John Moore—whose loss was deplored by the whole army and felt by me as having deprived me of the best of friends—and at last to have gained this distinction by such a recommendation was indeed ample compensation for the bitter disappointment I had so many years laboured under."

Major-General Graham served in the disastrous Walcheren expedition, having taken part in the bombardment of Flushing, and he returned to England thoroughly disgusted with the mismanagement of the enterprise. He received his first independent command in February, 1810, when he obtained the command of the British garrison in Cadiz with the local rank of lieutenant-general. He reached his post on the 25th March, and immediately set about strengthening the position.

In December, 1810, Soult was withdrawn from the vicinity of Cadiz to co-operate with Massena in Estremadura. The force under Victor engaged in the blockade of Cadiz, nevertheless, in February, 1811, had a strength of about 20,000 men. Graham therefore considered that it would be extremely difficult to force the French lines by a direct frontal attack; and a naval expedition composed of British and Spanish troops sailed from Cadiz on 21st February. The British contingent, passing its destined port in a gale of wind, landed at Algesiras and marched to Tarifa, arriving there on the afternoon of the 24th. The strength and detail of the British force at Tarifa on the 25th were as follows:—Two squadrons German horse, 180 sabres. Major Busche; detachment of artillery, Major Duncan; detachment of engineers, Captain Birch; brigade of guards with detachment 95th Rifles, 1,221 bayonets, Brigadier-General Dilkes; 28th, 67th, and 87th regiments, with two companies Portuguese, 1,764 bayonets. Colonel Wheatly;

flank battalion of detachments 95th Rifles and two companies 47th regiment, 594 bayonets, Lieutenant-Colonel A. Barnard; two companies of 9th, 28th, and 82nd regiments, 475 bayonets, Lieutenant-Colonel Brown, 25th Regiment; Company Royal Staff Corps, 33 bayonets. Lieu- tenant Read: total of sabres and bayonets, 4,314, with 10 guns. This force is described by Napier as "all good and hardy troops, their commander a daring old man, and of ready temper for battle."

On the 27th the Spanish captain-general La Peña landed at Tarifa with 7,000 Spanish troops; and Graham, to preserve unanimity and flatter Spanish pride, ceded to him the chief command, although this was contrary to his instructions. On the following day a march of twelve miles carried the allied army over the ridges between the plains of San Roque and those of Medina and Chiclana; and being within four leagues of the enemy's positions, the force was reorganised. The advance-guard was entrusted to Lardizabel; the centre was commanded by the Prince of Aglona; the reserve, consisting of the British troops and the two Walloon regiments, was given to Graham; and the cavalry was under Colonel Whittingham, a British officer in the Spanish service. Victor had to maintain his lines of blockade; but he was able, nevertheless, to hold in position some 9,000 of good troops near Chiclana, where he awaited the unfolding of the project of the allies. In the first instance La Peña's objective seemed to point to Medina, and on the 2nd March his advanced guard stormed Casa Vieja, where he was reinforced by General Beguines with 1,600 infantry and several hundred irregular cavalry. With a strength, then, all told of quite 13,000 men, he bent towards the coast and drove the French from Vejer de la Frontera. After a long and straggling night march which greatly wearied the troops, he continued his movement, and on the morning of the 5th, after a skirmish in which his advanced guard of cavalry was routed by a French squadron, he reached with the head of his force the height of Barrosa. Before the whole of the long straggling column had come up. La Peña, without disclosing his own intentions or communicating in any way with Zayas, pushed forward Lardizabel straight to the mouth of the Santi Petri. Zayas had duly constructed his bridge connecting the mainland with the island, but on the night between the 4th and 5th he had been surprised and driven in by the French. Lardizabel, however, after some hard fighting in which 300 Spaniards fell, forced his way through the French posts and effected a junction with Zayas.

La Peña desired that the British contingent should follow Lardizabel, notwithstanding that, as the reserve, its place was in the rear: Graham, however, recognised the possible value of the Barrosa height and was fain that it should be held in strength. His argument was that Victor, the French commander, could not molest Lardizabel and Zayas in their position on the Almanza creek, since in attempting to do so he would expose his left flank to the allies holding the Barrosa height. Lascy, La Peña's chief of staff, roughly controverted this reasoning, and La Peña gave Graham the peremptory command to march to occupy the long narrow ridge of the Bermeja, through the pinewood on the slope in front of that position. With admirable self-control Graham obeyed the discourteous order, and moved in the prescribed direction; but he left on the Barrosa height the flank companies of the 9th[1] and 82nd regiments, under Major Brown of the 28th, to guard his baggage. Graham moved as ordered with the less reluctance, because of his impression that La Peña would remain on the Barrosa height with Aglona's division and the Spanish cavalry, and because also of his knowledge that another detachment was still behind in the vicinity of Medina. But Graham did not know of what poltroonery La Peña was capable. The British force had scarcely entered the wood in front of the Bermeja, when the Spanish commander suddenly and without even the courtesy of a notice, carried off with him his main body, and directing the cavalry to follow, hurried by the sea-road in the direction of the Santi Petri, leaving the Barrosa height covered with baggage protected only by a weak rear-guard of four guns and five battalions.

Barrosa—or, as the Spaniards call it, the Cerro de Puerco—is a low ridge trending inward until its farthest and loftiest extremity is about a mile and a half from the coast. It overlooks a high broken plain of small extent, bounded on the left, as one looks towards Cadiz, by the cliffs of the seashore, on the right by the forest of Chiclana, and directly in front by the pine-wood on the hither slope of the Bermeja. Victor had not as yet shown himself from his cover in the forest of Chiclana, and Graham, as he entered the Bermeja pine-wood, saw no adversary. But Victor was skilled in the ruse. He was waiting until Cassagne's infantry from Medina should come up; and, momentarily expecting its arrival, he felt so sure of success that his mass of cavalry had been directed on Vejer and other points to cut off the fugitives after the anticipated

---

1. It was in this battle that General Graham took favourable notice of Lieutenant Campbell of the 9th, afterwards Lord Clyde, then a lad of nineteen, for his conduct when left in command of the two flank companies of his regiment, when all the other officers had been wounded.

victory. He had fourteen guns and 9,000 excellent soldiers in three divisions, commanded respectively by Laval, Ruffin, and Villatte. The division under Villatte was posted on the extreme right on the Almanza Creek to cover the camp and watch the Spanish forces at Santi Petri and the vicinity; Laval's division was in the centre, with a reserve battalion of grenadiers out on the right flank; and the left consisted of Puffin's division, on the left flank of which were two reserve battalions of grenadiers and three squadrons of regular cavalry.

Cassagne had not yet arrived; but Victor, awake to the seeming opportunity, sallied out on to the plain and began the battle. Leading Ruffin's troops in person he climbed the rear of the Barrosa ridge, drove the Spanish rear-guard off the height in the direction of the sea, swept away the baggage and followers in all directions and took three guns. Major Brown, however, was a resolute man: he maintained a stout front, and, although unable to hold his ground against odds so overwhelming, he retired into the intervening plain slowly and in good order, and sent across it to Graham for orders. The general, then in the pine-wood, gave the laconic command, "Fight!" then he faced about and regained the plain with all speed, expecting to find La Peña with his main body and artillery on the Barrosa height. As he emerged from the wood the spectacle before him was in the nature of a sudden and great surprise. In front he beheld Ruffin's division, flanked by its two grenadier battalions, on the summit of the Barrosa height; down the slope towards the seaward the Spanish rear-guard and the baggage in full rout, the French cavalry in pursuit of the fugitives; Laval close on his own left flank, and La Peña—"nowhere"!

Well did Napier describe Graham as "a daring old man, and of ready temper for battle." In a situation of seemingly utter despair, he was cool and dauntless. Recognising that a retreat to the Bermeja would bring the enemy pell-mell with the allies on to that narrow ridge and must result in complete disaster, Graham resolved to spring to the attack, notwithstanding that the key of the battlefield was in possession of the enemy. Major Duncan with his 10 guns hurried across the intervening plain, and bringing up his right shoulder, poured a fierce fire into the face of Laval's column; while on his left Colonel Barnard with his detachments of riflemen and two companies of the 47th Foot, dashed forward at the double and hurried his gallant men against Laval's front, simultaneously shaken by Duncan's artillery fire. So sudden was the call to arms that there was no time to form regiments or brigades with any approach to regularity; but two separate

bodies were roughly and hurriedly thrown together. Wheatly with his three line battalions and with two companies of Portuguese, pushed forward in support of Barnard against Laval's front, already undergoing severe ravages from Duncan's guns. Laval's artillery in position on the left flank of his column retaliated furiously on Barnard and Wheatly as they hurried forward to get to close quarters, in the course of which advance they were suffering from the fire of Ruffin's batteries, which, from the edge of the Barrosa height, were taking them in flank. On both sides the infantry pressed forward eagerly, the musketry fire pealing louder as the interval became shorter. But as the hostile masses closed in one upon the other, a fierce and prolonged charge of the 87th Regiment overthrew at the bayonet-point the first line of Laval's troops; and though the latter struggled stoutly, they were dashed violently by the gallant Irishmen upon the second French line, with the result that Laval's column was broken by the shock and sullenly retired, the reserve battalion of grenadiers which had been posted on the right alone remaining to cover Laval's retreat.

While Victor's centre was thus fighting hard with the ultimate result of being discomfited and forced to retreat, a bitter contest was being waged on his left with an issue not less disastrous. Major Brown had lost no time in acting on Graham's curt order to fight. With his improvised battalion of detachments he fell headlong upon the face of Ruffin's column, posted as it was on the summit of the Barrosa height; and although nearly half of his command went down under the enemy's volleys, he stubbornly maintained the fight until Dilkes's brigade of Guards, which had hurried across the plain, scrambled through a deep ravine and never stopping even for a moment to re-form the battalions, came up. Without halting, and with but little order, but full of ardour for fighting, the Guards charged up towards the summit, where Ruffin's column grimly waited for the assault. At the very edge of the ascent the gallant opponents met each other in close and bitter strife; and a fierce, and for some time doubtful, combat raged. The contest was sanguinary; but the dauntless perseverance of the brigade of Guards, and the brave hardihood of Brown's battalion and of Norcott's and Acheson's detachments, overcame every obstacle. Finally, Ruffin himself and Colonel Chaudron Rousseau, who commanded the two battalions of reserve grenadiers, fell mortally wounded; then the English bore strongly forward and their slaughtering fire forced the French from off the height with the loss of three guns and many men.

The discomfited French divisions, retiring concentrically from the respective points of the recent fighting, presently gathered *en masse*, and with a gallant resolution endeavoured to reconstruct their formations and renew the struggle; but the steady and crushing fire of Duncan's guns rendered any such attempt impossible. Victor withdrew from the field with his broken and discomfited troops; and the conquerors, who had been for four-and-twenty hours under arms without food, were too much exhausted to engage in a pursuit.

During those fierce infantry combats on and about the Barrosa height, La Peña looked on with a strange indifference, sending no assistance of any sort to his gallant ally, nor even menacing Villatte's

division, which was within easy reach of him and comparatively weak. It was without any orders from him that the two regiments of Walloon Guards, the regiment of Ciudad Real, and some guerilla cavalry, came up at the close of the action. Whittingham, it was true, was an officer in the Spanish service; but he was an Englishman, and in command of 800 regular cavalry; yet he remained supine while his countrymen were fighting out a mortal combat. No stroke was struck by a Spanish sabre that day, although the French cavalry did not exceed 250 men; and although it was evident that Whittingham's force, by sweeping round Ruffin's left, would have rendered Victor's defeat utterly ruinous. That this might have been so was evidenced by the conduct of Colonel Frederick Ponsonby, who subsequently fell at Waterloo; and who, carrying away from the ignoble Whittingham 150 German Hussars belonging to the British contingent, charged and overthrew the French squadrons in their defeat, captured two guns, and assailed Rousseau's chosen grenadiers.

The actual fighting in the battle of Barrosa lasted only an hour and a half. During that period of time 4,000 British soldiers defeated a French army having a strength of at least 9,000 men. The action was exceptionally bloody in proportion to the strengths engaged. Fifty officers, 60 sergeants, and 1,100 rank and file were killed or wounded on the British side; the French loss exceeded 2,000 officers and men. The trophies of the victory were six guns and an eagle; 400 prisoners fell into the possession of the victors. After the battle had ended, Graham still remained some hours on the height of Barrosa, in the hope that La Peña would at last awake to the prospect of glory opened to him by the success of the British arms. He had been largely reinforced from Cadiz by fresh troops, and before him were the remnants of the French troops retreating in utter disorder on Chiclana. But soldierly feeling did not live in the breast of the Spanish dastard who posed as an officer; and Graham, no longer able to endure the scene, left La Peña on the Bermeja and filed the British troops over the bridge into the Isla.

Subsequently, in an address to the Cortes, La Peña had the insolence to claim the victory for himself: maintaining that the arrangements previous to the battle were made with the knowledge and approbation of the English general, and that the latter's retreat to the Isla was the real cause of the failure. Graham, disgusted by those unworthy and untruthful statements, wrote a letter to the British envoy at Cadiz in which he exposed the misconduct of La Peña; he refused

with contempt the title of *grandee* of the first-class voted to him by the Cortes; and when the chief of staff of La Peña used expressions relative to the action which were personally offensive to Graham, the latter promptly enforced an apology with his sword. Having thus shown himself superior to his opponents at all points, the gallant old man relinquished his command to General Cooke, and joined Lord Wellington's army.

Graham in 1811 was sixty-three years of age, but there was any

amount of fighting still in him. When Wellington advanced in the spring of 1813 towards the Ebro, Graham commanded his left wing during its long and difficult march through the mountainous region of Tras-os-Montes and onward to Vittoria, in which memorable battle he took an important part. He was entrusted with the task of reducing the strong fortress of San Sebastian. On the day of its reduction the stern old man concentrated the cannonade of fifty pieces immediately over the heads of the British troops gathered at the base of the breach, strewing the rampart with the mangled bodies of the French defenders. His last military service was at Bergen-op-Zoom in 1814, which unfortunately miscarried. In May of the same year Sir Thomas Graham was created Baron Lynedoch of Balgowan, with a pension of £2,000 a year. He lived in full haleness of body and mind to a very great age. In the spring of 1843, he presided at the annual dinner attended by the surviving officers who had served under him at Barrosa. In autumn of the same year, he was shooting over a moor which he had rented in Forfarshire. When at length the tough and brave old warrior succumbed in November, 1843, he was on the verge of attaining his ninety-sixth year.

ALSO FROM LEONAUR
AVAILABLE IN SOFTCOVER OR HARDCOVER WITH DUST JACKET

A HISTORY OF THE FRENCH & INDIAN WAR *by Arthur G. Bradley*—The Seven Years War as it was fought in the New World has always fascinated students of military history—here is the story of that confrontation.

WASHINGTON'S EARLY CAMPAIGNS *by James Hadden*—The French Post Expedition, Great Meadows and Braddock's Defeat—including Braddock's Orderly Books.

BOUQUET & THE OHIO INDIAN WAR *by Cyrus Cort & William Smith*—Two Accounts of the Campaigns of 1763-1764: Bouquet's Campaigns by Cyrus Cort & The History of Bouquet's Expeditions by William Smith.

NARRATIVES OF THE FRENCH & INDIAN WAR: 2 *by David Holden, Samuel Jenks, Lemuel Lyon, Mary Cochrane Rogers & Henry T. Blake*—Contains The Diary of Sergeant David Holden, Captain Samuel Jenks' Journal, The Journal of Lemuel Lyon, Journal of a French Officer at the Siege of Quebec, A Battle Fought on Snowshoes & The Battle of Lake George.

NARRATIVES OF THE FRENCH & INDIAN WAR *by Brown, Eastburn, Hawks & Putnam*—Ranger Brown's Narrative, The Adventures of Robert Eastburn, The Journal of Rufus Putnam—Provincial Infantry & Orderly Book and Journal of Major John Hawks on the Ticonderoga-Crown Point Campaign.

THE 7TH (QUEEN'S OWN) HUSSARS: Volume 1—1688-1792 *by C. R. B. Barrett*—As Dragoons During the Flanders Campaign, War of the Austrian Succession and the Seven Years War.

INDIA'S FREE LANCES *by H. G. Keene*—European Mercenary Commanders in Hindustan 1770-1820.

THE BENGAL EUROPEAN REGIMENT *by P. R. Innes*—An Elite Regiment of the Honourable East India Company 1756-1858.

MUSKET & TOMAHAWK *by Francis Parkman*—A Military History of the French & Indian War, 1753-1760.

THE BLACK WATCH AT TICONDEROGA *by Frederick B. Richards*—Campaigns in the French & Indian War.

QUEEN'S RANGERS *by Frederick B. Richards*—John Simcoe and his Rangers During the Revolutionary War for America.

AVAILABLE ONLINE AT **www.leonaur.com**
AND FROM ALL GOOD BOOK STORES

ALSO FROM LEONAUR
AVAILABLE IN SOFTCOVER OR HARDCOVER WITH DUST JACKET

JOURNALS OF ROBERT ROGERS OF THE RANGERS *by Robert Rogers*—The exploits of Rogers & the Rangers in his own words during 1755-1761 in the French & Indian War.

GALLOPING GUNS *by James Young*—The Experiences of an Officer of the Bengal Horse Artillery During the Second Maratha War 1804-1805.

GORDON *by Demetrius Charles Boulger*—The Career of Gordon of Khartoum.

THE BATTLE OF NEW ORLEANS *by Zachary F. Smith*—The final major engagement of the War of 1812.

THE TWO WARS OF MRS DUBERLY *by Frances Isabella Duberly*—An Intrepid Victorian Lady's Experience of the Crimea and Indian Mutiny.

WITH THE GUARDS' BRIGADE DURING THE BOER WAR *by Edward P. Lowry*—On Campaign from Bloemfontein to Koomati Poort and Back.

THE REBELLIOUS DUCHESS *by Paul F. S. Dermoncourt*—The Adventures of the Duchess of Berri and Her Attempt to Overthrow French Monarchy.

MEN OF THE MUTINY *by John Tulloch Nash & Henry Metcalfe*—Two Accounts of the Great Indian Mutiny of 1857: Fighting with the Bengal Yeomanry Cavalry & Private Metcalfe at Lucknow.

CAMPAIGN IN THE CRIMEA *by George Shuldham Peard*—The Recollections of an Officer of the 20th Regiment of Foot.

WITHIN SEBASTOPOL *by K. Hodasevich*—A Narrative of the Campaign in the Crimea, and of the Events of the Siege.

WITH THE CAVALRY TO AFGHANISTAN *by William Taylor*—The Experiences of a Trooper of H. M. 4th Light Dragoons During the First Afghan War.

THE CAWNPORE MAN *by Mowbray Thompson*—A First Hand Account of the Siege and Massacre During the Indian Mutiny By One of Four Survivors.

BRIGADE COMMANDER: AFGHANISTAN *by Henry Brooke*—The Journal of the Commander of the 2nd Infantry Brigade, Kandahar Field Force During the Second Afghan War.

BANCROFT OF THE BENGAL HORSE ARTILLERY *by N. W. Bancroft*—An Account of the First Sikh War 1845-1846.

AVAILABLE ONLINE AT **www.leonaur.com**
AND FROM ALL GOOD BOOK STORES

ALSO FROM LEONAUR
AVAILABLE IN SOFTCOVER OR HARDCOVER WITH DUST JACKET

AFGHANISTAN: THE BELEAGUERED BRIGADE by G. R. Gleig—An Account of Sale's Brigade During the First Afghan War.

IN THE RANKS OF THE C. I. V by Erskine Childers—With the City Imperial Volunteer Battery (Honourable Artillery Company) in the Second Boer War.

THE BENGAL NATIVE ARMY by F. G. Cardew—An Invaluable Reference Resource.

THE 7TH (QUEEN'S OWN) HUSSARS: Volume 4—1688-1914 by C. R. B. Barrett—Uniforms, Equipment, Weapons, Traditions, the Services of Notable Officers and Men & the Appendices to All Volumes—Volume 4: 1688-1914.

THE SWORD OF THE CROWN by Eric W. Sheppard—A History of the British Army to 1914.

THE 7TH (QUEEN'S OWN) HUSSARS: Volume 3—1818-1914 by C. R. B. Barrett—On Campaign During the Canadian Rebellion, the Indian Mutiny, the Sudan, Matabeleland, Mashonaland and the Boer War Volume 3: 1818-1914.

THE KHARTOUM CAMPAIGN by Bennet Burleigh—A Special Correspondent's View of the Reconquest of the Sudan by British and Egyptian Forces under Kitchener—1898.

EL PUCHERO by Richard McSherry—The Letters of a Surgeon of Volunteers During Scott's Campaign of the American-Mexican War 1847-1848.

RIFLEMAN SAHIB by E. Maude—The Recollections of an Officer of the Bombay Rifles During the Southern Mahratta Campaign, Second Sikh War, Persian Campaign and Indian Mutiny.

THE KING'S HUSSAR by Edwin Mole—The Recollections of a 14th (King's) Hussar During the Victorian Era.

JOHN COMPANY'S CAVALRYMAN by William Johnson—The Experiences of a British Soldier in the Crimea, the Persian Campaign and the Indian Mutiny.

COLENSO & DURNFORD'S ZULU WAR by Frances E. Colenso & Edward Durnford—The first and possibly the most important history of the Zulu War.

U. S. DRAGOON by Samuel E. Chamberlain—Experiences in the Mexican War 1846-48 and on the South Western Frontier.

AVAILABLE ONLINE AT **www.leonaur.com**
AND FROM ALL GOOD BOOK STORES

ALSO FROM LEONAUR
AVAILABLE IN SOFTCOVER OR HARDCOVER WITH DUST JACKET

THE 2ND MAORI WAR: 1860-1861 *by Robert Carey*—The Second Maori War, or First Taranaki War, one more bloody instalment of the conflicts between European settlers and the indigenous Maori people.

A JOURNAL OF THE SECOND SIKH WAR *by Daniel A. Sandford*—The Experiences of an Ensign of the 2nd Bengal European Regiment During the Campaign in the Punjab, India, 1848-49.

THE LIGHT INFANTRY OFFICER *by John H. Cooke*—The Experiences of an Officer of the 43rd Light Infantry in America During the War of 1812.

BUSHVELDT CARBINEERS *by George Witton*—The War Against the Boers in South Africa and the 'Breaker' Morant Incident.

LAKE'S CAMPAIGNS IN INDIA *by Hugh Pearse*—The Second Anglo Maratha War, 1803-1807.

BRITAIN IN AFGHANISTAN 1: THE FIRST AFGHAN WAR 1839-42 *by Archibald Forbes*—From invasion to destruction-a British military disaster.

BRITAIN IN AFGHANISTAN 2: THE SECOND AFGHAN WAR 1878-80 *by Archibald Forbes*—This is the history of the Second Afghan War-another episode of British military history typified by savagery, massacre, siege and battles.

UP AMONG THE PANDIES *by Vivian Dering Majendie*—Experiences of a British Officer on Campaign During the Indian Mutiny, 1857-1858.

MUTINY: 1857 *by James Humphries*—Authentic Voices from the Indian Mutiny-First Hand Accounts of Battles, Sieges and Personal Hardships.

BLOW THE BUGLE, DRAW THE SWORD *by W. H. G. Kingston*—The Wars, Campaigns, Regiments and Soldiers of the British & Indian Armies During the Victorian Era, 1839-1898.

WAR BEYOND THE DRAGON PAGODA *by Major J. J. Snodgrass*—A Personal Narrative of the First Anglo-Burmese War 1824 - 1826.

THE HERO OF ALIWAL *by James Humphries*—The Campaigns of Sir Harry Smith in India, 1843-1846, During the Gwalior War & the First Sikh War.

ALL FOR A SHILLING A DAY *by Donald F. Featherstone*—The story of H.M. 16th, the Queen's Lancers During the first Sikh War 1845-1846.

AVAILABLE ONLINE AT **www.leonaur.com**
AND FROM ALL GOOD BOOK STORES

ALSO FROM LEONAUR
AVAILABLE IN SOFTCOVER OR HARDCOVER WITH DUST JACKET

THE FALL OF THE MOGHUL EMPIRE OF HINDUSTAN *by H. G. Keene*—By the beginning of the nineteenth century, as British and Indian armies under Lake and Wellesley dominated the scene, a little over half a century of conflict brought the Moghul Empire to its knees.

LADY SALE'S AFGHANISTAN *by Florentia Sale*—An Indomitable Victorian Lady's Account of the Retreat from Kabul During the First Afghan War.

THE CAMPAIGN OF MAGENTA AND SOLFERINO 1859 *by Harold Carmichael Wylly*—The Decisive Conflict for the Unification of Italy.

FRENCH'S CAVALRY CAMPAIGN *by J. G. Maydon*—A Special Correspondent's View of British Army Mounted Troops During the Boer War.

CAVALRY AT WATERLOO *by Sir Evelyn Wood*—British Mounted Troops During the Campaign of 1815.

THE SUBALTERN *by George Robert Gleig*—The Experiences of an Officer of the 85th Light Infantry During the Peninsular War.

NAPOLEON AT BAY, 1814 *by F. Loraine Petre*—The Campaigns to the Fall of the First Empire.

NAPOLEON AND THE CAMPAIGN OF 1806 *by Colonel Vachée*—The Napoleonic Method of Organisation and Command to the Battles of Jena & Auerstädt.

THE COMPLETE ADVENTURES IN THE CONNAUGHT RANGERS *by William Grattan*—The 88th Regiment during the Napoleonic Wars by a Serving Officer.

BUGLER AND OFFICER OF THE RIFLES *by William Green & Harry Smith*—With the 95th (Rifles) during the Peninsular & Waterloo Campaigns of the Napoleonic Wars.

NAPOLEONIC WAR STORIES *by Sir Arthur Quiller-Couch*—Tales of soldiers, spies, battles & sieges from the Peninsular & Waterloo campaingns.

CAPTAIN OF THE 95TH (RIFLES) *by Jonathan Leach*—An officer of Wellington's sharpshooters during the Peninsular, South of France and Waterloo campaigns of the Napoleonic wars.

RIFLEMAN COSTELLO *by Edward Costello*—The adventures of a soldier of the 95th (Rifles) in the Peninsular & Waterloo Campaigns of the Napoleonic wars.

AVAILABLE ONLINE AT **www.leonaur.com**
AND FROM ALL GOOD BOOK STORES

ALSO FROM LEONAUR
AVAILABLE IN SOFTCOVER OR HARDCOVER WITH DUST JACKET

AT THEM WITH THE BAYONET by *Donald F. Featherstone*—The first Anglo-Sikh War 1845-1846.

STEPHEN CRANE'S BATTLES by *Stephen Crane*—Nine Decisive Battles Recounted by the Author of 'The Red Badge of Courage'.

THE GURKHA WAR by *H. T. Prinsep*—The Anglo-Nepalese Conflict in North East India 1814-1816.

FIRE & BLOOD by *G. R. Gleig*—The burning of Washington & the battle of New Orleans, 1814, through the eyes of a young British soldier.

SOUND ADVANCE! by *Joseph Anderson*—Experiences of an officer of HM 50th regiment in Australia, Burma & the Gwalior war.

THE CAMPAIGN OF THE INDUS by *Thomas Holdsworth*—Experiences of a British Officer of the 2nd (Queen's Royal) Regiment in the Campaign to Place Shah Shuja on the Throne of Afghanistan 1838 - 1840.

WITH THE MADRAS EUROPEAN REGIMENT IN BURMA by *John Butler*—The Experiences of an Officer of the Honourable East India Company's Army During the First Anglo-Burmese War 1824 - 1826.

IN ZULULAND WITH THE BRITISH ARMY by *Charles L. Norris-Newman*—The Anglo-Zulu war of 1879 through the first-hand experiences of a special correspondent.

BESIEGED IN LUCKNOW by *Martin Richard Gubbins*—The first Anglo-Sikh War 1845-1846.

A TIGER ON HORSEBACK by *L. March Phillips*—The Experiences of a Trooper & Officer of Rimington's Guides - The Tigers - during the Anglo-Boer war 1899 - 1902.

SEPOYS, SIEGE & STORM by *Charles John Griffiths*—The Experiences of a young officer of H.M.'s 61st Regiment at Ferozepore, Delhi ridge and at the fall of Delhi during the Indian mutiny 1857.

CAMPAIGNING IN ZULULAND by *W. E. Montague*—Experiences on campaign during the Zulu war of 1879 with the 94th Regiment.

THE STORY OF THE GUIDES by *G.J. Younghusband*—The Exploits of the Soldiers of the famous Indian Army Regiment from the northwest frontier 1847 - 1900.

AVAILABLE ONLINE AT **www.leonaur.com**
AND FROM ALL GOOD BOOK STORES

ALSO FROM LEONAUR
AVAILABLE IN SOFTCOVER OR HARDCOVER WITH DUST JACKET

ZULU:1879 *by D.C.F. Moodie & the Leonaur Editors*—The Anglo-Zulu War of 1879 from contemporary sources: First Hand Accounts, Interviews, Dispatches, Official Documents & Newspaper Reports.

THE RED DRAGOON *by W.J. Adams*—With the 7th Dragoon Guards in the Cape of Good Hope against the Boers & the Kaffir tribes during the 'war of the axe' 1843-48'.

THE RECOLLECTIONS OF SKINNER OF SKINNER'S HORSE *by James Skinner*—James Skinner and his 'Yellow Boys' Irregular cavalry in the wars of India between the British, Mahratta, Rajput, Mogul, Sikh & Pindarree Forces.

A CAVALRY OFFICER DURING THE SEPOY REVOLT *by A. R. D. Mackenzie*—Experiences with the 3rd Bengal Light Cavalry, the Guides and Sikh Irregular Cavalry from the outbreak to Delhi and Lucknow.

A NORFOLK SOLDIER IN THE FIRST SIKH WAR *by J W Baldwin*—Experiences of a private of H.M. 9th Regiment of Foot in the battles for the Punjab, India 1845-6.

TOMMY ATKINS' WAR STORIES: 14 FIRST HAND ACCOUNTS—Fourteen first hand accounts from the ranks of the British Army during Queen Victoria's Empire.

THE WATERLOO LETTERS *by H. T. Siborne*—Accounts of the Battle by British Officers for its Foremost Historian.

NEY: GENERAL OF CAVALRY VOLUME 1—1769-1799 *by Antoine Bulos*—The Early Career of a Marshal of the First Empire.

NEY: MARSHAL OF FRANCE VOLUME 2—1799-1805 *by Antoine Bulos*—The Early Career of a Marshal of the First Empire.

AIDE-DE-CAMP TO NAPOLEON *by Philippe-Paul de Ségur*—For anyone interested in the Napoleonic Wars this book, written by one who was intimate with the strategies and machinations of the Emperor, will be essential reading.

TWILIGHT OF EMPIRE *by Sir Thomas Ussher & Sir George Cockburn*—Two accounts of Napoleon's Journeys in Exile to Elba and St. Helena: Narrative of Events by Sir Thomas Ussher & Napoleon's Last Voyage: Extract of a diary by Sir George Cockburn.

PRIVATE WHEELER *by William Wheeler*—The letters of a soldier of the 51st Light Infantry during the Peninsular War & at Waterloo.

AVAILABLE ONLINE AT **www.leonaur.com**
AND FROM ALL GOOD BOOK STORES

ALSO FROM LEONAUR
AVAILABLE IN SOFTCOVER OR HARDCOVER WITH DUST JACKET

OFFICERS & GENTLEMEN *by Peter Hawker & William Graham*—Two Accounts of British Officers During the Peninsula War: Officer of Light Dragoons by Peter Hawker & Campaign in Portugal and Spain by William Graham .

THE WALCHEREN EXPEDITION *by Anonymous*—The Experiences of a British Officer of the 81st Regt. During the Campaign in the Low Countries of 1809.

LADIES OF WATERLOO *by Charlotte A. Eaton, Magdalene de Lancey & Juana Smith*—The Experiences of Three Women During the Campaign of 1815: Waterloo Days by Charlotte A. Eaton, A Week at Waterloo by Magdalene de Lancey & Juana's Story by Juana Smith.

JOURNAL OF AN OFFICER IN THE KING'S GERMAN LEGION *by John Frederick Hering*—Recollections of Campaigning During the Napoleonic Wars.

JOURNAL OF AN ARMY SURGEON IN THE PENINSULAR WAR *by Charles Boutflower*—The Recollections of a British Army Medical Man on Campaign During the Napoleonic Wars.

ON CAMPAIGN WITH MOORE AND WELLINGTON *by Anthony Hamilton*—The Experiences of a Soldier of the 43rd Regiment During the Peninsular War.

THE ROAD TO AUSTERLITZ *by R. G. Burton*—Napoleon's Campaign of 1805.

SOLDIERS OF NAPOLEON *by A. J. Doisy De Villargennes & Arthur Chuquet*—The Experiences of the Men of the French First Empire: Under the Eagles by A. J. Doisy De Villargennes & Voices of 1812 by Arthur Chuquet .

INVASION OF FRANCE, 1814 *by F. W. O. Maycock*—The Final Battles of the Napoleonic First Empire.

LEIPZIG—A CONFLICT OF TITANS *by Frederic Shoberl*—A Personal Experience of the 'Battle of the Nations' During the Napoleonic Wars, October 14th-19th, 1813.

SLASHERS *by Charles Cadell*—The Campaigns of the 28th Regiment of Foot During the Napoleonic Wars by a Serving Officer.

BATTLE IMPERIAL *by Charles William Vane*—The Campaigns in Germany & France for the Defeat of Napoleon 1813-1814.

SWIFT & BOLD *by Gibbes Rigaud*—The 60th Rifles During the Peninsula War.

AVAILABLE ONLINE AT **www.leonaur.com**
AND FROM ALL GOOD BOOK STORES

ALSO FROM LEONAUR
AVAILABLE IN SOFTCOVER OR HARDCOVER WITH DUST JACKET

ADVENTURES OF A YOUNG RIFLEMAN *by Johann Christian Maempel*—The Experiences of a Saxon in the French & British Armies During the Napoleonic Wars.

THE HUSSAR *by Norbert Landsheit & G. R. Gleig*—A German Cavalryman in British Service Throughout the Napoleonic Wars.

RECOLLECTIONS OF THE PENINSULA *by Moyle Sherer*—An Officer of the 34th Regiment of Foot—'The Cumberland Gentlemen'—on Campaign Against Napoleon's French Army in Spain.

MARINE OF REVOLUTION & CONSULATE *by Moreau de Jonnès*—The Recollections of a French Soldier of the Revolutionary Wars 1791-1804.

GENTLEMEN IN RED *by John Dobbs & Robert Knowles*—Two Accounts of British Infantry Officers During the Peninsular War Recollections of an Old 52nd Man by John Dobbs An Officer of Fusiliers by Robert Knowles.

CORPORAL BROWN'S CAMPAIGNS IN THE LOW COUNTRIES *by Robert Brown*—Recollections of a Coldstream Guard in the Early Campaigns Against Revolutionary France 1793-1795.

THE 7TH (QUEENS OWN) HUSSARS: Volume 2—1793-1815 *by C. R. B. Barrett*—During the Campaigns in the Low Countries & the Peninsula and Waterloo Campaigns of the Napoleonic Wars. Volume 2: 1793-1815.

THE MARENGO CAMPAIGN 1800 *by Herbert H. Sargent*—The Victory that Completed the Austrian Defeat in Italy.

DONALDSON OF THE 94TH—SCOTS BRIGADE *by Joseph Donaldson*—The Recollections of a Soldier During the Peninsula & South of France Campaigns of the Napoleonic Wars.

A CONSCRIPT FOR EMPIRE *by Philippe as told to Johann Christian Maempel*—The Experiences of a Young German Conscript During the Napoleonic Wars.

JOURNAL OF THE CAMPAIGN OF 1815 *by Alexander Cavalié Mercer*—The Experiences of an Officer of the Royal Horse Artillery During the Waterloo Campaign.

NAPOLEON'S CAMPAIGNS IN POLAND 1806-7 *by Robert Wilson*—The campaign in Poland from the Russian side of the conflict.

AVAILABLE ONLINE AT **www.leonaur.com**
AND FROM ALL GOOD BOOK STORES

ALSO FROM LEONAUR
AVAILABLE IN SOFTCOVER OR HARDCOVER WITH DUST JACKET

OMPTEDA OF THE KING'S GERMAN LEGION by *Christian von Ompteda*—A Hanoverian Officer on Campaign Against Napoleon.

LIEUTENANT SIMMONS OF THE 95TH (RIFLES) by *George Simmons*—Recollections of the Peninsula, South of France & Waterloo Campaigns of the Napoleonic Wars.

A HORSEMAN FOR THE EMPEROR by *Jean Baptiste Gazzola*—A Cavalryman of Napoleon's Army on Campaign Throughout the Napoleonic Wars.

SERGEANT LAWRENCE by *William Lawrence*—With the 40th Regt. of Foot in South America, the Peninsular War & at Waterloo.

CAMPAIGNS WITH THE FIELD TRAIN by *Richard D. Henegan*—Experiences of a British Officer During the Peninsula and Waterloo Campaigns of the Napoleonic Wars.

CAVALRY SURGEON by *S. D. Broughton*—On Campaign Against Napoleon in the Peninsula & South of France During the Napoleonic Wars 1812-1814.

MEN OF THE RIFLES by *Thomas Knight, Henry Curling & Jonathan Leach*—The Reminiscences of Thomas Knight of the 95th (Rifles) by Thomas Knight, Henry Curling's Anecdotes by Henry Curling & The Field Services of the Rifle Brigade from its Formation to Waterloo by Jonathan Leach.

THE ULM CAMPAIGN 1805 by *F. N. Maude*—Napoleon and the Defeat of the Austrian Army During the 'War of the Third Coalition'.

SOLDIERING WITH THE 'DIVISION' by *Thomas Garrety*—The Military Experiences of an Infantryman of the 43rd Regiment During the Napoleonic Wars.

SERGEANT MORRIS OF THE 73RD FOOT by *Thomas Morris*—The Experiences of a British Infantryman During the Napoleonic Wars-Including Campaigns in Germany and at Waterloo.

A VOICE FROM WATERLOO by *Edward Cotton*—The Personal Experiences of a British Cavalryman Who Became a Battlefield Guide and Authority on the Campaign of 1815.

NAPOLEON AND HIS MARSHALS by *J. T. Headley*—The Men of the First Empire.

AVAILABLE ONLINE AT **www.leonaur.com**
AND FROM ALL GOOD BOOK STORES

ALSO FROM LEONAUR
AVAILABLE IN SOFTCOVER OR HARDCOVER WITH DUST JACKET

COLBORNE: A SINGULAR TALENT FOR WAR by *John Colborne*—The Napoleonic Wars Career of One of Wellington's Most Highly Valued Officers in Egypt, Holland, Italy, the Peninsula and at Waterloo.

NAPOLEON'S RUSSIAN CAMPAIGN by *Philippe Henri de Segur*—The Invasion, Battles and Retreat by an Aide-de-Camp on the Emperor's Staff.

WITH THE LIGHT DIVISION by *John H. Cooke*—The Experiences of an Officer of the 43rd Light Infantry in the Peninsula and South of France During the Napoleonic Wars.

WELLINGTON AND THE PYRENEES CAMPAIGN VOLUME I: FROM VITORIA TO THE BIDASSOA by *F. C. Beatson*—The final phase of the campaign in the Iberian Peninsula.

WELLINGTON AND THE INVASION OF FRANCE VOLUME II: THE BIDASSOA TO THE BATTLE OF THE NIVELLE by *F. C. Beatson*—The final phase of the campaign in the Iberian Peninsula.

WELLINGTON AND THE FALL OF FRANCE VOLUME III: THE GAVES AND THE BATTLE OF ORTHEZ by *F. C. Beatson*—The final phase of the campaign in the Iberian Peninsula.

NAPOLEON'S IMPERIAL GUARD: FROM MARENGO TO WATERLOO by *J. T. Headley*—The story of Napoleon's Imperial Guard and the men who commanded them.

BATTLES & SIEGES OF THE PENINSULAR WAR by *W. H. Fitchett*—Corunna, Busaco, Albuera, Ciudad Rodrigo, Badajos, Salamanca, San Sebastian & Others.

SERGEANT GUILLEMARD: THE MAN WHO SHOT NELSON? by *Robert Guillemard*—A Soldier of the Infantry of the French Army of Napoleon on Campaign Throughout Europe.

WITH THE GUARDS ACROSS THE PYRENEES by *Robert Batty*—The Experiences of a British Officer of Wellington's Army During the Battles for the Fall of Napoleonic France, 1813.

A STAFF OFFICER IN THE PENINSULA by *E. W. Buckham*—An Officer of the British Staff Corps Cavalry During the Peninsula Campaign of the Napoleonic Wars.

THE LEIPZIG CAMPAIGN: 1813—NAPOLEON AND THE "BATTLE OF THE NATIONS" by *F. N. Maude*—Colonel Maude's analysis of Napoleon's campaign of 1813 around Leipzig.

AVAILABLE ONLINE AT **www.leonaur.com**
AND FROM ALL GOOD BOOK STORES

ALSO FROM LEONAUR
AVAILABLE IN SOFTCOVER OR HARDCOVER WITH DUST JACKET

BUGEAUD: A PACK WITH A BATON by *Thomas Robert Bugeaud*—The Early Campaigns of a Soldier of Napoleon's Army Who Would Become a Marshal of France.

WATERLOO RECOLLECTIONS by *Frederick Llewellyn*—Rare First Hand Accounts, Letters, Reports and Retellings from the Campaign of 1815.

SERGEANT NICOL by *Daniel Nicol*—The Experiences of a Gordon Highlander During the Napoleonic Wars in Egypt, the Peninsula and France.

THE JENA CAMPAIGN: 1806 by *F. N. Maude*—The Twin Battles of Jena & Auerstadt Between Napoleon's French and the Prussian Army.

PRIVATE O'NEIL by *Charles O'Neil*—The recollections of an Irish Rogue of H. M. 28th Regt.—The Slashers—during the Peninsula & Waterloo campaigns of the Napoleonic war.

ROYAL HIGHLANDER by *James Anton*—A soldier of H.M 42nd (Royal) Highlanders during the Peninsular, South of France & Waterloo Campaigns of the Napoleonic Wars.

CAPTAIN BLAZE by *Elzéar Blaze*—Life in Napoleons Army.

LEJEUNE VOLUME 1 by *Louis-François Lejeune*—The Napoleonic Wars through the Experiences of an Officer on Berthier's Staff.

LEJEUNE VOLUME 2 by *Louis-François Lejeune*—The Napoleonic Wars through the Experiences of an Officer on Berthier's Staff.

CAPTAIN COIGNET by *Jean-Roch Coignet*—A Soldier of Napoleon's Imperial Guard from the Italian Campaign to Russia and Waterloo.

FUSILIER COOPER by *John S. Cooper*—Experiences in the 7th (Royal) Fusiliers During the Peninsular Campaign of the Napoleonic Wars and the American Campaign to New Orleans.

FIGHTING NAPOLEON'S EMPIRE by *Joseph Anderson*—The Campaigns of a British Infantryman in Italy, Egypt, the Peninsular & the West Indies During the Napoleonic Wars.

CHASSEUR BARRES by *Jean-Baptiste Barres*—The experiences of a French Infantryman of the Imperial Guard at Austerlitz, Jena, Eylau, Friedland, in the Peninsular, Lutzen, Bautzen, Zinnwald and Hanau during the Napoleonic Wars.

AVAILABLE ONLINE AT **www.leonaur.com**
AND FROM ALL GOOD BOOK STORES

ALSO FROM LEONAUR
AVAILABLE IN SOFTCOVER OR HARDCOVER WITH DUST JACKET

CAPTAIN COIGNET *by Jean-Roch Coignet*—A Soldier of Napoleon's Imperial Guard from the Italian Campaign to Russia and Waterloo.

HUSSAR ROCCA *by Albert Jean Michel de Rocca*—A French cavalry officer's experiences of the Napoleonic Wars and his views on the Peninsular Campaigns against the Spanish, British And Guerilla Armies.

MARINES TO 95TH (RIFLES) *by Thomas Fernyhough*—The military experiences of Robert Fernyhough during the Napoleonic Wars.

LIGHT BOB *by Robert Blakeney*—The experiences of a young officer in H.M 28th & 36th regiments of the British Infantry during the Peninsular Campaign of the Napoleonic Wars 1804 - 1814.

WITH WELLINGTON'S LIGHT CAVALRY *by William Tomkinson*—The Experiences of an officer of the 16th Light Dragoons in the Peninsular and Waterloo campaigns of the Napoleonic Wars.

SERGEANT BOURGOGNE *by Adrien Bourgogne*—With Napoleon's Imperial Guard in the Russian Campaign and on the Retreat from Moscow 1812 - 13.

SURTEES OF THE 95TH (RIFLES) *by William Surtees*—A Soldier of the 95th (Rifles) in the Peninsular campaign of the Napoleonic Wars.

SWORDS OF HONOUR *by Henry Newbolt & Stanley L. Wood*—The Careers of Six Outstanding Officers from the Napoleonic Wars, the Wars for India and the American Civil War.

ENSIGN BELL IN THE PENINSULAR WAR *by George Bell*—The Experiences of a young British Soldier of the 34th Regiment 'The Cumberland Gentlemen' in the Napoleonic wars.

HUSSAR IN WINTER *by Alexander Gordon*—A British Cavalry Officer during the retreat to Corunna in the Peninsular campaign of the Napoleonic Wars.

THE COMPLEAT RIFLEMAN HARRIS *by Benjamin Harris as told to and transcribed by Captain Henry Curling, 52nd Regt. of Foot*—The adventures of a soldier of the 95th (Rifles) during the Peninsular Campaign of the Napoleonic Wars.

THE ADVENTURES OF A LIGHT DRAGOON *by George Farmer & G.R. Gleig*—A cavalryman during the Peninsular & Waterloo Campaigns, in captivity & at the siege of Bhurtpore, India.

AVAILABLE ONLINE AT **www.leonaur.com**
AND FROM ALL GOOD BOOK STORES

ALSO FROM LEONAUR
AVAILABLE IN SOFTCOVER OR HARDCOVER WITH DUST JACKET

THE LIFE OF THE REAL BRIGADIER GERARD VOLUME 1—THE YOUNG HUSSAR 1782-1807 by Jean-Baptiste De Marbot—A French Cavalryman Of the Napoleonic Wars at Marengo, Austerlitz, Jena, Eylau & Friedland.

THE LIFE OF THE REAL BRIGADIER GERARD VOLUME 2—IMPERIAL AIDE-DE-CAMP 1807-1811 by Jean-Baptiste De Marbot—A French Cavalryman of the Napoleonic Wars at Saragossa, Landshut, Eckmuhl, Ratisbon, Aspern-Essling, Wagram, Busaco & Torres Vedras.

THE LIFE OF THE REAL BRIGADIER GERARD VOLUME 3—COLONEL OF CHASSEURS 1811-1815 by Jean-Baptiste De Marbot—A French Cavalryman in the retreat from Moscow, Lutzen, Bautzen, Katzbach, Leipzig, Hanau & Waterloo.

THE INDIAN WAR OF 1864 by Eugene Ware—The Experiences of a Young Officer of the 7th Iowa Cavalry on the Western Frontier During the Civil War.

THE MARCH OF DESTINY by Charles E. Young & V. Devinny—Dangers of the Trail in 1865 by Charles E. Young & The Story of a Pioneer by V. Devinny, two Accounts of Early Emigrants to Colorado.

CROSSING THE PLAINS by William Audley Maxwell—A First Hand Narrative of the Early Pioneer Trail to California in 1857.

CHIEF OF SCOUTS by William F. Drannan—A Pilot to Emigrant and Government Trains, Across the Plains of the Western Frontier.

THIRTY-ONE YEARS ON THE PLAINS AND IN THE MOUNTAINS by William F. Drannan—William Drannan was born to be a pioneer, hunter, trapper and wagon train guide during the momentous days of the Great American West.

THE INDIAN WARS VOLUNTEER by William Thompson—Recollections of the Conflict Against the Snakes, Shoshone, Bannocks, Modocs and Other Native Tribes of the American North West.

THE 4TH TENNESSEE CAVALRY by George B. Guild—The Services of Smith's Regiment of Confederate Cavalry by One of its Officers.

COLONEL WORTHINGTON'S SHILOH by T. Worthington—The Tennessee Campaign, 1862, by an Officer of the Ohio Volunteers.

FOUR YEARS IN THE SADDLE by W. L. Curry—The History of the First Regiment Ohio Volunteer Cavalry in the American Civil War.

AVAILABLE ONLINE AT **www.leonaur.com**
AND FROM ALL GOOD BOOK STORES

ALSO FROM LEONAUR
AVAILABLE IN SOFTCOVER OR HARDCOVER WITH DUST JACKET

LIFE IN THE ARMY OF NORTHERN VIRGINIA by *Carlton McCarthy*—The Observations of a Confederate Artilleryman of Cutshaw's Battalion During the American Civil War 1861-1865.

HISTORY OF THE CAVALRY OF THE ARMY OF THE POTOMAC by *Charles D. Rhodes*—Including Pope's Army of Virginia and the Cavalry Operations in West Virginia During the American Civil War.

CAMP-FIRE AND COTTON-FIELD by *Thomas W. Knox*—A New York Herald Correspondent's View of the American Civil War.

SERGEANT STILLWELL by *Leander Stillwell*—The Experiences of a Union Army Soldier of the 61st Illinois Infantry During the American Civil War.

STONEWALL'S CANNONEER by *Edward A. Moore*—Experiences with the Rockbridge Artillery, Confederate Army of Northern Virginia, During the American Civil War.

THE SIXTH CORPS by *George Stevens*—The Army of the Potomac, Union Army, During the American Civil War.

THE RAILROAD RAIDERS by *William Pittenger*—An Ohio Volunteers Recollections of the Andrews Raid to Disrupt the Confederate Railroad in Georgia During the American Civil War.

CITIZEN SOLDIER by *John Beatty*—An Account of the American Civil War by a Union Infantry Officer of Ohio Volunteers Who Became a Brigadier General.

COX: PERSONAL RECOLLECTIONS OF THE CIVIL WAR--VOLUME 1 by *Jacob Dolson Cox*—West Virginia, Kanawha Valley, Gauley Bridge, Cotton Mountain, South Mountain, Antietam, the Morgan Raid & the East Tennessee Campaign.

COX: PERSONAL RECOLLECTIONS OF THE CIVIL WAR--VOLUME 2 by *Jacob Dolson Cox*—Siege of Knoxville, East Tennessee, Atlanta Campaign, the Nashville Campaign & the North Carolina Campaign.

KERSHAW'S BRIGADE VOLUME 1 by *D. Augustus Dickert*—Manassas, Seven Pines, Sharpsburg (Antietam), Fredricksburg, Chancellorsville, Gettysburg, Chickamauga, Chattanooga, Fort Sanders & Bean Station.

KERSHAW'S BRIGADE VOLUME 2 by *D. Augustus Dickert*—At the wilderness, Cold Harbour, Petersburg, The Shenandoah Valley and Cedar Creek..

AVAILABLE ONLINE AT **www.leonaur.com**
AND FROM ALL GOOD BOOK STORES

ALSO FROM LEONAUR
AVAILABLE IN SOFTCOVER OR HARDCOVER WITH DUST JACKET

THE RELUCTANT REBEL by *William G. Stevenson*—A young Kentuckian's experiences in the Confederate Infantry & Cavalry during the American Civil War..

BOOTS AND SADDLES by *Elizabeth B. Custer*—The experiences of General Custer's Wife on the Western Plains.

FANNIE BEERS' CIVIL WAR by *Fannie A. Beers*—A Confederate Lady's Experiences of Nursing During the Campaigns & Battles of the American Civil War.

LADY SALE'S AFGHANISTAN by *Florentia Sale*—An Indomitable Victorian Lady's Account of the Retreat from Kabul During the First Afghan War.

THE TWO WARS OF MRS DUBERLY by *Frances Isabella Duberly*—An Intrepid Victorian Lady's Experience of the Crimea and Indian Mutiny.

THE REBELLIOUS DUCHESS by *Paul F. S. Dermoncourt*—The Adventures of the Duchess of Berri and Her Attempt to Overthrow French Monarchy.

LADIES OF WATERLOO by *Charlotte A. Eaton, Magdalene de Lancey & Juana Smith*—The Experiences of Three Women During the Campaign of 1815: Waterloo Days by Charlotte A. Eaton, A Week at Waterloo by Magdalene de Lancey & Juana's Story by Juana Smith.

TWO YEARS BEFORE THE MAST by *Richard Henry Dana. Jr.*—The account of one young man's experiences serving on board a sailing brig—the Penelope—bound for California, between the years 1834-36.

A SAILOR OF KING GEORGE by *Frederick Hoffman*—From Midshipman to Captain—Recollections of War at Sea in the Napoleonic Age 1793-1815.

LORDS OF THE SEA by *A. T. Mahan*—Great Captains of the Royal Navy During the Age of Sail.

COGGESHALL'S VOYAGES: VOLUME 1 by *George Coggeshall*—The Recollections of an American Schooner Captain.

COGGESHALL'S VOYAGES: VOLUME 2 by *George Coggeshall*—The Recollections of an American Schooner Captain.

TWILIGHT OF EMPIRE by *Sir Thomas Ussher & Sir George Cockburn*—Two accounts of Napoleon's Journeys in Exile to Elba and St. Helena: Narrative of Events by Sir Thomas Ussher & Napoleon's Last Voyage: Extract of a diary by Sir George Cockburn.

AVAILABLE ONLINE AT www.leonaur.com
AND FROM ALL GOOD BOOK STORES

ALSO FROM LEONAUR
AVAILABLE IN SOFTCOVER OR HARDCOVER WITH DUST JACKET

ESCAPE FROM THE FRENCH by *Edward Boys*—A Young Royal Navy Midshipman's Adventures During the Napoleonic War.

THE VOYAGE OF H.M.S. PANDORA by *Edward Edwards R. N. & George Hamilton, edited by Basil Thomson*—In Pursuit of the Mutineers of the Bounty in the South Seas—1790-1791.

MEDUSA by *J. B. Henry Savigny and Alexander Correard and Charlotte-Adélaïde Dard* —Narrative of a Voyage to Senegal in 1816 & The Sufferings of the Picard Family After the Shipwreck of the Medusa.

THE SEA WAR OF 1812 VOLUME 1 by *A. T. Mahan*—A History of the Maritime Conflict.

THE SEA WAR OF 1812 VOLUME 2 by *A. T. Mahan*—A History of the Maritime Conflict.

WETHERELL OF H. M. S. HUSSAR by *John Wetherell*—The Recollections of an Ordinary Seaman of the Royal Navy During the Napoleonic Wars.

THE NAVAL BRIGADE IN NATAL by *C. R. N. Burne*—With the Guns of H. M. S. Terrible & H. M. S. Tartar during the Boer War 1899-1900.

THE VOYAGE OF H. M. S. BOUNTY by *William Bligh*—The True Story of an 18th Century Voyage of Exploration and Mutiny.

SHIPWRECK! by *William Gilly*—The Royal Navy's Disasters at Sea 1793-1849.

KING'S CUTTERS AND SMUGGLERS: 1700-1855 by *E. Keble Chatterton*—A unique period of maritime history-from the beginning of the eighteenth to the middle of the nineteenth century when British seamen risked all to smuggle valuable goods from wool to tea and spirits from and to the Continent.

CONFEDERATE BLOCKADE RUNNER by *John Wilkinson*—The Personal Recollections of an Officer of the Confederate Navy.

NAVAL BATTLES OF THE NAPOLEONIC WARS by *W. H. Fitchett*—Cape St. Vincent, the Nile, Cadiz, Copenhagen, Trafalgar & Others.

PRISONERS OF THE RED DESERT by *R. S. Gwatkin-Williams*—The Adventures of the Crew of the Tara During the First World War.

U-BOAT WAR 1914-1918 by *James B. Connolly/Karl von Schenk*—Two Contrasting Accounts from Both Sides of the Conflict at Sea D uring the Great War.

AVAILABLE ONLINE AT **www.leonaur.com**
AND FROM ALL GOOD BOOK STORES

ALSO FROM LEONAUR
AVAILABLE IN SOFTCOVER OR HARDCOVER WITH DUST JACKET

IRON TIMES WITH THE GUARDS by *An O. E. (G. P. A. Fildes)*—The Experiences of an Officer of the Coldstream Guards on the Western Front During the First World War.

THE GREAT WAR IN THE MIDDLE EAST: 1 by *W. T. Massey*—The Desert Campaigns & How Jerusalem Was Won---two classic accounts in one volume.

THE GREAT WAR IN THE MIDDLE EAST: 2 by *W. T. Massey*—Allenby's Final Triumph.

SMITH-DORRIEN by *Horace Smith-Dorrien*—Isandlwhana to the Great War.

1914 by *Sir John French*—The Early Campaigns of the Great War by the British Commander.

GRENADIER by *E. R. M. Fryer*—The Recollections of an Officer of the Grenadier Guards throughout the Great War on the Western Front.

BATTLE, CAPTURE & ESCAPE by *George Pearson*—The Experiences of a Canadian Light Infantryman During the Great War.

DIGGERS AT WAR by *R. Hugh Knyvett & G. P. Cuttriss*—"Over There" With the Australians by R. Hugh Knyvett and Over the Top With the Third Australian Division by G. P. Cuttriss. Accounts of Australians During the Great War in the Middle East, at Gallipoli and on the Western Front.

HEAVY FIGHTING BEFORE US by *George Brenton Laurie*—The Letters of an Officer of the Royal Irish Rifles on the Western Front During the Great War.

THE CAMELIERS by *Oliver Hogue*—A Classic Account of the Australians of the Imperial Camel Corps During the First World War in the Middle East.

RED DUST by *Donald Black*—A Classic Account of Australian Light Horsemen in Palestine During the First World War.

THE LEAN, BROWN MEN by *Angus Buchanan*—Experiences in East Africa During the Great War with the 25th Royal Fusiliers—the Legion of Frontiersmen.

THE NIGERIAN REGIMENT IN EAST AFRICA by *W. D. Downes*—On Campaign During the Great War 1916-1918.

THE 'DIE-HARDS' IN SIBERIA by *John Ward*—With the Middlesex Regiment Against the Bolsheviks 1918-19.

AVAILABLE ONLINE AT **www.leonaur.com**
AND FROM ALL GOOD BOOK STORES

ALSO FROM LEONAUR
AVAILABLE IN SOFTCOVER OR HARDCOVER WITH DUST JACKET

FARAWAY CAMPAIGN by F. James—Experiences of an Indian Army Cavalry Officer in Persia & Russia During the Great War.

REVOLT IN THE DESERT by T. E. Lawrence—An account of the experiences of one remarkable British officer's war from his own perspective.

MACHINE-GUN SQUADRON by A. M. G.—The 20th Machine Gunners from British Yeomanry Regiments in the Middle East Campaign of the First World War.

A GUNNER'S CRUSADE by Antony Bluett—The Campaign in the Desert, Palestine & Syria as Experienced by the Honourable Artillery Company During the Great War.

DESPATCH RIDER by W. H. L. Watson—The Experiences of a British Army Motorcycle Despatch Rider During the Opening Battles of the Great War in Europe.

TIGERS ALONG THE TIGRIS by E. J. Thompson—The Leicestershire Regiment in Mesopotamia During the First World War.

HEARTS & DRAGONS by Charles R. M. F. Crutwell—The 4th Royal Berkshire Regiment in France and Italy During the Great War, 1914-1918.

INFANTRY BRIGADE: 1914 by John Ward—The Diary of a Commander of the 15th Infantry Brigade, 5th Division, British Army, During the Retreat from Mons.

DOING OUR 'BIT' by Ian Hay—Two Classic Accounts of the Men of Kitchener's 'New Army' During the Great War including *The First 100,000* & *All In It*.

AN EYE IN THE STORM by Arthur Ruhl—An American War Correspondent's Experiences of the First World War from the Western Front to Gallipoli-and Beyond.

STAND & FALL by Joe Cassells—With the Middlesex Regiment Against the Bolsheviks 1918-19.

RIFLEMAN MACGILL'S WAR by Patrick MacGill—A Soldier of the London Irish During the Great War in Europe including *The Amateur Army, The Red Horizon & The Great Push*.

WITH THE GUNS by C. A. Rose & Hugh Dalton—Two First Hand Accounts of British Gunners at War in Europe During World War 1- Three Years in France with the Guns and With the British Guns in Italy.

THE BUSH WAR DOCTOR by Robert V. Dolbey—The Experiences of a British Army Doctor During the East African Campaign of the First World War.

AVAILABLE ONLINE AT www.leonaur.com
AND FROM ALL GOOD BOOK STORES

ALSO FROM LEONAUR
AVAILABLE IN SOFTCOVER OR HARDCOVER WITH DUST JACKET

THE 9TH—THE KING'S (LIVERPOOL REGIMENT) IN THE GREAT WAR 1914 - 1918 *by Enos H. G. Roberts*—Mersey to mud—war and Liverpool men.

THE GAMBARDIER *by Mark Severn*—The experiences of a battery of Heavy artillery on the Western Front during the First World War.

FROM MESSINES TO THIRD YPRES *by Thomas Floyd*—A personal account of the First World War on the Western front by a 2/5th Lancashire Fusilier.

THE IRISH GUARDS IN THE GREAT WAR - VOLUME 1 *by Rudyard Kipling*—Edited and Compiled from Their Diaries and Papers—The First Battalion.

THE IRISH GUARDS IN THE GREAT WAR - VOLUME 1 *by Rudyard Kipling*—Edited and Compiled from Their Diaries and Papers—The Second Battalion.

ARMOURED CARS IN EDEN *by K. Roosevelt*—An American President's son serving in Rolls Royce armoured cars with the British in Mesopatamia & with the American Artillery in France during the First World War.

CHASSEUR OF 1914 *by Marcel Dupont*—Experiences of the twilight of the French Light Cavalry by a young officer during the early battles of the great war in Europe.

TROOP HORSE & TRENCH *by R.A. Lloyd*—The experiences of a British Lifeguardsman of the household cavalry fighting on the western front during the First World War 1914-18.

THE EAST AFRICAN MOUNTED RIFLES *by C.J. Wilson*—Experiences of the campaign in the East African bush during the First World War.

THE LONG PATROL *by George Berrie*—A Novel of Light Horsemen from Gallipoli to the Palestine campaign of the First World War.

THE FIGHTING CAMELIERS *by Frank Reid*—The exploits of the Imperial Camel Corps in the desert and Palestine campaigns of the First World War.

STEEL CHARIOTS IN THE DESERT *by S. C. Rolls*—The first world war experiences of a Rolls Royce armoured car driver with the Duke of Westminster in Libya and in Arabia with T.E. Lawrence.

WITH THE IMPERIAL CAMEL CORPS IN THE GREAT WAR *by Geoffrey Inchbald*—The story of a serving officer with the British 2nd battalion against the Senussi and during the Palestine campaign.

AVAILABLE ONLINE AT **www.leonaur.com**
AND FROM ALL GOOD BOOK STORES

www.ingramcontent.com/pod-product-compliance
Lightning Source LLC
Chambersburg PA
CBHW031624160426
43196CB00006B/264